Cecilia Diaz Gruessing, MA

Mystical GODDESS DRAMA

RECREATING THE MYSTERIES OF:
Maria Lionza-Venezuela
Inanna-Sumeria

Demeter and Persephone - The Eleusinian Mysteries
St. Sara La Kali - Black Madonna - Queen of the Gypsies
St. Cecilia Patron Saint St. of Celestial Music
The Muses and the Maenads - Ancient Greece

Copyright ©2024 by Cecilia Anne Gruessing, M.A. .

Published by Cecilia Anne Gruessing

and Wanda Miller

ISBN   979-8-991-9680-0-3(softcover)
ISBN   xxx-x-xxxxxx-xx-x (hardcover)
ISBN   xxx-x-xxxxxx-xx-x (ebook)

All rights reserved. No part of this book may be reproduced or transmitted in any form or by any means, electronic or mechanical, including photocopying, recording, or by any information storage and retrieval system without express written permission from the author, except in the case of brief quotations embodied in critical reviews and certain other non-commercial uses permitted by copyright law.

This book is a work of fiction. Names, characters, places, and incidents are the product of the author's imagination or are used fictitiously. Any resemblance to actual locales, events, or persons, living or dead, is purely coincidental.

Printed in the United States

Mystical GODDESS DRAMA

A compilation of Mythical Plays

Cecilia Anne Gruessing, M.A.

"Mystical Goddess Drama" represents a pioneering fusion of contemporary sacred dance and theater, encapsulating the essence of innovative playwriting. This collection of six musical plays offers a compelling reinterpretation of ancient mythology, presenting archetypal gods and goddesses in modern settings. By addressing universal themes and human dramas, the work appeals to broad audiences, ensuring relevance and appeal for different demographics.

The thorough historical research, supported by bibliographies and referenced prose, lends the book an academic rigor that enhances its credibility and depth. This scholarly foundation not only enriches the narratives but also provides a valuable resource for educators, students, and theater professionals. Significantly, the author's focus on the feminine psyche stands out, offering complex and challenging roles for both women and men. This emphasis on female perspectives and experiences fills a critical gap in dramatic literature, responding to the growing demand for diverse and inclusive storytelling. The alternative mystical and feminine approach provides a fresh perspective in theater and film production, inviting creators to explore innovative storytelling techniques and narratives.

Additionally, "Mystical Goddess Drama" is more than a collection of plays; it serves as a conduit to the mystical and esoteric traditions of ancient civilizations. The book takes readers on a captivating journey through ancient mysteries, connecting past wisdom with contemporary consciousness. This dual role as a theatrical work and a guide to ancient wisdom makes it a unique and invaluable asset, appealing to both theater enthusiasts and those interested in mystical traditions.

"Mystical Goddess Drama" offers several compelling advantages:

1. Innovative Content: Blends sacred dance, theater, and mythology in a novel format.

2. Educational Value: Supported by historical research and bibliographies, making it suitable for academic settings.

3. Diverse Perspectives: Focuses on the feminine psyche, filling a niche in dramatic literature.

4. Broad Appeal: Relevant to both theater professionals and general readers interested in mythology and mysticism.

5. Unique Selling Proposition: Combines theatrical narratives with ancient wisdom, creating a multifaceted reading experience.

In summary, "Mystical Goddess Drama" is a transformative work that enriches the field of contemporary dramatic literature and meets the growing demand for diverse, innovative, and educational content. Its acquisition would not only enhance any collection but also engage a wide range of readers and theater practitioners.

Cecilia Anne Gruessing, M.A.

DEDICATION

This book is dedicated to my mother, ***Josephine Grace Diaz Gruessing….*** the mother goddess in my life, who enabled so much of my freedom as an artist and humanitarian. Her love and support will never be forgotten as part of the divine and feminine fabric of my life, and my three adopted daughters. Thank you, Mom….

Mystical Goddess Drama

Cecilia Anne Gruessing, M.A.

MYSTICAL GODDESS DRAMA–

Play descriptions

I have worked in dance, theater, rock and roll, Broadway musicals, music video, and entertainment venues all my life. I have now artistically framed my fascination with archetypes of ancient history who keep reappearing in modern times, in the form of theatrical manuscript with this book.

And within those ancient epochs I have discovered that all performance takes root in ancient shamanism: the calling of spirit; the performance of ritual and ceremony; and in modern times, the best theater and dance. Within these six plays there are various themes in which dance, poetry, ritual, music, drama and song weave their way through sacred human mysteries that have been honored for centuries.

Ceil Gruessing

1. **The Mysteries of Maria Lionza** – A bi-lingual musical drama written about the Goddess cult of Maria Lionza in Venezuela. This musical play is structured around the mysteries of the Catholic rosary and tracks the real life of this great woman who lived during the Spanish conquest of Latin America. Maria Lionza arrives in spirit with her racial triumvirate, El Negro Felipe, and the great Chief Guacaipuro, through the transport of mediums and ancient rituals which still take place today in Venezuela. The musical follows her life and the miracles she performs. The author lived and worked inside the culture of these healers and is familiar with several of the characters within this pantheon of many global, ancestor spirits. She believes that this practice of Ancestor worship is the root of all dance and theater.

2. **The Mysteries of Inanna** – The great Sumerian Goddess Inanna is the first of all historically recorded goddesses. She precedes and sets the stage for Ishtar and Astarte, and all the water and mother goddesses who follow them, all the way up to our Virgin Mary. Within The Epic of Gilgamesh and recently translated cuneiform tablets, we discover many stories about Inanna. One in particular describes the Descent of Inanna into the underworld where she must die at the hand of her underground sister Ereshkigal, and then be reborn again to return to her throne alongside her lover,

Dumuzzi. The author uses the seven circuit Hopi labyrinth as a floor design to structure the musical descent of a modern, Iraqi Miss Universe, who must give up her crown because of differences she has with her Uncle Sadam Hussein. It is a dramatic musical following Inanna's descent as she gives up her individual female powers to the seven great planetary leaders along the way. Her exchange and death by hanging at the hands of the underworld queen Ereshkigal, is the VERY FIRST in a long line of sacrifice and dismemberment stories…their death, and their rebirth. The portal guardian characters and their dramas with Inanna are fascinating archetypal journeys for a powerful woman on her journey to and from leadership.

3. St. Sara la Kali, Queen of the Gypsies – The Goddess Kali is powerful and difficult to digest for many people. Her image is frightening. But her reputation is important to all women. The story of St. Sara La Kali is a Black Madonna story held sacred by the Gypsies, who originally migrate out of India with the inspiration of several Hindu deities like Kali and Tara. This conflated goddess, St. Sara La Kali, guides the gypsy caravans fearlessly on their homeless journeys. In May, there is a famous tradition for all gypsies to converge on St. Maries de la Mer in Comargue, France, where they celebrate the pilgrimage of the three Maries from Jesus's crucifixion to the shores of France. Below the present-day church is a sanctuary for St. Sara La Kali, to whom they pray earnestly for health, love and prosperity.

This is also the story of ethnic cleansing during the Serbian war in Yugoslavia, with the spiritual and musical connection between the gypsies, the refugees, and a team of American missionary belly dancers. They are all on their way to St. Maries de la Mer for the great Gypsy festival where they carry the saints to the sea…. much like the Hindu puja. The American dancers call attention to women and their traditions in the ancient world. This script includes drama, dance, culture and the fusion of poetry and music.

4. Sacred Journey -The Eleusinian Mysteries – taken from the Greek myth of Demeter and Persephone. It has been modernized with its location in modern Greek reality and migrates into the mythical landscape of the Eleusinian mysteries. According to the myth, Persephone is abducted and raped by the God Pluto who keeps her underground after her consumption of a pomegranate. Demeter's grief is so great that all agricultural life stops while she wanders the earth looking for her lost daughter. The author's version of this famous Greek myth reincarnates the characters in a modern setting and incorporates the seasonal fate of Persephone, and the repetition of this myth as part of the initiation into the Eleusinian mysteries. It is a short musical fairytale which would be ideal for stage or film.

5. St. Cecilia's Circle of Lost Souls –This allegorical fantasy has autobiographical qualities as it follows the fate of a deluded theater director who runs a hostel for lost souls in an old church, under the pretense of a performing arts school. Here the live-in artists are marginal street characters with very little connection to the world other than their rehearsals with the director/mistress, Ceci Ningun. St. Cecilia, patron saint of music, and a martyr for her dedication to Jesus, is the namesake of the main character.

It is the Day of the Dead festival, and one of the dancers is pregnant, and gives birth to a child to the sound of bulldozers as the city comes in to flatten the artistic slum. This too is a musical, with clown like characters struggling with their tragedies.

6. The Muses and The Maenads – Grace & Fury is a story about a modern day, refined school for girls in San Francisco, modeled on the Greek concept of the nine Muses. These girls study high level academics and the performing arts. Their Director, Paul (Apollo), and his sister, Misha (Artemis), run the school with Apollonian principals. During a fund raiser for the school, the Muses will dance, and various modern-day philanthropists like Tony Pythagoras, Frank Hesiod, Robert Plato, and Bill Euripides come to donate money and dance with the Muse students. Then a very dramatic and Nietzschean tragedy takes place. Paul's rock star crazy brother, Dion (Dionysus), crashes the party with his wild entourage of savage, rock n roll back up singers and musicians, the Maenads, and the clash of polarities makes for great musical drama. This is a great vehicle for dance and choreography.

Mystical Goddess Drama

TABLE OF CONTENTS

The Mysteries of Maria Lionza 1

The Mysteries of Inanna 133

St. Sara la Kali Queen of the Gypsies 179

Sacred Journey 269

St. Cecilia's Circle of Lost Souls 303

The Muses and The Maenads 344

Cecilia Anne Gruessing, M.A.

INTRODUCTION

I am proud of this dramatic material. It originated as plays written with documented research and historical footnotes. I did this as dramatic work, instead of writing traditional research papers, for a master's degree in philosophy and religion at California Institute of Integral Studies in San Francisco, Ca. I am eternally grateful to the school for their acknowledgement of my talent as a thespian and scholar.

With a BA in Dance/Theater, from Antioch College, in Yellow Springs, Ohio, during the sixties, the connection I have between art and spirit has always been strong. I have learned all the ropes as a professional choreographer, director, stage manager, and costume designer in the many aspects of show business. As a tr-lingual teacher of dance and theater arts, I have had students from every age, nationality, class, race, and walk of life all over the world.

During my 40 years in the business of education, it has been impossible to create an academic interdisciplinary field of study between the performing arts, and religion and philosophy. No university accepts this as a legitimate curriculum and field of study. Most performers in the USA have no idea that the roots of all the arts began as ritual and ceremony and offerings to the higher powers, where spiritual energy creates the magic of performance. As commercial as my experience has been teaching children, working in music video, musical theater, fashion, TV, or film . . . I have never been able to explore the bridge between performance and ritual as a creative class/workshop . . . exploring both technique, choreography, and playwriting in the context of ritual, ceremony, and mythmaking. Yet, how many times have I heard a director say, "put some spirit in it!"

CIIS gave me that opportunity. Here you have my formal contribution to SACRED DANCE AND THEATER in the form of a compilation of sacred musical plays. These are plays whose characters and stories have been taken from mythical discourse and literature . . . and then transformed into modern characters with the same karma as the mythical heroines, to live out their destinies in a modern world. In all the plays there is occasionally a fine line between the two worlds, where the modern character actually becomes the god, they are imitating in a dreamlike context.

Many of the plays talk about the shamanic practice of mediumship in which a person takes the spirit of an ancient ancestor or God into their body. I have seen this practice in Venezuela where "brujos" become possessed and allow that spirit to speak through them. "The Mysteries of Maria Lionza" is all about my experience with spirit. It is the best theater I have ever seen in my life. It is the roots of dance and theater and is part of all ritual and ceremonial culture from third world cultures around the globe. It is called Ancestor Worship and Shamanism. The correlation to nature and agricultural cycles forms another interesting part of the ritual and mythmaking in this spiritual practice. The common factor is dance, music, prayer, and drumming which take a shaman (artist) into a magical and dramatic trance in which their body is possessed by spirit. Clearly it is the origin of dance and acting. My master's in philosophy and religion was spent researching this very topic. My entire life as a dancer and choreographer has been spent trying to put that magic into my work . . . that moment of the suspension of disbelief, when the performer, is truly captivated by their character, beyond the ego of performance . . . completely in the hands of the persona in their body. These are the performances that rivet any audience.

*   *   *

All of these plays are designed for a lyricist and composer to complete their eligibility for production. I seek someone who is musically inspired by the material in these plays, and who wants to create the scores. I put this desire in the hands of the publisher, with the blessing of spirit wings.

I also hope to find a producer who appreciates the magical femininity of this material, as it reflects ancient myths and calls attention to the universal roles of archetypal women throughout time. I would love to see this material on stage, in amphitheaters, on movie screens, to bring more female consciousness to the public eye. This should include fashion, great music, talented singer/dancers, and top of the line production. However, I believe this work, as it exists in script form also speaks for itself as written entertainment and research material.

I must remember to thank all the men and women I have met along the way who have helped me learn about art and life. We are all mosaics of our predecessors, our ancestors, our teachers and our cultural heroes.

Then there is my family. My Mother, Josephine Gruessing, has been the source of great love and security for me over the years. She has also supported the arrival of my three beautiful, adopted daughters who have returned with me from Honduras, where I spent the last 10 years teaching dance and theater, and working with abandoned children.

Jazmin, Angie Nicolle, and Roxana are the lights of my life and the true inspiration behind everything I do now. The greatest work of art a woman can possibly put on the planet is a happy and healthy child. These girls, and how I got custody and visas for them, are the subjects of a musical about them which will be my next book " Si Dios Quiere." (God Willing)

My father, Joseph Gruessing, also appears in St. Cecilia's Circle of Lost Souls as a homeless angel… He lost his life to cancer and was the motive for seeking a cure to cancer in my work with Maria Lionza in Venezuela. He was very supportive of my interest in the performing arts, a truly kind and generous man. Finally, I must thank my daughters' Godfather, DeLouis Hurwits in Italy, who has helped me support them since leaving the orphanage. "It takes a Village" to save lives.

And for this reason, I make dance and theater… to unite the village, so the village saves lives and creates the fabric of society for the children who come after us. I pray that we all learn to live in peace and under the leadership wings of intelligent people who provide for everybody, including art and the people who make art.

I hope you benefit from the academic research and documentation included in this endeavor. Enjoy the work.

Ceil Gruessing, MA.   Oct 8, 2014
Richmond, Va.

The Mysteries of Maria Lionza

Cecilia Anne Gruessing, M.A.

The Mysteries of Maria Lionza

**A Latin American Musical derived from the legend
and practice of Spiritism with Maria Lionza in Venezuela**

With the structural guidance of:

**The Joyful the Glorious and The Sorrowful
Mysteries of the Catholic Rosary**

Ceil Gruessing— November 1999
Written for Charlene Spretnak and The Virgin Mary Class
California Institute of Integral Studies, San Francisco, Ca.

INTRODUCTION

The following text is a play called "The Mysteries of Maria Lionza". It is about a goddess/legend of a woman named Maria Lionza, who actually lived. It was originally written for a graduate class about the Virgin Mary, and her migration to various parts of the world. I have dramatized the impact of 15th and 16th century events in Spain that helped transport the "Virgin Mary" to Latin America and particularly Venezuela. I also write about the effects of the Spanish conquest on both the native indigenous and African slaves at that time. The Holy Queen Maria Lionza is in fact one of the many Latin American ambassadora's of the Virgin Mary (like Guadelupe in Mexico) and is the central character of this mystery play.

This work is structured in 15 scenes based on the development of the three- part mysteries in the Catholic rosary. In Act I, I have described the historical circumstances of Maria Lionza's birth as "The Joyful Mysteries". In "the Sorrowful Mysteries" (Act II) I look at the Spanish Conquest of Venezuela, using blatant parallel symbolism of the imasculanization of the Third World male and the exploitation of Latin American resources, to the Crucifixion of Christ and the fear of his magical message of peace. I conflate the crucifixion with the decapitation of a great Venezuelan Indian Chief under captivity, Tamanaco.

Act III, as the "Glorious Mysteries" will portray present day worship of Maria Lionza in Venezuela, and Maria's physical death, her ascent to heaven and her famous Coronation.

Maria Lionza is the queen of "Las Tres Potencias" (the three powers) in Venezuela, where she and the Indian Chief Guaicaipuro, and the Afro-Cuban liberator of the Slaves, Negro Felipe, work together in spiritual triumvirate to heal, guide, inspire, and accelerate the evolution of all sentient beings. One cannot help but note this parallel triple concept with the Catholic trinity.

This religious practice has been defined by a practice Alan Kardec calls "Espiritismo" (also called ancestor worship), in which departed ancestors, leaders, and healers, as well as animals, and nature spirits descend into the bodies of mediums (Brujos or Curanderos). They talk, see, and heal through those bodies, while the mediums are "asleep" and out of their bodies. I researched and videotaped this activity for three years, during which I made some very significant relationships with Venezuelan devotees and mediums, and most dramatically, with a huge pantheon of spirits from history. As a choreographer and thespian, I firmly believe that theater and dance grew out of this ancient practice of "ancestor worship" and shamanism. Basically, a good performer has the "spirit", and is so convincing or riveting in their delivery, that you actually believe that the character they are portraying is inside of their body. Again, I declare that the work of Las Tres Potencias and their pantheon of characters is the best theater I have ever seen. I was fortunate enough to have conversations with several of these spirits during all night sessions. My "protector's" name is Tamanaco, a great Indian chief who was part of the resistance to the Spanish Conquest. Maria Lionza herself, ceremoniously crowned me as her god daughter. I am proud of these friendships, difficult as it may be for many to understand.

Maria clearly claims the spiritual hearts of many followers. In Caracas there is a famous statue of her that rivets the imagination, sculpted by Alejandro Colon. Naked and straddling a danza-tapir, a lion/ boar looking animal, Maria raises her arms with fearless energy holding a female pelvis bone high above her head. (*page 1*)

I have enjoyed writing about the Virgin Mary and the Queen Maria Lionza in the theatrical form, because I am truly interested in what they represent as role models for women. I realize the benefits of "Organic Inquiry" amongst primary sources (local publications and musical tapes about prayer and natural cures which I bought on the street). I also credit first-hand experience as a patient of the healing ceremonies with the curanderos, as well as my own artistic intuition and creativity that allowed this work to emerge in this radical style.

This free form expression is especially radical in Act I and II, with the apparitions of the Virgin Mary and her moral disapproval of the imperialistic, Spanish dominion in the new world. I don't believe this has been properly confronted by Catholicism and religious history. The perspective from which the Virgin Mary speaks, predicting the birth of Maria Lionza in the Americas, clearly reflects a collective female voice that has been silent and frustrated for so long over the issues of war and violence. (Why don't Popes straight out condemn all acts of war? Why does the bible speak of military victories in the name of God?) I welcome this opportunity to examine what happened in Latin America with the Spanish Conquest, as I am interested in the subsequent tri-racial cultural mix of their spiritual music and beliefs.

Act III will use the Glorious Mysteries to bring us into modern times with the cult practice of Maria Lionza and her Tres Potencias in Venezuela and on her Mountain sanctuary of Sortes (suerte- luck); in Chivicoa. Here the government has reserved a sacred river and ground for her devotees to practice on national park land. My memories of being inside that world of La Montana de Sortes are still vivid.

Act III also addresses the physical death of Maria Lionza and her ascension to heaven where she continues her work in spirit to this day. This play has been supported by spirit, and it is as artist and shaman that I write it in her behalf as historical fiction.

Thank you for the opportunity to follow my mission as a spiritual artist.

Ceil Gruessing— October 1999— San Francisco, Ca.

BACKGROUND

I have chosen to write in theatrical form, about this Goddess- spirit from Venezuela called "Maria Lionza" with connections to the study of the Virgin Mary and her cult in Spain during the XV and XVI centuries. Several aspects of research were used to write this manuscript, from legends to written material, to primary and secondary source interviews, and personal experience. With this background material, you will have a better idea where this magical, nature-based practice comes from.

Pre-Colombian shamanism and mythology reveals a mother water goddess, YARA, amongst the Northern Amazonian tribes of the Tupari. She is portrayed as a mermaid, accompanied by snakes, who lures a young Indian chief into the water where he becomes initiated by his aquatic intercourse with a Spanish woman. Yara also reveals the importance of the flute, the reeds, and the secret memory of an ancient matrilineal history. Some references say that Maria Lionza was initially called "Yara", born in the province of Yaracuy, before she was given the name Maria.

For many people, Maria Lionza is considered "a myth", legend, or another aspect of the Virgin Mary. There are many different stories of her origin, which generally define her as an indigenous descendent on the paternal side of the Caquetio tribe in

Niragua, the daughter of Chief Guare of Yaracuy, the granddaughter of Chief Chilua and the great granddaughter of Chief Yare. They were all famous leaders and warriors from Venezuelan history. Her mother was Spanish. Folklore has Maria descending from the pre-Columbian goddess Yara, and because of her green watery eyes, she was considered a strange, evil, magical being who had to be sacrificed to a great monster/anaconda from the lagoon to protect the tribe. She escapes this tragedy and survives, to become a mythical goddess and hermit-queen of the jungle and its inhabitants. She was later named Maria to connect her to the Catholic church. The legends vary within these parameters.

In reference books she is also conflated with The Virgin of Coromoto, who is Venezuela's Patron Saint, born the same day, October12 (also on the day Columbus discovered America, and also called the Dia de la Rasa). Clearly, the church has merged with the indigenous cultures to change history and control the masses.

With a very sincere desire to track down Maria Lionza's real roots as a human being, and to validate my actual conversations with her in spirit regarding her past, I have chosen the most logical of the stories which fits the true history of her birth. Through very grass roots Spanish literature, I have discovered an account of Maria's mother, Princess Ana Carolina del Prado de la Talavera de la Reina, back in 15th century Spain. Despite all the supernatural legends, I have gone with Maria Lionza's authentic, primary source description (by interview), stating that her mother was the daughter of a Royal Spanish Encomendero immigrant couple, and her father was an indigenous Venezuelan Indian, Chief Guare. Her controversial birth in the new Caribbean world as Spanish royalty, mixed with indigenous blood, leads her to become the Queen of The Three (racial) Powers (Las Tres Potencias). This triumvirate legitimized the beginning of the melting pot which exists today between the Spanish Castilians, the West Africans (El Negro Felipe) who came with the slave trade, and the Indigenous native Venezuelans (Chief Guaicaipuro).

Maria Lionza was destined for "queenship" in the new melting pot world, because of her mixed blood and exotic beauty (green eyes, dark hair) despite fear of her strange blood. She eventually renounced her family and chose to live as a hermit in the jungle with her animals, and became the protectoress of the indigenous peoples, and all living things, providing safety for all endangered species, and condemning murder of any kind upon her land. The Natives eventually accepted her with love despite her clear eyes. The Church wanted her myth to submit to their prescriptions of the Virgin Mary, so the Mission Friars introduced Maria Lionza with obligatory love at an opportune time when spiritual survival from the Spanish conquistadores was only possible through worshipping a mix of their Catholic Mary, the Virgin de Coromoto and their Nature/Earth deities. Maria Lionza provided the connection, although in present day, the church does not acknowledge her and considers her an Indian legend. Maria, however, continues to use Catholic rituals in her prayers and healing.

In 1492 as Spain was taking over many parts of Latin America. After expelling the Moors from their territory, and creating a Catholic Reign of Terror, the powerful rule that King Ferdinand and Queen Isabella created many reasons to migrate to the New Land…… mainly freedom.

The Cult of the Virgin Mary was very popular in Spain, with many villages having their own "Nuestra Señora", or "Virgin" protectoress who had appeared to some villager and demanded the construction of a church on the spot. In Toledo, Spain there were many Basilicas, Hermitages, and Sanctuaries of "Our Lady" around which regular celebrations and ceremonies took place, often mixing cultures with Arabic traditions, music, and temple architecture leftover from Moorish influences. Yet despite the strength of the Spanish Inquisition, pagan practices still survived, often combining the worship of the earth mother for agricultural fertility and healing purposes, with the benevolent mystique of the Virgin Mary, who promised them salvation if they worked hard, accepted Jesus, prayed the Rosary, and gave to the church.

Outside Toledo, Spain is a hermitage called "Ermito de Nuestra Virgen del Prado de la Talavera de la Reina", constructed sometime in the late 15th century. There Nuns manufactured and painted ceramic pottery by day and called upon the Virgin by night in their sacred groves with songs and dances, incantations, and infusions of herbs, candles, and prayers clearly tied to previous pagan rites.

Here is where Maria Lionza has her maternal Royal Spanish roots, as her mother Ana Carolina del Prado de la Talavera de la Reina was born there to Doña Herminia and Don Juan de la Talavera de Nivar. They came to Venezuela around 1572 to take advantage of the Encomienda System which basically enforced Spanish military law through Spanish entrepreneurs who farmed, mined, or bred animals, and employed/exploited local Indians to work for them in exchange for residence on their own land. Upon coming of age, La Srta Ana Carolina falls uncontrollably in love with a Caquitios Indian Chief named Guare, father of Maria.

Meanwhile, atrocities have taken place all through Venezuela as the conquistadores ruthlessly destroy and exploit villages and tribes. Dozens of famous Venezuelan Indian chiefs go down in the line of duty to their people, including my own protector, el Cacique Tamanaco. Guaicaipuro, being the main native representative in Maria Lionza's trinity court, plays a major role in the final resistance. The invaders were merciless. There are many legends about brave natives who fought to the end, defending their land and people. A smallpox plague brought in by the Spanish also wiped out about two thirds of the indigenous population by 1590. Those natives who remained were now combined with the slave labor created by African immigration into Latin America. Here we meet the other third of Maria Lionza's trinity, El Negro Felipe, a Cuban liberator of African slaves.

Maria de La Onza del Prado de la Talavera de Nivar is born on October 12, 1591, in the deep Yaracuy jungle to hide the fact that she is the illegitimate daughter of a Spanish immigrant. Ana Carolina, and a Venezuelan Indian Chief. Chief Guare's tribe considers her bad luck because of her light-colored eyes, and that her mother comes from royal, Spanish, conquista blood. Ana's parents will not offer inheritance to a half breed child unless the indigenous father becomes a Spanish count under the crown, and a Catholic under the church.

In 1591 there is the legend of the of Ana Carolina meeting a Venezuelan Indian Chief in the river, where they fall in love, and create Maria. Her eventual magical powers are eventually conflated with the Virgin of Coromoto— Protectress of Venezuela, or Patron Saint under the Catholic church. In 1653 a parish was built in Nirgua, over an ancient matrilineal sacred site, called "La Parroquia de Nuestra Señora Maria de la Onza del Prado de la Talavera de la Reina", where she was conceived.

According to channeled material (Santiago de Jesus Rodriguez Moreno) Maria's mother Ana, puts a Negra Hamurapi in charge of Maria while she grows up in the jungle enveloped by nature, insisting that she must be simultaneously trained in the catechism of the Catholic Church. The mother and father promise to return for the baby Maria, after Ana Carolina formally marries Guare in the church. Maria develops supernatural powers in the wild, including particular healing qualities acquired from the Yaracuy River water, and the ability to talk to animals. She takes her name, Maria de la Onza from the onza (lion), which she rides, also called a danta, or a tapir. She dedicates herself to nature and all living things. The plight of the natives against the Spanish becomes her reclusive fight, to maintain her sacred mountain where the natives could take refuge from the Spanish conquerors. It is recorded in Ponce de Leon's journals that he met with her and that HE gave her the name Maria de la Onza del Prado de la Talavera de Nivar, in hopes of winning her back over to the Spanish Monarchy by reclaiming her blood. But she refused and condemned the barbaric slaughter of the native Venezuelan people and the African Slaves, despite her familial connection to the Spanish conquistadores.

Maria takes on the central role of her Trilogy platform of the Three Races, or the Three Powers (Las Tres Potencias or Poderosos) by joining the spirits of Chief Guaicaipuro, and the Great Liberator of the slaves, Negro Felipe. She translates the Christian trilogy of the Father, Son, and Holy Ghost into a fusion of the African, European, and indigenous powers with her prayers, and takes refuge in nature. Here she reigns, allowing no murder of any kind, incorporating more and more courts of spirits.

Maria also is a virgin, despite the attentions of a Spanish soldier, who was madly in love with her, whom she had to reject because she felt emotionally scarred by her own people's selfish and opportunistic ways. She was ashamed to be instrumental in any way for the violence of this Spanish imperialist bloodline. She could only devote herself to nature and healing, and the protection of the humble, subaltern population who had taken her in.

According to Angelina Pollak-Eltz (1987), who is a leading, published scholar on Maria Lionza's cult, the first center under her name was opened in the early 1900s in Caracas by a known curandero and espiritista (healer and trance medium). The cult grew in popularity during the twentieth century amongst the lower class. Moreover, the Venezuelan Dictator General Gomez (1908- 1935), was a devotee of the practice, and also had a mistress who was a priestess of the cult. Marcos Perez Jimenez (1950-1958), another Venezuelan Dictator also participated in the practice.

These ideological, fascist regimes brought great support to a distinctive cultural phenomenon that is still part of the Venezuelan identity.

Maria Lionza's cult became very visible in the 1940's, between the wars, and reinforced its roots with the African Yoruban faith called "Santeria", thereby cementing the racial integration of all the aboriginal and Espiritista practices. The government set aside several acres, six hours east of Caracas, in Chivicoa, Yaracuy, as National Park, called "The Mountain of Maria Lionza", or "Sortes" (Suerte - luck). Devotees come on pilgrimages every weekend to bathe in the healing waters of the Yaracuy River, and to pay their respects to Maria Lionza and her pantheon of nature spirits and ancestors. One comes with their "Brujo" and tribe for three days to set up an altar, sleep under the stars, and pray for miracles. Here, spirits will descend into the bodies of mediums, initiates, or sick patients, to heal or transfer messages to the people. Spirits descend through the permission of God and Maria Lionza. One must pray to her first, for her intercession, and endorsement towards a spiritual encounter with a particular spirit whose specialty might resolve their potentially magical connection to Dios Poderoso and be healed. Sacred space, altars, candles, flowers, music, cigars (tobaccos or hache), baths, and offerings are blessed and conjured to supply truth and abundance, health and love, happiness, and understanding as part of the performance package.

Because I actually studied this practice for three years, I want to convey the mystical aspects of the experience through dramatic events connected to my personal, experiential knowledge. There was also a limited amount of academic information written about the cult. Most of my research, including religious Spanish History in the XV and XVI centuries, is my attempt to ground the story. I have intuitively constructed this script around my own personal acquaintance and interviews with this Holy Queen Mother Maria, and what she told me about her family history…. as well as my experiences witnessing the descent of many spirits under her wing in Venezuela. The Spanish conquest is not mystical and is unpleasantly necessary to the story as history marches on in patriarchal audacity. The chosen sequence of theatrical and musical events delivers what I consider to be a mythic, and folkloric dedication to Maria Lionza and to the Virgin Mary.

It is a pity the great archaea-mythologist Maria Gimbutas did not get to do her research in Latin America. Her Matrilineal/ Goddess formula tends to fit into many of the symbols of birds, chevrons, triangles, and snake designs, left by South and Central American Neolithic ancestors and shamans. This includes findings by Colombus of female clay idols. Goddesses of the maternal waters are also predominant and filter down to present day mother cult folklore all over the Central and South American continent. And what remains in 21st century, subaltern Latino culture is still the solace of a Queen/Mother/Goddess, who loves every living thing, and embraces the rich as well as the sick and poor. Come to her for love, for forgiveness, for healing, in poverty and abundance, in happiness, or death. Learn how to be humble and pray, to recite the rosary, to confess your sins, and the Queen Mother will always listen.

From my personal experience of being in Maria Lionza's presence, hearing her sing the Ave Maria in the bodies of mediums, watching her sip red wine, listening to her wisdom and compassion, being humbled by her blessing of ceremonial Coronation, and being ordained as her Goddaughter, I am humbled by all the warmth and incredible magic. I was finally embraced for my spiritual merit in her court. I am truly honored by the experience and knowing and believing in the actual previous earthly existence of Maria Lionza, enables me to validate her practice. Again, I must declare, that it was the best "theater" I have ever seen in my life. For these reasons, I embody her in the medium of theater, which was born of the rituals of the Ancient Goddess. I thank you Oh Holy Mother, Queen and Saint, Goddess and Virgin, Maria Lionza.

    Ceil Gruessing
    1999, San Francisco, Ca.

SCENE BREAKDOWN

ACT I

THE JOYFUL MYSTERIES

1. **THE ANNUNCIATION**— An indigenous Amazonian shaman calls the Goddess of the Waters, Yara to heal a barren woman. Yara announces the birth of a warrior and promises the later birth of a Goddess savior. (1480) .... *page 16*

2. **THE VISITATION**— (Outskirts of Toledo, Spain, 1580) The Apparition of the Virgin del Prado de la Talavera de la Reina at a Nun's hermitage (by the same name), who blesses Anna Carolina del Prado de la Talavera as the future mother of Maria Lionza, Goddess of Peace .... *page 19*

3. **THE NATIVITY**— 1591— Anna Carolina falls in love with a Venezuelan Chief Guare, and they conceive "Yara/Maria" within their polarity................................. *page 25*

4. **THE PRESENTATION**— September 1591 — Making proper birth arrangements for a problematic half-breed.. *page 27*

5. **FINDING THE BLESSED CHILD**— Maria del Prado de la Talaverra de la Reina (eventually known as Maria Lionza) is born on October 12, 1591 in sacred waters under the vigilance of the Virgin of Coromoto (Patron Saint of Venezuela often identified with Maria Lionza) .... *page 32*

Cecilia Anne Gruessing, M.A.

ACT II

THE SORROWFUL MYSTERIES

1. **THE AGONY IN THE GARDEN**— (1493—Toledo, Spain)—
   The Virgin Mary observes High Holy Mass
   with disgrace as Queen Isabella, King Ferdinand,
   Christopher Colombus, Tomas de Torquemada,
   and Pope Sixtus celebrate the Inquisition and
   the Conquest of the New World.. *page 39*

2. **THE SCOURGING AT THE PILLAR**— 1490's— "Fields of Blood"
   — A "Conquista Ballet, abstractly danced to the
   formal verbal declaration of domination from
   King Ferdinand and Queen Isabella to the
   Indigenous peoples of the New World .... *page 43*

3. **THE CROWN OF THORNS**— (1580)
   Mary appears on an "Encomienda— Mission"
   for captured natives and African slaves run by
   "Encomendros" and Friars - to witness their
   humiliating exploitation as prisoner/workers .... *page 45*

4. **CARRYING THE CROSS**— Mary watches the
   persecution of the great Venezuelan
   Chief Tamanaco as a gladiator in front
   of his own tribe .... *page 54*

5. **THE CRUCIFIXION**— The Transformation
   — Mary returns the decapitated body of Tamanaco
   to the Goddess Yara and her primordial waters.
   Maria Lionza emerges on her "onza" (tapir) to resist
   the Spanish Conquest into the 17th century .... *page 55*

ACT III

THE GLORIOUS MYSTERIES

1. **The Resurrection**— Semana Santa, A Spiritual Session in Catia, Caracas, Easter, 1995 .... page 63

2. **The Ascension**— Pilgrimage to Maria Lionza's Mountain of Sortes; from Caracas to Chivicoa, Yaracuy— May, 1995 .... page 81

3. **The Descent of the Spirit**—Tongues of Fire and the "trabajos" of the Brujos— Maria Lionza's Altar high atop Sortes .... page 90

4. **The Assumption**— FLASHBACK/Transport to Maria's last living day in Nirgua, Yaracuy, August 15, 1653 .... page 108

5. **The Coronation**— October 12, 1995. Dia de la Raza— Maria Lionza's Birthday in Sortes —A Celebration of her Love and Wisdom .... page 115

Cecilia Anne Gruessing, M.A.

ACT I—

THE JOYFUL MYSTERIES

Characters

- **Tupari Shaman**— Pre-Columbian witchdoctor
- **Native Woman**—Young woman trying to become pregnant
- **8 native priestesses**, dancers
- **Yara**— Pre-Columbian Goddess of the waters, origin Brazil
- **8 Spanish nuns**— 16th century
- **8 humble Spanish pilgrims**
- **Doña Herminia del Prado de la Talavera**— wealthy noble— 30
- **Don Juan del Prado de la Talavera**– wealthy merchant/husband
- **Ana Carolina del Prado de la Talavera**— 12-year-old daughter
- **Ana Carolina**— 27
- **Sister Fe**
- **Sister Caridad**
- **Sister Esperanza**
- **Caquetio warrior Chief Guare**— 28
- **La Negra Hamurapi**— 30 ish African slave nanny
- **Black Virgin Mary**
- **Virgin of Coromoto**— same as Mary

The Mysteries of Maria Lionza

Scene 1— The Annunciation
— Pre-Colombian Ceremony invoking YARA, 1480

There is darkness. In the distance we can hear the approaching sound of a reed flute and a drum. The performance area becomes illuminated with the entrance of an aboriginal, Tupari shaman carrying a torch, followed by "the patient" (a young woman), and a string of women who spiral into a circle and begin to sing and dance as the Shaman prepares his sacred ground. A three-tiered universe is portrayed with the ceremony taking place on the earthly plane, which is suspended between the celestial vault (looks like an inverted bowl), and the subterranean waters, and connected by a large central tree (the axis mundi) and sacred caves.[1] The song about Yara[2] has been passed down into Portuguese even though their original songs were in Tupi.

CANTO da YARA	**(Ronaldo Barbosa)[3]**
Canta e encanta sereia dos lagos	*Sing and enchant mermaid of the lakes*
Yara dos rios	*Yara of the rivers*
Tua beleza e a propria melodia	*Your beauty is a melody in itself*
Brota das aguas e invade a floresta em sinfonia	*Make water bloom and invade nature*
Encanto que surge ao luar	*Enchantment that surges from this place Symphonically*
Que envolve o pesdador	*That involves the fisherman*
Que seduz o navegador	*That seduces the boatman*
E Inspira o chamane	*And inspires the shaman*
Voz sonora infinita	*Infinite sounding voice*
Brasa ou calor	*ember of heat Everything*
Tudo em volta e	*Everything becomes*
Fogo, incenso, fumo e fervor	*fire, incense, smoke and fervor*
Canta minha sereia	*Sing my siren*
Yara dos rios	*Yara of the rivers*
E quando voce para, para, para, para ouvir	*It is when you stop to listen*

E quando voce pensa em voltar nao ha mais tempo	*You think there is no more time*
Tudo fica tao distante de voce	*Everything remains so far from you*
O canto de sereia seduziu voce	*The song of the siren seduces you*
Um canto caprichoso seduziu voce	*The capricious song seduces you*

The shaman positions the woman on a mat of leaves near the central tree. He wears tight, feathered, encircling ligatures, or bands on his forehead, upper arms, lower legs, and waist, which enhance his physical power. He shakes his maraca to clear the area around the patient. He begins to play his flute, when the women finish their song to YARA, echoing the melody of their song. He then uses the flute as a straw on the top of the patient's head, and then on her navel.[4] He takes a special wooden spatula and makes himself vomit. Then he positions himself on his "duho", a carved wooden ceremonial seat with the legs of a jaguar, where he will snort the fine, cinnamon colored cohoba powder,[5] and from his hunched "thinker" position, he will call the great Goddess YARA.

Shaman: I, Tupari shaman, call to the forces of the great universe to open the door to this young woman's curse of barrenness. I ask the spirits of nature to lead me to the cause of her imbalance, and to the plant or animal who can cure this disease. Please bring us the power of the great Goddess YARA, whose love and protection the Tupari people cannot live without. Oh, great Goddess of the dark waters, please bless this woman with your presence, your miraculous remedies, your strength and protection, your beautiful fertility, and your all-powerful love. Yara, Yara, Yara . . . .

Kaleidoscopic vision takes over as the Shaman becomes dizzy. The dancers begin to reflect this shift and become jaguars who guide the Shaman into his own feline body language and direct him to a plant. Then, the guaraguao eagle arrives— a celestial bird which takes him through the tree to the celestial heavens where he sings and dances ecstatically with the eagle. And finally, the raw, gypsy-like voice of YARA shatters the ambiance, and the shaman is drawn back to the earth plane, near his patient, flat on his back. On the nearby shoreline, YARA emerges from the subterranean waters with her powerful wailing lament. She is half woman, half fish/anaconda.

YARA: Hello, my people, I am Yara. I am clearly moved by your devotion to my powers. This beautiful woman is physically capable of making a child. The man who is the elected father has not appeased the spirit of a jaguar he killed without permission.

This is forbidden in my world. I cannot permit the entrance of this very important female goddess soul at this time, because the blood is not right.[6] As your protectoress I had hoped that she would carry my natural powers into your village, but I must wait for another virgin mother, whose spirit has no blood stain. I will, however, give your patient, a young boy, who will become a great brave chief named Tamanaco.[7] You will need this great leader, and many others, because there are invaders coming from the other side of the world— white men with arms of fire who will try to destroy you and take your land. They carry a great wooden cross— do not be fooled by this cross, for it is the symbol of your death. We have been blessed by many moons of peace, and now this vision brings me great sadness.

However, there is a peaceful Goddess coming, who will have the blood of many tribes in her veins, and she will come to show the many-colored people how to love one another. But now, I must give your people a warrior, of which you will need many, to stand up to the great white man.

Now, bring me the young woman, and let's fill her up.

Yara breaks into more of her wailing lament, which is accompanied by the sound of rain, water and waves. The shaman brings the patient to Yara who encircles her in the water, with her long, anaconda tail, and the women once again begin to sing and dance for Yara. The young girl begins to dance in the rain, to celebrate her newborn fertility, and the scene ends with a violent storm and the sounds of thunder and lightning.

* * *

Scene 2— The Visitation
— The Hermitage of the Virgin del Prado de la
Talavera de la Reina, 1575
(in the rural outskirts of Toledo, Spain)[8]

A procession of nuns in white habits carrying flowers, enters a monastery garden where there is a colorful fountain made of the old painted Moorish ceramic style brought by the Arabs in the 11th century.[9]

The fountain is at one end of the garden, with a statue of a dark Virgin and child. She has a vivid bleeding heart on her chest. Baby Jesus holds a ceramic globe of the earth in his hand. Pilgrims, who are clearly of the lower class, begin to arrive carrying flowers. They have come from the village in a long procession including singers and dancers, and a few bulls.[10]

CON FLORES A MARIA[11]

Venir y vamos todos	*We are all coming and going*
con flores a porfia	*with intended flowers*
con flores a Maria	*with flowers for Maria*
que Madre Nuestra es	*who is Our Mother*
1. De nuevo aqui nos tienes	*Once again you have us, purest virgin,*
purisima doncella mas que la luna	*purer than the beautiful moon,*
bella, prostrados a tus pies. (2x)	*prostrated at your feet.*
2. Venimos a ofrecerte las flores	*We come to offer you flowers from this*
de este suelo, con cuanto amor y	*soil with so much love and longing*
anhelo, Señora, Tu lo ves (2X)	*Señora, you see this.*

The pilgrims encircle the fountain around the Virgin, leaving their flowers. They begin to pray, kneeling with their rosaries, blessing themselves with the holy water.[12] *They begin to recite their prayers.*

"Por la senal de la Santa Cruz, de nuestros enemigos libranos, Señor Dios nuestro. En el nombre del Padre, y del Hijo, y del Espiritu Santo. Amen

ACTO DE CONTRICION— Yo confieso antes de Dios poderoso y antes de ustedes, hermanas, que he pecado mucho de pensamiento, palabra, obra y omision; por mi culpa, por mi culpa, por mi gran culpa. Por eso ruego a santa Maria, siempre virgen, a los angeles, a los santos, y a ustedes, hermanas, que intercedan por mi antes de Dios nuestro Señor.

AVE MARIA— Dios te salve, Maria, llena eres de gracia, el Señor es contigo; bendita tu eres entre todas las mujeres, y bendito es el fruto de tu vientre, Jesus. Santa Maria, Madre de Dios, ruega por nosotros los pecadores, ahora y en la hora de nuestra muerte. Amen."

Local spectators, the sick, and miracle seekers are congregating. All begin to sing in.

HYMN TO THE VIRGIN QUEEN (Saint Bernard 1120-40)

"O savior Virgin, Star of the Sea
Who bore for child the Son of Justice
The source of Light,
Virgin always Hear our praise!

Queen of Heaven who have given
Medicine to the sick, Grace to the devout,
Joy to the sad, Heaven's light to the world

And hope of salvation;
Court royal Special Virgin
Grant us cure and guard

Accept our vows, and by prayers
Drive all griefs away!

(Henry Adams piece)[13]

The Countess Doña Herminia del Prado de la Talavera enters the garden with her young daughter, Ana Carolina del Prado de la Talavera, who is about 12 years old. They are definitely overdressed and unexpected for the night's dark mysteries. A nun greets her.

Sister Fe: Señora del Prado de la Talavera! We were not expecting you this evening. This is a service for the sick and poor. Is there something I can do for you?

Doña Herminia: I'm very sorry to surprise you like this sister, but I believe that my daughter is very ill, and the physicians cannot determine the source of the disease.

Sister Fe: What are her symptoms?

Doña Herminia: It is some kind of epilepsy they say, that comes on when she is tired, and lately it seems to be occurring more and more often. She seems tortured by images of hellish worlds where people are being slaughtered like animals. I am so afraid it is consuming her. Look at her, my poor darling, she is so exhausted and confused, what with our move to the new world coming next week. I can't bear to take her on the boat like this. Sister, please help me. She is such a precious soul, and our only child who must carry on our name in Venezuela.

Sister Esperanza: We all love sweet Ana Carolina, and it saddens my hearts to hear of this affliction. Let me take her to the Virgin.

Doña Herminia waits in the background, while Ana Carolina joins the others lighting candles around the dark Virgen del Prado de la Talavera de la Reina.[14] They begin to sing another prayer to Mary, when some of the sick break down and weep uncontrollably in their petitions for healing and happiness. The nuns invoke the presence of spirit with a libretto style prayer, overlapped by individual prayers and petitions for healing.

ANCIENT PRAYER TO THE VIRGIN[15]

We turn to you for protection,	*Pedimos protection*
holy Mother of God.	*Madre de Dios sagrada*
Listen to our prayers	*Oiga nuestras oraciones*
and help us in our needs.	*Ayudanos con nuestros necessidades*
Save us from every danger	*Guardenos de cada peligro*
glorious and blessed Virgin.	*Oh, mi virgin gloria y bendita.*

(PRESENCIA DEL ESPIRITU)[16]

Santa Maria, Madre del Señor Jesus y nuestra	*Holy Mother Mary, Jesus's mother & ours*
obtennos la presencia vivificante del Espiritu	*Give us the living presence of the spirit*
y la gracia de andar siempre por los caminos de Dios	*and the grace to walk with God*
por tu bondadosa intercesion	*For your blessed intercession*
Consigue que estemos libres de las tristezas presentes	*Continue to keep us free of the present sadness*
pilgrim # 1: de las acechanzas del enemigo,	*from enemy attacks*
pilgrim # 2: de las flaquezas en la lucha,	*from the scars of life's battle*
piligrm # 3: de la pobreza y el hambre	*from poverty and hunger*
pilgrim # 4: de la plaga y muerto temprano	*from the plague and early death*
Y para cuando seamos convocados por el Padre	*And when we are called by the father*
consigue para nosotros las alegrias sin fin— Amen	*Find us happiness without end. Amen*

A crescendo builds during these passionate requests for help and salvation. Suddenly, Ana Carolina begins to convulse and roll on the floor in front of the statue of the Virgin. Out of nowhere we hear a voice singing Ave Maria. Doña Herminia and the nuns come to Ana's aid, who is faint.

Herminia: Mi hija, que pasa?

Sister Esperanza: Is it just me, or does the air seem fragrant with roses?

Sister Caridad: Dios Mio, the Virgin is crying!!!!

She Points to the statue.

Anna Carolina revives and begins to glow with marvel as she focuses on the weeping statue of Mary. Mary steps out from behind the statue.

Ana Carolina: Mama, she is calling me. She wants me to go to her.

Doña Herminia: Go my child, and listen well, for you are the only one who can see or hear her.

Sister Fe: What does she say Carolina? Why is she weeping?

Sister Esperanza: I swear I smell roses . . . .

Ana Carolina: She says that— *(The crowd freezes)*

Mary *(The statue is replaced by an actress who takes over the light)*:
"I weep over the horrors of the present world. I weep over the lies of the people who themselves forge the weapons of destruction. I weep over the selfish ingratitude of God's children"[17]

Ana Carolina: What have we done Holy Mother?

Mary begins to weave a path among all the frozen pilgrims as she speaks with Ana Carolina.

Mary: Our leaders have gone too far with the Inquisition. Too many people have died unnecessarily, in the name of the church— the Moors, the Jews, the pagans . . . This violence cannot bring peace. And it does not stop.

Ana Carolina: Mother, please tell me what we should do . . .
I am going crazy from the mad killing. I can see these pictures in my nightmares, of these horrible, bloody deaths, of poor innocent brown people!!! I cannot stand to go to sleep, to see any more of this pain and massacre— this must surely be hell!!

Mary: You are seeing the truth and violent ignorance of the Spanish Conquistadores throughout the New World. Your particular visions are of Venezuela where the men are being murdered, tortured, impaled on sticks. Some are being ripped apart by wild dogs; and the rest of the population will die from smallpox. Teresa of Avila has had similar visions. We have been merciless once again in the name of the cross and my precious Father God. This is why I weep.

Ana Carolina: But holy mother, my queen, can you explain why I must see these tortures? I am going to Venezuela, and I never want to see this.
How can we stop this torture Holy Mother, Blessed Queen? What can I do?

Mary: Sweet child of such purity and innocence, come let me hold you close to my bleeding heart. Now listen child ... because your family is moving to America ... because of your innocence, you have been chosen to conceive a child by the seed of an indigenous man from the New World. Your daughter will have my heart, and she will be a queen, and a savior for a new Holy Trinity in the New World. She will be miraculously endowed with the understanding and the powers of Mother Nature, through the Goddess Yara of the Waters, in the deep Amazon jungles of the new world. Remember my words, for your road will be that of an "eccentric" pioneer for peace in the New World where crossbreeding will clearly be considered taboo. But your child will be one of my saints. I promise you. And you must promise me that she will be brought up under the doctrine and morality of the Catholic Church and our Lord Jesus Christ as you have been trained.

Ana Carolina: I promise to do as you say, Mother. Thank you for your blessings. I will honor your wishes and pray the rosary daily. Please stay with me always. *Ana Carolina reaches up and dries Marias tears with her hair.*

Mary: I will come through you, my child. And I have removed your sensitivity to the pain of the Conquista, so that you can cultivate peace with your influence as a citizen of the Spanish Crown. This act is endorsed by my son, as he well knows the torturous pain of his own death and wishes that no one suffers oppression ever... anywhere... in his name.

Ana Carolina: Oh Glory Glory!!!!!

The crowd comes to life: HALLELUJAH!!!!!

Ana Carolina: *Announcing to the crowd as it recovers from a mystical sleep...*
The Holy Mother will now heal all of you in this hour.

Doña Herminia embraces Anna Carolina.

Doña Herminia: In the name of God, Holy child, tell me what happened?

Ana Carolina: I have been healed Mother, and I cannot wait to set foot in the New World. We must leave these people to their privacy with the holy Mother. Let us go.

Doña Herminia: Of course, darling.

Somewhat awestruck, she makes the sign of the cross to the Virgin, thanks the nun, and leaves with Ana Carolina. The Nuns sing a reprise of the last song to the Virgin as others take their prayers on their knees, and line up for the magic spot to be seen by the Virgin.

Scene 3— The Nativity
— The Conception of Yara/Maria

This scene is performed entirely to music as a dramatic ballet between ANA CAROLINA, at the age of 27, and a young Caquetio indigenous warrior named GUARE.[18] Cacique Guare enters with his band of hunters and they come to the river where they do many things— fish, make fire, fashion arrows, eat, and nap. Ana Carolina is proper and mature now, yet still overdressed for a hot day in the Venezuelan jungle, fanning herself vigorously to keep off flies and beads of sweat. She sees the river and decides immediately to disrobe and take a refreshing dip in the cool waters.

Ana Carolina immerses herself in a tranquil river pool and begins to sing out loud sonnets to the Moon Goddess.

> **"Benevolent nourisher; great Nature's key**
> **Belongs to no divinity but thee ...**
> **Thine is the task to unlock the virgin**

**With births you sympathize, though pleased to see the numerous offspring of fertility.
When racked with nature's pangs and distress
Sex invokes thee, as the soul's sure rest ..."**[19]

Cacique Guare wakes up and sees this beautiful, strange, white woman in the river, and assumes it is YARA. She is beautiful, and he is overtaken by her aquatic bliss. Surely this is Yara, Goddess of the Waters. He calls to her and moves closer to a rock, where he sits and further observes her. Ana is startled, yet not naked.

Her song ceases, and he asks her to continue. She gets out of the water, and he begins to sing madly, calling out like a fool on the rock in his native tongue, although this is **Hildegard Bingen**.

> **Guare:** "Hail to you, O greenest, most fertile branch!
> You budded forth amidst breezes and winds
> in search of the knowledge of all that is holy.
> When the time was ripe
> your own branch brought forth blossoms.
> Hail greetings to you!
> The heat of the sun exudes sweat from you like the balsam's perfume.
> In you, the most stunning flower has blossomed
> and gives off its sweet odor to all the herbs and roots,
> which were dry and thirsting before your arrival.
> Now they spring forth in fullest green!
> Because of you, the heavens give dew to the grass,
> the whole Earth rejoices; Abundance of grain comes from
> Earth's womb and on its stalks and branches the bird's nest.
> And, because of you, nourishment is given to the human family and
> great rejoicing to those gathered round.
> And so, in you O gentle Virgin is every fullness of joy".[20]
>
> I want you beautiful woman!!!

Ana Carolina: *(laughing)* I know!!!

He dives into the water and arrives at her side in seconds flat.

Guare: You are like my water Goddess Yara. Do you know her?

Ana: No, I don't believe so ... do you know my Goddess Maria?

Guare: No, but I want to know you.

They dance subtly at first, circling each other like animals. They are so different, but she likes his strength, his innocence, his ardent focus. He is mystified by Ana; he likes to look at her, to smell her, to laugh at her ways, and to marvel at her elaborate clothing, used to frame, conceal, and display all parts of her magnificent porcelain body. He lifts her, and she likes it. He carries her into the water, and an underwater duet begins, where they symbolically release and consummate their love through a sacramental marriage duet, which ends in a not so immaculate conception in the water.

Scene 4 — The Presentation and Purification
— The Half breed Savioress needs a "manger"

Doña Herminia and Don Juan del Prado de la Talavera are sitting at either ends of an elegant European lunch table in their hacienda in Tocuyo, Venezuela. The Negra Hamurapi is serving them. 1591.

Don Juan: I cannot stay long for this meeting. There are problems with the Indians and the new slaves at the Encomienda[21] mission and I must go resolve them.

Doña Herminia: Juan, we must resolve this very major problem with Ana Carolina and her, her . . . .

Don Juan: Her fiancé, Herminia ... Yes, I know. They will be married as soon as I can arrange for his title with the Queen as "Conte de la Coruna."

Herminia: And meanwhile ... their child will be born any minute and we will be the shame of the pueblo .. I can't even imagine what the child will look like.

Juan: She will look like you and me and these pagan savages and there is nothing we can do about it.

Herminia: Please Juan, I don't feel she is safe to have the child here. Everyone is waiting like flies on honey to find out who the father is.

Ana Carolina enters very pregnant, hot and bothered.

Herminia: There you are my child. How are you feeling this afternoon?

Ana Carolina: Oh mother, I feel like I'm carrying the world, and there is absolutely no position in which I find myself comfortable. Have you seen William yet?

Juan: Oh, are we calling him William now? What happened to El Grand Cacique Guare del Tribu Caquetios?

Ana Carolina: This is the name we've decided upon.

Juan: And what will you name your son?

Ana Carolina: Father, it is a girl, as the Virgin told me herself, whom we shall call Maria in her honor.

Herminia: The Virgin spoke to her at the hermitage in Spain and told her that she would carry a Goddess in her womb.

Juan: Maria del Prado de la Talavera de la Reina . . . Well, I guess we can't argue with the Virgin Mary, can we???

Guare enters wearing European clothing in awkward fashion. Ana Carolina runs to greet him.

Guare: I'm sorry I'm late. My tribe has moved deeper into the forest near the healing waters of the Yaracuy River[22]. I have been with our curandero who believes these waters hold a remedy for the smallpox. My mother is sick along with so many others in my tribe.

Ana Carolina: Oh, I am so sorry William, for I do so much want her to meet our baby. I want to go there and meet your mother. Feel her William, she is always dancing; she will be strong like you.

Guare: And beautiful like you, my flower.

Herminia: Please sit down and join us for lunch William.

Juan: So, how are your workers doing in the mines William?

Guare: I'm sorry sir, but I cannot speak the truth.

Juan: You can speak the truth with me Guare.

Guare: Sir, they don't understand how the white man can take their land away from them, and then make them work for you, while you take the profit. They are also discouraged by the plague that has killed so many of us, and they do not like your God.[23]

Juan: That's enough Guare ... Heathens!!! What about progress?
Do these people want to be stuck in the past forever?

Ana Carolina: Must we discuss this now Father??

Herminia: Yes, let's talk about the baby.

Ana Carolina: Yes, our precious, special child ... I cannot wait to hold her.

Herminia: Ana, your father and I feel that it would be safer for you to have the child outside the village. *Silence strikes the table.*

Ana Carolina: But why Mother?

Herminia: Because you are not married, and this is not good for the family or the child.

Ana Carolina: But mother, our marriage status will not dictate the birth of this baby. How much longer can we keep our love a secret?

Guare: Excuse me Ana ... *(addressing Juan)* I want very much to
marry your daughter Sir. But I have also been warned about bringing a child with clear eyes into my tribe.[24] (fn salazar pg55) They believe it is bad luck, and they have already moved farther into the jungle near the Yaracuy River, to escape your people. I am in a difficult position, but I want to do what is right for the child.

Juan: And how do you think our people will feel about it? You cannot marry my daughter unless you become a Catholic and that's final.

Ana Carolina: He is the father of my child and that's enough marriage for me. I love him.

Herminia: Ana, think what you are saying! We are civilized remember.

Guare: I can take Ana to a special place in Yaracuy, in the jungle, high on a mountain above my people, where she will be surrounded by nature. There is a small shrine to Yara there where she will be comfortable. *(footnote found on page 31)*

Negra Hamurapi: Señora, I will go with Ana. I am a midwife, and I can care for her and the child there. I have heard of this sacred place.

Juan: I believe this is an excellent solution.

Ana Carolina: Oh Negra, do you think the Holy Mother will watch over us?

Negra Hamurapi: She is with you all the time, as I will be. Do not worry.

Herminia: Oh, what a relief! This surely makes me feel better.

Juan: Then it is settled. William, I will arrange your patronage to the crown at once, and then after the marriage you can bring the child back to Tocuyo, provided of course, that you convert to the Catholic church.

Guare: I am doing what I can to adapt to your culture. Give me time . . . I will take the women to see my mother at daybreak, and then on to the sanctuary. Our child will be born in paradise near holy river waters. This will please the Goddess Yara, and maybe she will bring the rain so that my flower won't be so hot and uncomfortable.

Juan: Ask Yara if she wouldn't mind raining on the crops as well. The farmers are going out of business with this drought.[25] *(He rises from the table to leave)* So now that the baby problem is 'somewhat' settled I must go to the Encomienda and resolve more problems. Please excuse me.

He kisses Anna Carolina, shakes Guares hand, and leaves; Guare and Anna leave.

Negra Hamurapi: Then I shall prepare Lady Ana for the trip Señora?

Herminia: Thank you Hamurapi . . . what would we do without you?

Negra Hamurapi: Señora, this baby has already been blessed by the spirit.

Herminia: You must promise me that the child will be trained in the full Catechism of the church, as Ana was. This is very important to us.

Negra Hamurapi: I understand Señora, and as I have raised Ana, I will raise your granddaughter under the grace of the Holy Mother, and her son, our Lord Jesus Christ.[26]

    Herminia: Amen que se sea.

*In Nirgua, Yaracuy in the 17th century (1653) a parish was founded with the name of "Nuestra Señora Maria de la Onza de Prado de Talavera de Nivar" on the site of an ancient indigenous sanctuary.

http://www.nodo50.ix.org/SODEPAZ/21art8.htm— ARTICULO 8 CUADERNOS N 21 (in Spanish)

The Virgin of Coromoto

Scene 5 — Finding the blessed child in the "Temple"
— The Virgin of Coromoto Guanare, Venezuela.
in the Ravine near the Tu cupido river- September 8, 1591

Guare, Ana Carolina, and the Negra Hamurapi are walking in the jungle. They come to the river. Ana Carolina is very pregnant, and they have taken a break to water themselves and the horses.

Guare: This is the holy water place, where my people come to pray and heal.

Ana: Can we bathe in the water? I'm so hot, and the water looks so refreshing.

Negra: How I wish it would rain? Feels like months since we've had a drop.

Guare: And the river is low, but high enough to bathe. I will water the horses. Watch out for snakes.

Negra: Señora Ana, let us say a quick prayer, if you wouldn't mind?

Ana: Of course, mi nodriza *(nursemaid)*.

Anna Carolina and la Negra Hamurapi kneel on the riverbank and pray

> "Soul of Mary, sanctify me.
> Heart of Mary, inflame me.
> Hands of Mary, support me.
> Feet of Mary, direct me.
> Immaculate eyes of Mary, look upon me.
> Lips of Mary, speak for me.
> Sorrows of Mary, strengthen me.
> O Mary, hear me
> In the wound of the Heart of Jesus, hide me.
> Let me never be separated from thee.
> From my enemy defend me.
> At the hour of death, call me.
> And bid me come to thine Immaculate Heart
>
> That thus I may come to the Heart of Jesus
> and there will the saints praise you
> For all eternity." Amen[27]

Anna Carolina disrobes within 10 seconds and descends in o the water.

Ana: Oh, my baby likes this and so do I. Venga mi Negra, Quita su ropa!

Negra: If you insist dear Ana, I won't decline the invitation in this heat.

Ana: Oh, this is like heaven, I never want to leave this river. O mi Negra, I am just too tired to meet his mother now. Can't we just stay here forever?

Negra: Ana my sweet, you carry his people's blood in your belly, and he wants you to know and like them. Can you blame him?

Ana: Of course not, I love William with all my heart. I hope his mother likes me.

Negra: Ana, your people have killed off most of his people, in one way or another. He is trying to make peace between enemies, and the world sits on his shoulders.

Ana: Well, I've got the world in my womb, and I hope I can get back up on that horse again.

Negra: Señora, I promise to make you comfortable in the mountain shrine.

Ana: Negra, I have never told you of the vision of the Virgin I had in Spain when I was a young girl telling me this would all happen with William. She told me that this would all happen, and that our baby would be a pioneer queen for peace in Venezuela. Santa Maria is with me all the time, and she will come to the shrine on the mountain to bless the child there.

Negra: Yes, I too believe that baby Maria will be a beautiful child with supernatural powers; and I promise you that I will care for her as if she were my own.

Ana: *(sadly)* You promise to hold her close to you a lot, and to sing to her, the way you sang to me, and to teach her the rosary . . . . you know? . . . .

Negra: Ana, I know what to do.

Ana: I know you know what to do, and I love you Negra . . . you always fix everything. God Bless You. Now, can you stop me from weeping?

Hamurapi splashes her face with water and makes her laugh.

Ana: Hamurapi, do you smell roses?

Guare returns from watering the horses and hears a divine female voice singing Ave Maria. He looks deeper into the ravine and sees a blaze of golden burning light rise up, inside which floats the Virgin Mary (As the Virgin of Coromoto) seated on her throne with Jesus on her lap holding a blue ball with a golden cross on it. She is singing and waving the three colored (blue, yellow, red) flag of Venezuela. Guare is spell bound. And the Virgin Mary speaks to him.

Virgin of Coromoto: You must collect your people and leave the forest. Go to the white men in order to be blessed and receive the water on the forehead so as to be able to enter heaven.[28]

She says this to him in his native language. This infuriates Guare. He cannot help but reject her commands.

Guare: Why must you touch every part of our lives? Why can we not worship our own God? Please let me keep what is my own true spirit!!!!!

This shouting causes YARA to arrive as turbulence in the river, bringing on thunder and rain. Ana Carolina begins to scream.

Ana Carolina: Oh Santa Madre, help me, my water has broken.

Negra: Come on hija, push! The river water is warm. This is the way my mother taught me in Africa.

Ana: William, help me! *(she prays)* Dios me salve, Reina, Madre de misericordia, vida, dulzura y esperanza mia . . . . Dios me salve

Guare: *(supporting her)* Look my flower, there they are . . . Both my Yara and your Maria have come to bless our baby.

Ana: Oh, dulce Santissima Madre, gracias . . . .. gracias . . . Oh, I feel another contraction!! . . . Deme sus bendeciones por favor en el nombre del

Padre, Hijo, y Espiritu Santo.

Negra: Come on Ana, push!!! I can see the head. Come on mujer!!

Ana: *(screaming)* Ayuda me MADRE!!!!

Negra: *(quoting yet shouting from the Song of Solomon)* "She brought forth like a strong man with desire, and she bore according to the manifestation . . . And acquired with great power!!!"[29]

Ana: *(letting out a final, award-winning scream)* MADRE!!!!!

Virgin of Coromoto: Tranquila mi hija, Estoy aqui contigo! I am here to protect you and bring light to you and your royal baby. Bendeciones . . . I bring to you a sacred daughter, from my purest heart. This child, Maria, will have her own mission as the Queen of the Three Powers (Las Tres Potencias). This will be her Spiritual trinity in Venezuela for the three races— The indigenous Indian, the African immigrated slave, and the European Spanish settlers. The holy Father blesses her with the powers of the Catholic Church and gives her direct contact with the divine. She will heal and be a Queen of the people. She will be the Patron Saint of Venezuela.[30] And this ravine will forever be a source of healing water for all who touch it. She will be remembered in formal recorded history as The Virgin of Coromoto. I baptize her in the name of the Father, the Son, and the Holy Ghost. *(she disappears, and Ana passes out)*

Despite the rain and thunder, this burning image of the Virgin has riveted the attention of Anna and Guare, as they all sit together in bloody river water. Negra Hamurapi presents them with a beautiful baby girl with black hair and green eyes.

Negra: Ana Carolina, your baby Goddess is here.

Guare: Come back to us Ana, our child is here. *(he revives her)*

Ana: Dios mio, where was I? *She sees the child ...* Oh, Santa Maria. . . . she is just beautiful ...look Guare; she looks like you.

Guare: She has beautiful clear eyes like yours, and her spirit is strong ...Yes.

The clouds clear, and with the sun comes a rainbow. Indigenous voices begin to sing a song to Yara, and Guare's mother arrives with her singing tribe and descends the banks of the river to see the new baby with clear eyes.

> **SONG to Yara**
>
> **Cuenta la leyenda que cerca del horizonte**
> **Vive una reina encanta por la noche**
> **Ella es tan bella que ilumina las estrellas**
> **Fuerte es la magia que transmite su presencia**
> **Son espiritus que cuida tu cammino**
> **Llevandote siempre hacia el bien**
> **Si solo crees ella estara contigo**
> **La Diosa de Yara – Ayudales**   **Johans Guevara**

Guare begins to rock the baby to the song to Yara, who is passed to his own mother, back to Ana, and then is reluctantly handed to Hamurapi.

Guare's mother: You must go now Guare. Our people will not accept your woman, for her people have been the cause of all our sorrow. And it will take some time for the child with her clear eyes and light skin to be trusted.

Ana: But this is my child, my baby!!!

Negra: It is better that you go now. I will keep my promise to care for her.

Guare's mother: And I will guide her to Yara's sanctuary on the mountain.

Guare carries the reluctant, weeping Ana away and they leave together to return to Tocuyo. Yara appears from the water.

Yara: Oh, joy of all joys, finally I see the fruits of my own soul incarnated in such pure beauty. Oh, my sweet Princess, how you will solve the mystery.

Hamurapi and Yara sing to Maria on the shores of the river.

END OF ACT I

Cecilia Anne Gruessing, M.A.

The Mysteries of Maria Lionza

ACT II—

THE SORROWFUL MYSTERIES— MURDER OF THE INDIGENOUS SPECIES OR THE SPANISH CONQUISTA

Characters

- **Pope Sixtus IV**— Spanish 16th century pope
- **King Ferdinand**
- **King Isabella**
- **Christopher Columbus**
- **Torquemada**— Christian Monk
- **White Virgin Mary**
- **Bartholeme de las Casas**— Spanish Friar
- **Nectorio Maria**— Spanish Friar
- **Captain Pedro Alonzo**— Spanish Soldier
- **Captain Tapia**— Spanish soldier
- **7 Native Indians**
   Including Chief Tamanaco
   Chief Manaure
- **el Negro Felipe**— Liberator of the slaves
- **6 African Slaves**
- **Virgin Mary**— native indgenous blood
- **The female Indian**—Tivisay— daughter of Tamanaco
- **The male Indian**—Terapaima— son of Tamanaco

Scene 1— The Agony in the Garden
— Holy High Mass— Toledo, Carnival— 1493

A 15th Century Spanish Processional brings Ferdinand, Isabella, Colombus, Torquemada, and the Pope Sixtus IV down the isle of the big basilica. They all kneel in front of the pope while he splashes them with holy water. The congregation is full of members of the court.

O GENITRIX AETERNI— Processional Hymn

**"O bearer of the eternal word, virgin Mary,
what voice, what human tongue can praise you well enough?
You, new star of the sea, window to the lofty heavens,
ladder from earth to heaven, from the lowest to the highest.
You conceived eternity, you gave birth to your parent.
the maker came from what he made,
the creator from the creature."**[31]

**Mary delivers her dialogue as spirit, which only we (the audience/ reader) can see and hear.

Pope: Glory be to the Father and to the Son and to the Holy Ghost. As it was in the beginning, is now, and ever shall be, world without end. Amen.

The Kneeling Three: "Thou shalt sprinkle me, Lord, with hyssop and I shall be cleansed; thou shalt wash me and I shall be made whiter than snow."

Pope: Show us Lord your mercy.

Three: Halleluia!

Pope: And grant us Your salvation.

Three: Halleluia!

Pope: Let us pray. "Hear us Lord, Holy Father, almighty and eternal God; and graciously send your Holy Angel from heaven to watch over, to cherish, to protect, to abide with, and to defend all who dwell in this house. Through Christ our Lord. Amen."[32] *They get off their knees.*

Pope: Ladies and gentlemen, good Catholics, and members of the congregation; we gather here today to celebrate a very important milestone in the history of the Catholic Church on this year 1492. Spain now belongs to the Catholic Church and to no other previous conquerors. And we owe this to the unifying skills of our beloved King Ferdinand and Queen Isabella.
Not only have they reformed the clergy, but they also have united Spain politically through their royal marriage, they have engineered the Reconquista, and they have delivered the Spanish Inquisition all in the name of the Holy Roman Catholic Church. Citizens of Spain, I give you your King and Queen.

Ferdinand: I have just returned from Granada, victorious over the last Moorish bastion in the southeast, marking the end of a nine-year battle which cleanses our land of the Islamic culture for the first time in two hundred years.[33]

Mary's head rolls right off her statue body, and crashes to the floor. The spirit of Mary then appears near the altar, clearly annoyed by the hypocrisy of the situation. An altar boy scrambles to pick it up as the service continues. Mary's dialogue is only heard by the audience.

Mary: Let me tell you it was a blood bath, I was there!

Ferdinand: I am proud to have been part of the diplomacy and military strategy which has achieved this Reconquista. May I present to you your queen, Isabella.

Mary: Get ready for a really big show Ladies and Gentlemen.

Isabella: We are triumphant! We have accomplished our goal. Spain is religiously pure and belongs to the Church and there it will stay in the name of God, the Father, the Son, and the Holy Ghost.

Mary: Pobrecita, she thinks all she has to do is cross herself every five minutes!

Isabella: Our soil is now free from Moors, Jews, gypsies, witches, pagans, and even the Protestants.

Mary: In the name of which God are you free your highness?

Isabella: Remaining "Moriscos" have been given the choice of voluntary exile or conversion to Christianity.[34]

Mary: I don't remember them being offered a choice.

Isabella: We must make room for the many "Conversos" (converted ones) who will be coming into church. And now I would like to introduce you to my most effective prosecutor in this enterprise, Brother Tomas de Torquemada.[35]

Mary: Another misguided, yet opportunist Catholic soul…poor guy.

Torquemada: I have a deeply religious connection to the Catholic church, and I am proud to be working for both the Pope and the Monarchy in this endeavor. I myself descend from a Converso family. I believe that non-Catholics and insincere converts could destroy both our church and country. Over 2000 Jews, Moors, apostates and deviates have already been investigated, punished and converted in the name of our Holy Father.

Mary: Try abducted, burned at the stake, and murdered without trial!

Torquemada: Our tribunal is composed of inquisitors from the finest Franciscan and Dominican orders. The Spanish Inquisition will live on, until every land under Spanish rule prays under our God and accepts Jesus Christ as his savior. Amen

Isabella: Thank you, Brother Tomas. We must also now celebrate our territorial claims in the New World with a few words from the man who is making us rich after placing our Spanish flag in terra firma, a shrewd businessman and brilliant navigator, Admiral Christopher Colombus.

Colombus: America is beautiful!! She is the gold pot at the end of the rainbow! She has been claimed in the name of the Spanish crown, and it is paradise for Spaniards who wish to pioneer for the golden treasure of El Dorado. As far as the natives…

Mary: Wait until you see how he twists this.

Columbus: …..... "they were very friendly. I knew that they were a people who could be more easily freed and converted to our holy faith by love than by force. Our gifts gave them great pleasure and made them so much our friends that it was a marvel to see."[36]

"They will surely become Christians, for they are inclined to the love and service of Your Majesty and of the entire Castilian nation, and they try to help and share with us the things they have in abundance which we need. And they know no religion nor idolatry, except they all believe that the power and the good is in heaven. And they believed very strongly that I came, with these ships and people, from heaven, and with due respect they receive me everywhere, after they lose their fear. And this is not because they are ignorant, rather they are of keen wit, and they are men who sail all those seas, for the good account they give everything is a marvel. Wherever we go, they run from house-to-house shouting, "Come to see the people from heaven". And after they felt secure with us, all of them came, both men and women, for not even the elderly nor the young would stay behind, and all of them would bring something to eat and to drink, which they offered with marvelous love."[37]

Isabella: Ahh Columbus, how Spain treasures your brilliant courage!!

Colombus: Here is a virgin land to behold for all the world. I invite you to join in the splendor. You are welcome to behold all the gold and pearls, strange fruits, exotic herbs we have brought back with us. (*Pause*) Am I the only one who smells roses?

Mary: *(She walks right up to Columbus, even though he can't see her she says:* Yes, a virgin land with innocent people who will now be raped, pillaged, exploited, and murdered, in the name of your God, not mine.

Colombus: Your perfume is divine Isabella . . .

Isabella: *(faning away demurely)* Now Admiral Colombus, we do not want to lose our population entirely to America. After all, España IS the world power now. *(She smiles)* Thank you so much for your contribution to civilization. We'll talk later.

Mary: Congratulations Christopher, you are the inspiration for the Conquistadores bloody imperialism.

Isabella: And now we want to invite the Pope to deliver Eucharist to all the people in the Plaza outside, where we will enjoy the body and blood of Christ in the form of celebratory libations on the day of the "Diablos."[38] Let us count our sins in Carnival celebration!! Let us drink to the blood of Christ . . .

Mary: …. while you drain the blood of all people of color.

Isabella: *(Exiting the church)* …. And to the purity of España!!! VIVA ESPAÑA!!

Mary: Oh, my dear Queen, one day you and I will have to discuss the barbaric consequences of your actions. Forgive me Father for my sarcasm.

Carnival music can be heard from outside, as the church clears. Mary kneels in front of the altar and recites Psalm 42. There is a parade of devil dancers innocently prancing around the altar while Mary prays.

Mary: "Do me justice, O God, and fight my fight against an unholy people, rescue me from the wicked and deceitful human. For Thou, O God, art my strength, why hast Thou forsaken me? And why do I go about in sadness, while the greedy annoy me? Send forth Thy light and thy truth: for they have brought me to Thy holy hill and thy dwelling place." (Psalm 42) Give me the insight and the strength to understand this need for power and territory, and to protect those less powerful. Help me to forgive the sins of these greedy people, and to lead them out of the path of darkness. In your holy name my Father/God, show me the light.

The Devil dancers take over the altar, and Mary leaves. Lights fade.

Scene 2— The Scourging at the Pillar
— The Conquest of Venezuela

The following scene will be portrayed as a ballet, and not a beautiful ballet. In a few minutes the entire Spanish conquest of Venezuela will be danced dramatically as Spanish soldiers and Indigenous warriors' skirmish in bloody battle. Because of their firearms and horses, the Spanish have the clear advantage, although all of this will be abstracted in a dance confrontation of cultures, emotions, and painful machismo. There is much torturous "scourging at the pillar" which begins the actual crucifixion of the Third World man/woman/culture. Over the music, King Ferdinand and Queen Isabella will recite their message to the Arawak Indians as the battle ensues. Mary will float around blessing the wounded.

(This speech was originally delivered by Colombus to the Indigenous and has been adapted for the King and Queen in the first person.)

Ferdinand: "In the name of myself, King Ferdinand and our Queen Isabella of Spain, conquerors of barbarian nations, we notify you as best we can that our Lord God Eternal created Heaven and Earth and a man and woman from whom we all descend for all times and all over the world. In the 5,000 years since creation, the multitude of these generations caused men to divide and establish kingdoms in various parts of the world, among whom God chose the Pope as the leader of all Mankind, which means admirable and greatest Father, governor of all men. Those who lived at that time obeyed the Pope as Lord and superior King of the universe, and so did their descendants obey his successors and so on to the end of time.

ISABELLA: The late Pope gave these islands and mainland of the ocean and the contents here of to us, the King and Queen, as is certified in writing and you may see the documents if you should so desire.
Therefore, we as your Royal Highnesses are your lords and masters of this land and are acknowledged as such when this notice is posted, and we will be served willingly and without resistance. Many of our religious envoys have already been acknowledged and obeyed without delay, and all subjects unconditionally and of their own freewill are becoming Christians and thus will remain. We receive their allegiance with joy and benignity and decreed that natives be treated in this spirit like good and loyal vassals AND YOU ARE UNDER THE OBLIGATION TO DO THE SAME!!

FERDINAND: Therefore, we request that you understand this text, deliberate on its contents within a reasonable time, and recognize the Church and its highest priest, the Pope, as rulers of the Universe, and in their name, We, the King and Queen of Spain, as rulers of this land, allowing the religious fathers to preach our holy Faith to you. You owe compliance as a duty to the Spanish Crown and our officials will receive you with love and charity, respecting your freedom and that of your wives and sons and your rights of possession and we shall not compel you to baptism unless you, informed of the Truth, wish to convert to our holy Catholic Faith as almost all your neighbors have done in other islands, in exchange for which we have bestowed many privileges and exemptions.

ISABEL: Should you fail to comply, or delay maliciously in so doing, we assure you that with the help of God we shall USE FORCE against you, declaring war upon you from all sides and with all possible means, and we shall bind you to the yoke of the Church and of Their Highnesses; we shall enslave your persons, wives and sons, sell you or dispose of you as the King sees fit; we shall seize your possessions and harm you as much as we can as disobedient and resisting vassals. And we declare you guilty of resulting deaths and injuries, exempting the Crown. We hereby request that legal signatures be affixed to this text and pray those present to bear witness for us . . ."[39]

The choreography ends with lifeless Indians signing papers. Mary is visibly overwhelmed and sings a lament.

Scene 3 — The Crown of Thorns— Las Encomienda/Missiones

In a crude monastery in El Tocuyo near Barquisimetro, Venezuela in 1572 there is a statue of Mary standing on one side, and a sculpture of Jesus carrying the cross with his Thorn of Crowns on the other side of the altar.

Bartholome de las Casas[40] and Nectorio Maria[41] are two Friars whose duty it is to civilize the Indians and the African Slaves regarding clothing, behavior, and the ways of the church, feed them, and send them to manual labor everyday with their "Encomendros". Bartholeme is playing a passionate hymn to Mary on a humble organ, while Nectorio Maria arranges the benches for their new conquered students.

Bartholemew sings in romantic bliss, a song to Mary

The Mysteries of Maria Lionza

IN HER PATHS by Francis Thompson

> "And she has trod before me in these ways!
> I think that she has left here heavenlier days.
> And do I guess her passage, as the
> skies of Holy Paradise turn deeply holier,
> And, looking up with sudden new delight,
> One knows a seraph-wing has passed in flight
> The air is purer for her breathing,
> Sure!
> And all the fields do wear the beauty fallen from her;
> The winds do brush me with her robe's allure,
>
> Tis, she has taught the heavens to look sweet,
> and they do but repeat
> The heaven, heaven, heaven of her face!
>
> The clouds have studies going from her grace!
> Essence of old, essential pure as she
> For this is that Lady, and none other
> the man in me calls "Love"
> — the child calls "mother."[42]
> (IN HER PATHS by Francis Thompson

At a very passionate point in the music, the monastery door flings open, just violently enough to disturb the revelry Bartholemew has evoked in the sanctuary. A "Capitan Pedro Alonzo"[43] escorts a string of seven natives into the room. Their hands are tied, they are barely dressed, smeared with warpaint, they are angry, and they are told to sit.

Capitan Alonzo: *(shouting)* Sientense!!! you savage!!! Do you even know what a chair is?!!

They are mad, but they sit. One in particular (Cacique Tamanaco), is very rebellious.

Nectorio: That's quite all right Captain, we'll take it from here.

Capitan Alonzo: No, I don't trust this one. *(He indicates Tamanaco)*

Bartholeme: I have an idea, let's start with the uniform. *(He passes out Monks robes which they put on)* OK one for everybody. Nectorio, will you please hand out the crosses? Thank you . . . OK, now let's teach them how to do "The Sign of the Cross." *(He holds up the cross against his chest, and encourages them to imitate)* OK, follow me guys: The Father, The Son, and The Holy Ghost. Amen. Shall we do that again? *(It is repeated until they all get it)*

Nectorio: Very good, gentlemen.

Captain Alonzo: What seems to be this one's problem? *He indicates Tamanaco who is not participating, so the captain must force a robe on him, and stuffs the cross into his hands. Tamanaco is furious.*

Tamanaco: First you rape my land, then you kill my brothers with your firearms, next you take our women prisoner, and now you want me to pray to your God. What kind of God is this? You are crazy!! *(He spits)* I will kill you too!!

Captain Alonzo: I should dismember you right here— right now.

Bartolome: Please Captain Alonzo, we are in God's house.

Captain Alonzo: Tamanaco's the big chief.... the big strong, hold out tough guy, Cacique Tamanaco. *(He addresses Tamanaco)* I remember when you charged our men with conch horns.[44] *(Imagining himself there lustfully)* Then we responded, and your men were confused. *(addresses the others)* But then Tamanaco, gathering new inspiration from his men's unexpected disorder, provided gallant resolve and, with macana (machete) in hand, maintained the combat against that large number solely through his vindictiveness . . . So! That was then . . . How strong are you now Tamanaco? Let's you and I step outside for a while OK Chief?

Captain Alonzo and Tamanaco leave, and a string of African Slaves enters, all tied up. El Negro Felipe is among this group.[45]

The Africans are then lined up by Spanish Captain Tapia[46]. *They pass out robes and crosses.*

The Indians are looking at the Africans, and the Africans are completely overwhelmed. Bartholeme begins the introduction to a marching Hymn. Nectorio tries to lead the singing.

> **Onward Christian soldiers,**
> **Marching off to war . . .**
> **With the cross of Jesus,**
> **Going on before . . .**
>
> **Christ the Royal Master**
> **Leads against the foe**
> **Marching into battle,**
> **see those banners flow.**

The entire scenario becomes a farce, as the Natives and the Africans become more and more stunned by the experience. The effects are comical, yet tragic. Especially when Captain Alonzo returns with a beaten up Tamanaco.

Nectorio: I think that's enough exercise. Let's teach them the table manners.

Tables are pulled up, napkins and spoons are presented, and a fabulous soup which everybody likes. While they are on the soup line, they check each other out, and fumble with tables, chairs, spoons, and napkins. The Negro Felipe is kind and teaches some of the Natives how to use the spoon.

Negro Felipe: If I can teach Guaicaipuro how to drink from a glass, I can teach you how to sip soup!! *(they all sit down)*

Native Manaure: Do you know about Guaicaipuro?

Negro: *(pausing)* I guess the drum didn't get this far.

Bartholeme: Now we are all going to recite the Ave Maria . . . All together now, repeat after me, line by line.

The captain and the monk are now both on behavior modification detail, to force and teach them everything, including not to eat before they pray.

The Ave Maria - in Spanish

> **Dios te salve, Maria**
> **Llena eres de gracia**
> **El Señor es contigo**
> **y bendita Tu eres**
> **Entre todas las mujeres**
> **y bendito es el fruto**
> **de tu vientre, Jesus**
> **Santa maria, madre de Dios**
> **ruega por nosotros, los pecadores**
> **ahora y en la hora de nuestra muerte.**
> **Gracias Madres, por nuestra pan de cada dia....**
> **En el nombre de Dios Poderoso, el Hijo,**
> **y el Espiritu Santo.   Amen**

Manaure: Negro ... tell me what happened to Guacaipuro ...

Negro Felipe: I'll tell you later amigo.

Manaure: I must hear now, please .... Guacaipuro was like a brother to me.

Captain Tapia— He's finally dead!! That's what!! El Grand Cacique Guaicaipuro is dead!! I was there when we ambushed him, I heard his final words. We finally had him outnumbered and surrounded.

Manaure: Hey, Guaicaipuro was the greatest warrior in our land. He organized up to 2000 warriors under his command at a time. He was invincible!!!!

Negro Felipe: Listen hombre, I heard that Guaicaipuro fought to the end. I heard that he pulled out a sword he had taken over from Juan Rodriguez, and with 22 men, he held off the entrance to his village. The whole tribe flanked to his aid, wielding their macanas *(macetes)*. Most of them perished, and there was much lamenting and confusion until the soldiers, weary of the barbarian's defense, threw a firebomb into his house. As it began to spread, Guaicaipuro came to the door of his burning village and screamed:

GUAICAIPURO appears

Guaicaipuro: "Ay Spanish cowards! Because you lack courage to force me to surrender, you use fire to defeat me. I am the one you seek, Guaicaipuro, who never feared your haughty race. Since I am now in this position, though, kill me, and through my death be free of the terror I inspire in you."[47]

There is silence

Negro Felipe: And there he died by the sword of the Spanish invaders on his own land along with his last 22 warriors.

Captain Tapia: Are you trying to start trouble too?

Negro Felipe: My name is El Negro Felipe, and I am the son of the famous Liberator of the Slaves, El Negro Miguel, and I am working, as he did, for the absolute emancipation and freedom for people like us from people like you. And if you hang around long enough, I'll teach you some great songs about that. *(He smiles)* You have a tambor? I can make all these guys happy before they have to go off to your mine tomorrow, to sweat and haul rocks that make you rich.

Captain Alonzo: Ok ok… enough, Tapia. Take this idiot outside . . .

Bartolome: In the name of God Captain, we'll take over now.

Nectorio: We have some drums you can use left over from our last Encomienda.

Nectorio pulls out 2 primitive drums made out of logs, and a percussive piece of bamboo, called a "tiki-tiki", as is common in Barlovento with the Africans— El Negro and his boys get right on it. They organize the vocal and instrumental parts of an Afro-Venezuelan tambor song.

__Juan del Prado de la Talavera__ (the Encomendero of the Mission) and his daughter __Ana Carolina__ enter. Ana seems distant and somewhat lost, as she has given up her child to be raised in the new world. The friars go to greet Sr. Prado humbly, for their existence depends on him.

Bartholeme: How are you Señor Juan Encomendro del Prado de la Talavera? We were not expecting you until tomorrow.

Juan: Just checking on the new crew. How are things going here Nectorio? Everybody getting along?

Nectorio: As well as can be expected on the first day Sir.

Bartholeme: We have a gentleman here by the name of Negro Felipe who is about to entertain us with some music. *(He smiles)*

Ana Carolina: Oh Papa, we are just in time!!

Her mood has shifted when she sees the drums.

Juan: We cannot stay, my darling— tomorrow is a workday. Which is why I came . . . Nectorio, how many of them will be ready to work tomorrow?

Nectorio: All but one sir.

Captain Alonzo: Not to worry about this savage Chief Tamanaco. He will be at the mine by dawn with everybody else.

Bartholeme: *(quickly changing the subject)* Are we ready for the music?

El Negro: Listo y allegre.... Vamos! *The drumming begins.*

    LA NEGRA TOMASA (Traditional African/Venezuelan tambor)

> **Estoy tan enamorado de la Negra Tomasa**
> **que cuando se va de casa— que triste me pongo**
> (I am so in love with the Negra Tomasa, that when she leaves
> the house, it makes me so sad)
> **Lo mas' que me gusta la café, que ella me prepara**
> **Lo mas' que me gusta la comida, que ella cocina"**
> (I like the coffee she makes me— I like the food she cooks for me.)[48]

During this display, both the Natives and the Africans begin to dance. Even Ana Carolina gets carried away by the repetition and the heat. She is almost ecstatic, when suddenly....

Ana Carolina: Papa look!!!!! *She points to the statue of Mary, weeping blood. The music stops. Everybody becomes frozen and speechless, staring at Mary.*

Bartholeme: Holy Mother, Queen of Heaven, what is happening?

The Natives begin to sniff and describe the smell of sweet fragrant roses. Only Ana can understand the words of the Virgin now. Ana Carolina slowly tries to speak as she fixates on the Virgin's face and repeats the Virgin's words verbatim.

Ana: She weeps blood for the pain caused by the ball and chain (*Thorn of Crowns*) which sabotages and takes away the power and the strength of the Third World Man.

Nectorio: *On his knees crossing himself, he is clearly moved by the events, ignoring what Ana says.*
> **"O kindly mother of the redeemer,**
> **you who are still the open gate of**
> **heaven and the star of the sea;**
> **aid this fallen people which strives to rise;**
> **You who gave birth to your holy father,**
> **while Nature looked on in wonder."**
> *Advent antiphon Alma Redemptoris mater"*[49]

Mary: *(Heard only by Ana Carolina) Here* my child, the Universe brings you to see with your own eyes the beauty of these indigenous people, and how much they need a Queen to protect and unite them. Your daughter, Maria, will someday be this, Queen.

Ana Carolina: Oh, tell me mi Reina, how is my precious baby Maria? How I long for her.

Mary: Maria is under great care and love of her native Grandmother and La Negra Hamurapi.

Ana: It has been 15 years, Madre, I miss her so much.

Mary: You have made a humanitarian sacrifice for a larger cause dear Ana. With my power, Maria will triumph with the compassion of a holy mother, over the tyranny of these controlling Imperialists.

Ana: But she is lost in the jungle... so far away from me. *She breaks down.*

Mary: Weep not. She is surrounded by the love of nature and will come to represent the Holy trinity of the three races. Do not cry. You make me cry. I know your pain. I lost my son, but he still exists in spirit, as I do… and he gave his life for humanity.

Ana: I want so much to see her. But she will not leave her sanctuary.

Mary: Maria is beautiful and is becoming a beautiful young woman. Pray for her…

Ana: Yes, I remember when you told me I would carry a saint… when we were in Spain. And yet, I have been so confused about her welfare.

Mary: She is destined for God's work.

Ana: I am so sorry that I made you cry Santa Madre.

Mary: My heart bleeds for so many my child. I am glad you understand. All mothers make sacrifices for their children. So now… I have a job to do. Please tell these poor abused souls that I love them, and bless them all, and that I feel their suffering. I will bless them and take away their pain one by one. Please continue to pray the rosary every day and be strong.

Ana Carolina: Yes, mi Reina, I promise to be strong. *Ana wipes her tears and turns to address the slaves.*

The Holy Queen Mother told me to tell all of you that she loves you, and blesses you, and feels all of your suffering— And that the meek shall inherit the Earth. She will see you now.

Mary: Well, done my dear.

Ana Carolina: Thank you, Holy Mother. Now would it be possible for the others to be healed? They are in such pain.

Mary: Yes of course, ask Brother Bartholeme to play my song. Let's see if they accept my blessing.

Ana whispers to Bartholeme, who starts to play his mandolin, and a magical blaze of light appears in front of the statue of the Virgin. Everyone is spellbound as Mary's voice fills the air along with the smell of roses.

    MARY SONG— DE INNOCENTIBUS— **To the Innocents**

> **"Our King is eagerly ready**
> **to welcome the blood-witness of the Innocents.**
> **Angels gather in chorus singing highest praise**
> **yet the clouds cry out in pain over the Innocents' blood.**
> **Glory be to the Father, the Son and Holy Spirit.**
> **And the clouds cry out in pain over the Innocent's blood."**
>
> **Hildegard of Bingen**

Scene 4 — Carrying the Cross
— Tamanaco's Gladiator Death

Capitan Pedro Alonzo struts onto a dark barren stage holding a torch.

Pedro Alonzo: In the name of the Crown of Spain and the Holy Roman Catholic Church, I sentence you, Cacique Tamanaco to death, for innumerable crimes committed against her Majesty's people. We have planned a rather special execution to offer a, shall we say— diversion for your people, by testing the level of your courage. Inside a caged amphitheater you will fight in single combat, a war dog of singular bravery named Amigo. If you can defeat this beast, then you will be offered liberty and your life.

Tamanaco: I accept!

He stands in the circle waiting for the dog to be released on him, praying that his strong arm will bring a quick triumph. Seeing the animal come out to attack him, Tamanaco screams in Mariche language.

Tamanaco: "Today you will die at my hands, and Spaniards will learn that there is no danger in the world that can make a coward of Tamanaco."[50]

The dog, Amigo, turned on him with extreme ferocity, pawing at his chest, threw him to the ground within moments. There, the bloodstained dog rips Tamanaco's head from his body, using his claws. Mary walks on stage and kneels down near the bloody body of Tamanaco.

Mary: News of this gory spectacle, which caused horror even among those who had conceived it, spread quickly among the tribes. In order to avoid a similar fate, Natives pledged obedience to Pedro Alonso and the Crown. And, the rebellion of the Mariches, the most obstinate tribe of the great Cacique of Venezuela— Tamanaco, was thus suppressed. Here lies a beautiful man, who wanted only to protect his people and to live in peace on the Earth the creator gave him. May his brave soul rest in peace.

Scene 5— The Crucifixion
— The Transformation—

Mary remains in her pool of blood holding what's left of Tamanaco's body together. She wraps his body in her robe and sings AVE MARIA again. Tamanaco's two children, La India Tivisay, and his son, Terapaima, carry him to the water where the water goddess Yara waits for him, and takes him back into her arms.

Yara: "My altars are the mountains and the ocean, Earth, air, stars, all that springs from the great Whole, who hath produced, and will receive the soul." George Byron[51]

There is music and a sudden flight of butterflies over the water (Maria Lionza personally told me that whenever I see a butterfly, to know that she is visiting me.) This fluttering sound is followed by the beat of a hoofed, galloping animal, mixed with the sounds of forest animals. Slowly we hear the vocal strains of Ave Maria, this time sung by Maria Lionza (age 16) who enters naked and singing at the top of her lungs, astride her tapir (see photo), holding the bone of a female pelvis high above her head.

Maria de la Onza: I am Maria de la Onza, Maria de Leonza, Maria Lionza . . . I come to deliver and bless this beautiful soul, el gran Cacique Tamanaco. His courageous sacrifice made in the name of saving his people, has not been in vain. I am the incarnation of the Virgin Maria and Yara, Pre- Colombian Goddess of the Waters. Ponce de Leon chose to name me Maria de la Onza del Prado de la Talavera de la Reina de la Coruna, after my royal Spanish blood. I ride on the back of an onza, and from that I get my true name. Sometimes they think I am the Virgin of Coromoto. My mother was a Spanish immigrant, and my father was a native Caquetio who became Count William Guare de la Coruna and suffered much pain trying to live between both the worlds of the white man and his native people. I cannot split myself like that, so I have chosen my place in nature, on the mountain of Sortes in Chivicoa, Yaracuy. My mission is to unite the races by living harmoniously, to bring love and peace into the world, and to forbid all types of murder of animals, plants, or humans on my land.

I am the champion of the poor and the sick, and the disenfranchised. My mission is to enable people to fulfill their positive destinies, no matter how little they possess in this world—To correct disease through the forces and remedial plants of nature— and to accelerate the evolution of devoted souls towards enlightenment. I believe in God the Father, the Son and the Holy Ghost and they are my direct link to the divine along with all of the nature spirits of Mother Earth's sacred paradise. I have chosen to live my life as a hermit, deep within the jungle where I am protected by the Earth's creatures. I offer refuge to all pilgrims of any faith in my natural sanctuary, where they can come to be healed, or to be safe from the attack of malevolent forces.

I am, and always will be a Virgin, in a land where strong native men and women were raped, conquered and plagued by the white man's disease, along with African slaves who were also exploited. My people are in a state of modernity shock. They carry the blood of three races in a world that is still dominated by white Western culture. I now work with the great Chief Guaicaipuro and the Negro Felipe in an effort to make right these wrongs.

She continues: It is not Catholicism and the Church that the frustrated male and the disenfranchised, virgin female[52] are calling out to - It is me, their Queen Maria Lionza . . . I will relieve their pain. Come to my mountain and you will witness miracles never touched by the western world.

END ACT II

INTRODUCTION – ACT III
THE MYSTERIES OF MARIA LIONZA

Act III will take you through the Glorious Mysteries of the rosary to Maria Lionza's present day practice on the Mountain of Sortes, six hours east of Caracas in Chivicoa, Venezuela. Every Friday night pilgrims from all parts of Venezuela pile into buses and make the long weekend journey to this mountain to redeem their souls, find cures, determine criminals, get romantic advice, have healthy babies, have businesses blessed, and much more. Maria Lionza is the key to all of this in Venezuela, and after making the sign of the traditional Catholic cross, one must pray to her for tangible results.

In Act I, I established that Maria del Prado de la Talavera de la Reina was an actual living person (with a Spanish mother and Venezuelan Indian father) whose destiny brought her as a child to the feet of the Virgin Mary in apparition.

I now believe that some of the Virgins are really 'Mary' in all her different characters. Others were actual living holy women (like Maria Lionza), whose missions were to serve humanity in the flesh and spirit through the archetypal role model of the Virgin Mary. Some were beatified, and others remained, like the Black Madonnas, as part of the subaltern religion and mythology. The validity of thousands of apparitions of the Virgin Mary, in all her manifestations has not been confirmed by the Catholic church. This Maria is very real and truly accessible through the practice of "spiritism."

Maria Lionza is unique in that the church does not accept her revolutionary racial Trinity of the Three Powers (with the Negro Felipe and the Indian Chief Guacaipuro). This was born of the Native and African population after the Spanish Conquista and colonization in the 1500s. Despite the continued use of Catholic prayers and beliefs, the Cult of Maria Lionza is still ignored by the Catholic Venezuelan Church. However, you will see how her devotees still go to Mass as part of the practice.

The shamanic practices, prayers, and rituals included in this dramatic text are revealed exactly as I witnessed them over a period of three years while living in Venezuela and practicing with these priests and priestesses of Maria Lionza. The characters, Marion and Manuel, are two real mediums who taught me much of what I know and introduced me to a huge pantheon of spirits. Many of the scenes depicting spirit are true to my experience, including the scenes with Simon Bolivar, Tamanaco, and Dr. Jose Gregorio. (In fact, the late Hugo Chavez, who was commander of the Fuerzas Armadas, and a devotee of Maria Lionza's cult, became Venezuela's President as a result of a revolution I witnessed in 1992.)

Maria Lionza embodies the same qualities of love and compassion as the Virgin Mary and provides one more important blessing. One can actually talk to her and many of her holy helpers to get spiritual, medical, financial, or romantic support and counsel in times of crisis. She descends rarely, and usually in only the bodies of mediums of high light.

And although I am not a medium. there is no doubt that she is using me to speak as I write this manuscript, for it has poured out of me. I am honored that she actually crowned me in 1992 and christened me as her God child in a special ceremony before I left the country. I hope that my eyewitness experience is properly conveyed to you through the magic of this musical-drama format.

Most of the songs and the prophet's poetry I have transcribed and translated from a cassette tape that I bought at a Perfumeria in Chivicoa. In the archaeo-mythologist, Maria Gimbutas's research tradition, I've assimilated so much about Maria Lionza's connection to Yara, the pre- Colombian water goddess mermaid. From the poetry and songs on this tape, one can understand her beloved protection over nature's flora and fauna, and most of all the passionate devotion she inspires in thousands of her followers. The street paperbacks of prayers and oraciones have also been handy, including a plethora of spell books in the witchcraft tradition ("brujeria"), with recipes for special banos (baths), despojos (aura cleaner/ exorcizers), trabajos (magical artworks), and candle art.

I am grateful for the opportunity to be able to share this experience in the context of my studies with Charlene Spretnak and her investigation of "Mary, Queen of the West". I hope that the anthropological aspects of my research have been suitably presented in this artistic form to enhance the mystical and spiritual profoundness of my experience. Although this property would be better rendered on film, I can still imagine how I would mount it on stage. Depending on the feedback I get from producers to whom I plan to submit this play, I can imagine mounting it as a bi-lingual production for Latin American audiences to celebrate its rich existing cultural magic. My dream, of course, has always been to mount my work on Broadway. Always lighting candles…...

I hope you enjoy the work,

Cecilia Diaz Gruessing
12/1/99   San Francisco

The Mysteries of Maria Lionza

ACT III—

THE GLORIOUS MYSTERIES

Characters

- **Maria Lionza**— herself— half white/half native, long black hair, beautiful green eyes
- **Negro Felipe**— African man, dressed as a soldier, with stutter
- **Guaicaipuro**— Indian Chief— 40s
- **10 humble street people**— Catia barrio, Caracas
- **Poet/Prophet**— 50-year-old man
- **Marion**— 38-year-old indian woman, nurse, bruja, medium
- **Sophia**— 20-year-old daughter of Marion— also medium
- **Luis**— 22-year-old boyfriend of Sophia, drummer
- **Luz**— 8-year-old daughter of Sophia, granddaughter of Marion
- **Rafael**— 28-year-old boyfriend of Marion, drummer, medium

Clients:

- **Cero**— Afro-Latino man— 50s
- **Martin**— Cero's 20-year-old, alcoholic son, Afro-Latino
- **Hugo Chavez**— Military commander turned revolutionary— 35 ish
- **Cecilia**— gringa tourist 34— American blond
- **Rosita**— young pregnant Afro-Caribbean lady— 23
- **Veruska**— 25-year-old white beauty— Miss Venezuela
- **6 other clients:** Prophet, 2 drummers, musician, 2 women
- **Manuel**— thin white man, medium— 30
- **Ana Gonzalez**— 40-year-old woman patient
- **Jazmin** (played by Cecilia)— assistant of Maria Lionza
- **Yarita** (played by Veruska) - assistant of Maria Lionza

Cecilia Anne Gruessing, M.A.

Scene l— The Resurrection— Semana Santa & Easter Sunday — Catia, Caracas, Venezuela, April 1995

Scene 1— Calle del Barrio (Ghetto street)

The lights come up on the teeming market life of a Caracas urban street barrio, Catia, on Easter Sunday. The opening choreography presents a hybrid population, mixed with the Native Venezuelan Indigenous people, the African slave descendants, some Trinidadian (East Indian) influence, and the Criolle Caucasian Spanish. A backdrop-screen portrays a "perfumeria" with hanging herbs, religious regalia, and a sign saying "Perfumeria Las Tres Potencias" with the image of El Negro Felipe, the Holy Queen Maria Lionza, and El Cacique Guaicaipuro suspended over a Venezuelan flag. Standing in front of the store is a life size statue of Maria Lionza astride her danta. The store is flanked by a food market on one side, and a fabric store on the other. Above the Perfumeria, is a second-floor balcony one can reach by a downstairs doorway saying "Consultos Espirituales." It is ll am in the morning and the streets are lined with merchants selling everything from "hallacas" (Venezuelan holiday tamales) to last minute Easter regalia. Churchgoers are wearing their purple cotton robes over their ghetto best. The sound of salsa mixed with the street noise has provided the music for this stylized opening number. The mood switches with the distant sound of a slow, brass church band.

An eccentric street poet/prophet sits next to the statue of Maria preaching and singing to the church band back-up, with great urgency and drama:

Poet/prophet:

"The city is lost . . . .
And the anguished people run wild on the highways and the streets,
Desperately ... not knowing which way they are supposed to go ...
The crops don't matter,
the human being driving at your side doesn't matter
What's important is speed, and that there is triumph.
The pedestrian is no longer important

timidly waiting for a light that never will change
The accident of a possible friend doesn't matter-
-- Nor the hand of a beggar,
Nor the ball of a little boy,
Nor the smile of the flower girl,
Nor, well ...... nor love.

A big car passes ......

a small car passes the statue on the wide highway

Where she is seated on a danta,

nude to the sun, strong, firm and erect,

Mounted over the city, like a symbol of love,

She is nailed into the earth of her ancestors,

the real owners of this land...

those who were dispossessed of their homes, of their truth, of their culture ...

Maria Lionza is there—
in the middle of this terrible culture where love and the truth don't mean anything
Maybe that's why she is there, rising up
from the virgin earth with a woman's pelvis in her hand ...
Indian Goddess, like a wakeup call,
to remind us of our actual birth and ancestry."

(transcribed and translated from cassette tape)

A procession of Catholic church officers and purple clad congregation members slowly parades down the street, carrying three separate images of Jesus Christ and his Holy Mother: The first is Jesus wearing the crown of thorns, and his purple cloak, carrying the cross with Mary following; the second, is Jesus on the Cross with Mary at his feet; the third is Mary holding the dying Jesus in her lap (like the Pieta). The brass and percussion band is out of tune, playing a slow dirge to which people march in solemn procession en route to the Cathedral in the plaza, where Easter Mass will take place.

Scene 2— Inside the Centro de Las Tres Potencias
— (The Center of the Three Powers)

As soon as the parade passes, the street begins to change shape, the balcony over the Perfumeria empties, the backdrop lifts, and we go inside to Marion's mysterious sanctuary of magic, dominated by her multi-dimensional altar of spirits and animas where she will receive clients for spiritual consultations during this highest holy day of the year, Easter and the resurrection.

Marion's Altar

Marion's indoor/outdoor city apartment serves as her spiritual center (centro), her home, and as a menagerie for her pet birds, snakes, chickens, and dogs. She is a registered nurse and grandmother in her early fifties with her daughter Sophia, son-in-law Luis, granddaughter Luz, and young drummer lover, Rafael. She puts on some music as they transform from church attire to their "spiritual work clothes." They quickly wash down the altar and the busts. All three of these young people have been trained as mediums and bancos (assistants) and know the routine. Marion counts her cash from the altar, consults her list, and gets ready to send her team out on errands to buy altar paraphernalia and food.

> **Marion:** Pues....... Gracias a Dios that we went to the early Mass; we are expecting so many clients today, I'm a little backed up. SO, I've got the cash. We need: flores amarillos, incensio, candles, frutas, arroz, yucca (yam)/, and liquores— and fast because when this Mass lets out, we are going to have a line around the block with this full moon— Madre Gracias!

Marion looks up at the altar, crosses herself. Handing out cash as she designates buyers, she informs the group . . .

> **Marion:** Luz stays with me so we can clean up both physically and spiritually— the oldest and the youngest, right mi muchachita?
> *Little seven-year-old Luz jumps into her arms with enthusiasm.*
>
> **Rafael—** Marion, what kind of liquor?
>
> **Marion:** Let's see ...... Rum for Negro Felipe, Cocuy for our people, Anise for the Malandros, Aquardiente for the corte Africano . . ..
> what else?
>
> **Sophia:** Red wine of course for la Reina!
>
> **Marion:** Of course! How could I forget? And we need Holy water too, Ok? Please hurry...You can get most of it downstairs.

They all leave except little Luz, who begins to sweep, and clean the area while Marion washes down the altar and statues with a special concoction of ammonia, water, lemon, flowers, and special essencias. She talks to the statues as she tenderly washes them. She knows that the Negro Felipe does not like water, so he must be carefully dusted. She prays and conjures a cigar. Christ on the cross hangs high over the altar, with the next highest level being devoted to Maria, Felipe, and Guaicaipuro. The altar is eclectic and international including, Catholic Saints, Indians, Africans, Asians, leaders, doctors, and religious deities, known and unknown from all corners of the Earth. Marion crosses herself with a cigar.

> **Marion:** En el nombre de Dios Poderoso, el hijo, y el espiritu santo, yo pido permiso a mi Santa Reina Maria Lionza, el Libertador, el Negro Felipe, y el Gran C acique Indijeno Guaicaipuro, para conjurar este puro (tabaco), con intenciones de trabajar hoy, dia, sagrada de la Semana Santa— Pedir permiso de todos los Santos, espiritus, y animas que viven cercita, para darnos proteccion, amor, paz, evolucion, sabiduria, abundancia, y salud en nuestra viaje de la vida. Gracias, Amen.
>
> (In the name of God the Father, the Son, and the Holy Ghost, I Marion de la Luz, ask permission to my Holy Queen Maria Lionza, to the great liberator of the slaves, El Negro Felipe, and to the mighty Indian chief Guaicaipuro, to conjur this cigar, with intentions of working here today, this sacred day of Holy Week. I ask permission of all the Saints, spirits, and animals that live near, to give us protection, love, peace, evolution, knowledge, abundance, and health in our journey through life. Gracias and Amen)

After making the sign of the cross again, Marion lights the cigar and puffs smoke towards the four cardinal directions, observing the direction of the smoke and the designs of the cigar ashes. This is how Marion will determine if the spirits give her permission to work. She puffs away at the cigar as she begins to recite a special prayer to Maria Lionza, snapping her fingers throughout the oracion in the sign of the cross around the cigar smoke.

> **Marion:** In the name of God Almighty, I, Marion de la Luz ask permission to work in this hour and in this moment, to smoke this tobacco for the protection and help of all Sentient beings who come to this altar today.
> In the name of all the spiritual courts represented at this sacred altar, I ask your support and guidance on this holy day: I call Maria Lionza, all the saints of the Celestial Court and all of her "Don Juan" divas of the rivers, mountains, flora and fauna. I call all the great Caciques of the Venezuelan Indian Resistance; The political Pantheon of Simon Bolivar; The Seven African Powers of the Yoruba, Santeria cult; The

medical court of Dr. Jose Gregorio Hernanadez, Doctor of the poor. the ferocious court of the Vikings; the great North American Indian Chiefs; the court of the "malandros" (dead, repentant criminals); the great Buddhas, the Hindu deities, the Egyptian Kings and Queens, ancestors and angels. I ask you all to descend upon these innocent souls today with love, compassion, integrity, and healing wisdom. Amen que se sea.

(This geographical vortex seems to be unlimited in its ability to receive energy from different, epochs, nationalities, and life forms.)

Marion makes the sign of the cross with the smoked cigar, tosses it and Luz runs to study the position in which it fell on the floor, for this sign determines the absolute yes or no for the session.

Luz: Esta bien Abuela?

Marion: Yes, gracias, Reina. You see, Luz, how the cigar points straight at her. It's a GO, come on, let's make it beautiful!

The rest of the team returns, and goes to work fixing up the altar with fresh flowers, offerings of fruits, cake, cigars, liquor, special protection necklaces, etc. The bust of Maria Lionza is given fresh makeup and perfume. A big blue candle is lit in front of her, yellow for Guaicaipuro, red for Negro Felipe. (These are Venezuela's flag colors, representing the races.) The altar is being prepared as a "portal" to be crossed by spirits into our world.

Marion's young lover, Rafael begins to bang on the tambor, and the candles flicker madly as Marion prays to the sound of the drum.

"Oh, Milagrosa Reina Maria Lionza,
Virgin que sacrificaste tu esplendorosa belleza

Oh Miracle Queen, Maria Lionza
Virgin, sacrificing your
splendorous beauty

en aras del amor a Cristo	*in altars of love to Christ*
a cambio te concedio el don infinito	*who in exchange gave you the infinite gift*
de remediar, durar, socorrer, abogar	*to heal, to endure, to assist, to intercede,*
y consolar a tus semejantes en este mundo terrenal Pidote de rodillas y con infinita devocion	*& to console your people in this world I ask you on my knees with infinite devotion*
me concedas lo que aqui humildemente te ruego si es para bien y gloria vuestra.	*to grant me that which I humbly ask you in the name of your glorious goodness,*
Amen	*Amen.*
Maria Lionza, belleza infinita, hacedme bendita. Tu culto es la gloria, tu nombre es Maria	*Maria Lionza, infinite beauty, make me blessed...Your cult is glorious, your name is Maria*
Concedenos todo, en este gran dia..."	*Grant us everything in this great day.*

Pilgrim: "Tu amor es la antorcha que alumbra el camino de vuestra conciencia. Bendigame con tu luz de fe, de esperanza."

Translation (Your love is the anchor that illuminates the road of our consciousness. Bless me with your light, your faith and your hope.)

Pilgrim: "Reina Maria Lionza, por tu poder, por los Siete Potencias que te acompanan, no dejes que las estrellas me maldigan, no que el Cielo me borre la ilusion, ni que Satanas ni los brujos me destruyan este pobre corazon."

Translation (Queen Maria Lionza, for your power, for the Seven Powers that accompany you, don't let the stars malign me, don't let heaven erase my illusion, nor Satan, nor the Brujos destroy this poor heart[1].)

The devotees, clients and more drummers are arriving with the call of the drum.

Clients: *Cero, an older Black man, 56 years old*
Hugo Chavez, a Venezuelan Army commander, 42
Cecilia, a Gringa tourist, 35
Rosita, a young pregnant Afro/Latina woman, 19
Veruska, an exotic Miss Venezuela contestant, 25

More drummers arrive. Marion greets everyone and asks them to make their offerings in front of the altar as she brushes them with branches of rue, to distance any negative energy. She purifies them with the smoke of her conjured tobaccos. The bancos also help fumigate (smudge with tobacco) a line-up of clients who lift their palms and gaze mystically into the altar, swaying to the intoxicating beat of the drum, the repetition of the song, and the rhythm and "fuerza" (strength/ spiritual energy) in the room. They have all come from confession, Easter Mass & Communion, and are ready for some magic. Marion soon falls into an effortless transport, and without question, the first arrival is of Maria Lionza. The bancos prepare Maria Lionza's blue cape, her rose, crown and scepter, and a beautiful goblet of red wine. The drumming stops, and the crowd is silent as **she sings the Ave Maria**. *The real Maria Lionza is on the theatrical catwalk above.*

Maria Lionza (Marion as): *(after singing and getting dressed)* Maria Lionza les bendice a todos en el nombre de Dios, Jesus Christo, y el espiritu Santo. (ML blesses everyone in the name of God, Jesus, and the Holy Spirit.)

Rafael, Son in Law: Buenas Tardes Reina Madre. Bienvenido a su casa, y a nuestro centro humilde en el nombre de usted y Las Tres Potencias— con el Negro Felipe, y el gran cacique Guacaipuro.

(Good afternoon, Queen Mother, welcome to your home, and our humble center in your name and the name of the Three Powers, with the Negro Felipe and the Great Chief Guaicaipuro)

Maria: Gracias, Me alegre estar aqui contigos para celebrar la resurecion de Jesus Cristo. Y como hay mucho gente a servir hoy, te digo con todo mi corazon que estoy aqui para solucionar todas sus problemas con mi gran equipe de espiritus trabajadores de Dios, llena de fe y amor para ustedes.

(Thank you, I am happy to be here with you to celebrate the resurrection of Jesus Christ. And as there are many people to serve today, I tell you with all of my heart, that I am here to resolve all your problems with my great team of God's spiritual workers, who have much faith and love for all of you.)

A. SCENE WITH CERO

She begins to walk around the patients and blesses each one of them with a handshake that makes the sign of the cross. Approaching Cero, a middle-aged Black man

Maria (Marion): Dios, te bendice Señor .... Don't be nervous Señor Cero .... I'm here to help you.

Cero: Thank you, Reina. I am honored and grateful to be in your presence.

Maria: It's your son. I understand that he has a drinking problem.

Cero: Yes, Madre, and we are desperate, for he is gone again.

Maria: Tranquila mi hijo... he will be back. We know that with the invention of alcohol have come many good times, and also much disease of addiction. There is a remedy however, which will end his desire once and for all. You must bring him to my mountain to bathe in the holy waters of the river Yaracuy. Bring me 33 white candles and obtain the urine of a very old giant macho turtle, which when mixed in his food will cause him to lose all desire for alcohol. Guaicaipuro taught me this, and it worked for many victims of the bottle. I want your son to be healthy.

Cero: Thank you and God Bless you, Reina— you don't know how much grief he has brought to the family.

Maria: He is not a bad man. He is in pain. The alcohol shoots holes in his system and other negative energies and entities enter and dominate his weak ambition dictating his actions. If he is willing to be helped, we can do a "despojo" in one spiritual session. You must all pray the rosary and let him hear you. God bless you Cero, for trying to help your dear son.

Cero: Gracias Señora, my family is my life.

B. SCENE WITH THE GRINGA

Maria (Marion as): And now the Gringa, whom I have been watching. I have many things to say about your countrymen, but that is for another time mi hija. What can I do for you now?

Gringa: Excuse me mam, but I feel like I am dreaming. Could I be in an alternate reality?

Maria: No, of course not, I'm really here and so are you, everybody else, and all the spirits.... We are all God's children. Why would you doubt that?

Gringa: Well, this is all like the movies for me. An inexplicable miracle has brought me to your feet, even though I thought you were merely a legend. But my scholastic inquiry sees that you are absolutely here talking to me!

Maria: And now you know that I am very real indeed. Why do you suppose we are meeting?

Gringa: Well, I think it is because I just lost my father, Joseph Gruessing, to a long struggle with liver Cancer, after years of painful chemotherapy and operations. The doctors knew he was terminal, and still fried him with chemicals. And all through it, I knew he needed undiscovered herbal and spiritual healing, but there was no alternative. After he died, everything I did had no rational direction. The Universe just picked me up and brought me to you.

Maria: I'm truly sorry about your father. He was not ready to die, but he was very brave, and we are taking care of him. There is a cure for cancer in Venezuela, which you will have formally explained to you by Dr. Jose Gregorio Hernandez Rodriguez of our medical court. I can see your father now, and he is a very kind man, reaching out to you now, with so much love.

Gringa: Please tell him I love him, and I miss him so much. And that I thank him for everything he has done for me, and all his love and support. That I have never found a man as caring and thoughtful and intelligent as he was. I lost a hero.

Maria: Don't cry my child. He can hear you, and he is in the loving arms of Santa Lucia and the Virgin of Carmen. Gringa Cecilia listen. We want you to learn about our plants, our remedies. God has created so many sacred plants on this Earth, which are equipped with properties to combat the diseases of man. In spirit, we can see microscopically how these properties catalyze each other to eliminate many powerful viruses. Our 'mapurite'[2], a relative of your pokeweed, combined with some other plant and insect elements, can wipe out cancerous tumors and all trace of malignancy in the blood.

Gringa: Queen Maria ....Do you think I could learn enough about this plant to help someone heal without chemotherapy.

Maria: Absolutely . . . This is the whole idea sweet Gringa........ that we get helped and help others in the name of universal love. When you come to the mountain, I will introduce you to Dr. Jose Gregorio, and you will learn of the alternative, natural medicine of the tropics. He is a very special man, a great un beatified Saint.

Gringa: This is very important to me. Yes, I want to do everything, meet everybody, and go everywhere. Thank you very much for this opportunity. I can feel the chills all over my body.

Maria: Bless you my child, because so many are dying of this disease in your country, and this plant really works. You are a soul of alta luz, and your humanitarian destiny is grand. You will not be alone forever.

I promise to help you.

Gringa: Thank you so much Maria.

C. SCENE WITH HUGO CHAVEZ

Maria (Marion as): And here we have el Commandante Hugo Chavez Frias— what a pleasant surprise. I remember your grandfather, "Maisanta[3]," the last great warrior on horseback.

Chavez: And it is with his spirit that I come to you today mi Reina.

Maria: Tell me what's happening my son.

Chavez: My Queen thank you for indulging me. *(He bows and crosses himself)*

Maria: Tell me what is in your heart Hugo.

Chavez: "With an impotent vision I see before my eyes, that all the principals that have formed me, have been trampled by the corruption of my superiors, to whom I'm supposed to be subordinate, obedient, and loyal. But how can I be loyal to that which has not been loyal to my Patria? Or to the Bolivarian ideals that are the Democratic origin of our country and nationality?"[4] There is no water in the street, no telephones, no schoolteachers, no sanitation services . These are the symptoms of the incompetent authority which dominates Venezuela now.

Maria: We are all seeing this corruption, again, 300 years after the intense struggle of our liberator, Simon Bolivar who gave his life to free us from the continuing ignorance of European oppression. I am confused and troubled by the corruption and incompetence of your president, Carlos Andres Perez. It troubles me greatly along with the great Indian Chiefs and African Slaves who fought for the same independence before Simon Bolivar. I clearly admire and deeply sympathize with the compassion and bravery you have for Venezuela. However, I must defer these issues of revolution and violence to our great Libertador himself, as I cannot endorse violence of any kind. You must come to the mountain, and he will empower you to do what is right in the eyes of God and our country. Your path is righteous yet full of obstacles, but I can feel Simon begging me to speak to you about this coup.

Chavez: Can I not speak to him now, Maria?

Maria: The time is not right, you must assimilate more data towards your own potential, and he will be of more value to you upon your next meeting. Trust me Hugo . . . This is his territory. You know, both General Gomez in the 1920's and 30's used to come to me for advice, as well as the dictator Marcos Perez Jimenez, in the fifties, and I could never advise violence.

Chavez: Mi Reina, I am here to tell you that there will soon be a revolution, that will harm innocent citizens of this great country of mine, and I come to you for support, understanding, and spiritual counsel at this time.

Maria: First, I must tell you that your grandfather, Maisanta, is asking me to send you his strength and support at this very moment. You have dedicated yourself to a very dangerous and noble path, for which some day you will become the President of this great Republic. But you must gather your people with honest heart. I can see that you are serious about this Coup, but . . . . Clearly Hugo . . . you are not yet organized. We ask you to become crystal clear. Then our Liberator, Simon Bolivar will respond to your prayers. He waits for you at my mountain. I bless you Hugo Chavez Frias with all my heart.

Chavez: As you wish my Holy Queen, I respect this advice, for I know that this is as much a spiritual journey, as it is a political and military transformation for our country. This is my mission, and I need your help in whatever way you can give it. I embrace you with my love, mi Santa Madre.

Maria: And I thank you for the humble Venezolanos who so desperately need a leader.

D. SCENE WITH ROSITA

Maria (Marion as): Dios te bendice hermana. How many months pregnant, are you?

Rosita: Gracias Madre, tengo 5 meses, but I think there may be something wrong because I am bleeding so much. I am worried because this is my first baby, and I want so much for her to be healthy.

Maria: Your baby is a boy, and you must refrain from drinking coffee or any type of alcohol . . . Let me see *(she embraces Rosita's belly from behind)*

Rosita: I don't drink coffee or alcohol madre.

Maria: *(pause)* Then someone has struck you ....the father of this child has shown you violence. Why is this happening??

Rosita: Because he is poor and frustrated and does not want this baby.

Maria: This baby must live, and he will be beautiful and full of goodness. You need the work of la India Rosa.

Rosita: She is my protectress. *(She holds up her pink and red beaded India Rosa necklace)*

Maria: You too must come to our next pilgrimage to the mountain and my river, and there she will treat you. Your baby is fine, we must now strengthen your uterus. You will need to bring yucca (yam) for my "materia" (medium) to prepare a special syrup for you, 21 pink candles, and many yellow flowers. And you must leave this man and go to your mother. He does not deserve any paternal rights to this soul inside of you, crying for love and life. Give your baby the name of Jesus, and he will be protected under my power and the Holy Father's. I will arrange for the India Rosa to see you on the mountain. Rosita, corazon, I am here for you. Pray the rosary with your heart and soul.

Rosita: Si Señora, *(weeping)* Thank you for everything my Holy mother. Here is a rose from my garden.

Maria puts the rose in her hair.

E. SCENE WITH VERUSKA

Maria (Marion as): Maria te bendice....... Veruska, how are you? My how you've changed.

Veruska: I'm very well thank you Señora (*bowing humbly*)

Maria: And your mother?

Veruska: She asked me to give you this special apple cake, baked in your honor on Easter for your sacred resurrection.

Maria: Thank your mother for thinking of me. I'm very touched. Now what can I do for you, as we all bathe in the radiance of your incredible beauty?

Veruska: Thank you mi Reina . . . I still live in the barrio with my mother, although I have unfortunately not inherited her cooking abilities.

Maria: Oh, now that's too bad.

Veruska: However, I am being trained and groomed by a special agency in Caracas[5] who is preparing me to run for Miss Venezuela in 1997.

Maria: And perhaps Miss Universe next I predict. Veruska, you are a beautiful woman inside and out, and you will have all my blessings.

Veruska: Thank you Maria . . .

Maria: We all know that Venezuela makes Goddesses. Am I right? We have developed a particular sensuality and charm, inherited from our multi-racial, hybrid roots. And also, from our ancient South American mythology of beautiful water goddesses who use their dark exotic beauty, their light mystical eyes, their seductive voices, and their fish tails to hypnotize, fertilize, and make us want to love, with an urge to merge. We have "god mothers" of baseball teams; there are beauty queens in village holidays, of harvests, companies, and especially the Carnival Queens. Every last pueblo has an Immaculate Patron Saint. Even in prisons we crown beautiful, convicted women. Our matrilineal roots have created queens everywhere who inspire a liturgical respect. Tell me how are these beauty groomers cultivating your spirit my child?

Veruska: Maria, I cultivate my own spirit. And I have decided to advance my knowledge of the rainforests. I want to protect our country's natural resources, and to propose legislation to outlaw the murder of all animals, to promote national vegetarianism, to improve the sanitation system, to start recycling, and to develop an ecological consciousness with children in the public schools. I need your help, Maria. This will be my platform— my mission for my country.

Maria: Veruska, your beauty is exuberant like a tropical forest, but your inner beauty and spiritual compassion is what will really carry you. I advise you not to be too distracted by the romance of men. For this will inhibit your strength as a leader of people. Men's adoration of women's beauty and sexuality is paradoxical in Venezuela.[6] Many Latina women are underpaid, oppressed, single, uneducated, and battered. Therefore, you, with your Diva like beauty and spirituality, must become a role model which delicately balances the high role of Goddess, while elevating the value of oppressed Venezuelan women. This you must accomplish in tandem with your feminine approach to ecology, and the protection of our Mother Earth— It is the same thing my child. Do you see? We are all Goddesses.

... When you are ready for a spiritual baptism, I will develop your faculties as a medium— a destaparse para desarollarse, oiste? Next time . . . .

Veruska: *(clutching her heart)* Oh Mother, what would I do without you?

Maria: What would we do without you? Everybody, take a look at the next Miss Venezuela, 1997— Veruska Ramirez! *(She actually was a virgin and did win the title in 1997).*

Veruska: Gracias's madre, I will prepare myself for that opportunity to speak your words and hold your spirit..... Please honor me with your blessing for now and I will be eternally grateful.

Maria: Te bendigo con amor, belleza, inteligencia, moralidad, y fuerza, para desarollar la grand luz humanitariana que vive adentro su espiritu en el nombre de Dios Poderoso, hijo, y espiritu santo. Amen

(I bless you with love, beauty, intelligence, morality, and strength, so that you can develop the great humanitarian light that lives in your soul, in the name of the father, the son and the holy ghost)

Ahora, la musica por favor, porque hay muchos espiritus que quieren bajar en este momento para ayudar mi gente. Yo me quedo en espiritu, pero me voy de la materia ahora, para bienvenir sus otros invitados. Yo bendigo este altar sagrado con todo mi fuerza.

(Now, music please, because there are many spirits who want to come down in this moment to help my people. I will remain nearby, but I leave my medium now to make way for the other guests. I bless this sacred altar with all of my strength.)

Many people are waiting in line to be seen by spirit. The musicians now include singers, tamboristas (drummers), y tocares de Quatro (mandolin players).

Mandolin player: Please Maria wait! May I sing a song to the Reina?

Luis: Adelante hermano!!

The musician steps forward to sing to Maria Lionza.

MI REINA

De donde vienes, De donde eres	*From where do you come?* *Where did you come from?*
Por cual camino, llegaste al monte	*From which path did you arrive from the mountain?*
Desde al arriba, o de la horizonte, **Quisas del canto de la guaregre** **o de las flores del buccaral (2x)** **Mujer hermosa, de dulce encantos**	*From above, or from the horizon?* *Perhaps from the song of the eagle* *or from the flowers of buccaral (?)* *Beautiful woman, of sweet enchantment*
de ojos verdes por la manana **y azul intenso a la tardecer** **de tierna imagen, y aliento des flores** **Dejame que ponga un presente en tu altar** **y un ramo de rosas, blancas de Alipan (?)**	*with green eyes in the morning and* *intense blue in the afternoon* *of tender image, and breathing flowers* *. . . .* *Allow me to make a presentation at your altar.* *and a bouquet of roses, white from Alipan (?)*
Que traje esta manana **para ti mi Reina, Yaracuyana......"**	*that I brought you this morning . . . .* *Just for you my Queen from Yaracuy.*

(taken from cassette tape)

The scene fades as the next group of patients takes their position in front of the altar, and the tamboristas begin to pound out fire and fuerza.

Cecilia Anne Gruessing, M.A.

Scene 3 — The Ascension
— Pilgrimage to the Mountain of Sortes, Chivicoa
(40 days after the Resurrection) May 1995

Scene 3a— Street scene in front of Botanica

It is a Friday night, on the street in front of Marion's Centro in Catia, and the same drummers segue into a continuing rhythm session as they wait for the pilgrimage to begin. An old school bus is being loaded with duffle bags, kitchen gear, food, religious props and tools, musical instruments, blankets, and hammocks. The bus says "Centro Las Tres Potencias," with crude paintings of el Negro, Maria, and Guaicaipuro on the side. The five featured pilgrims, along with others, are ready for the journey. Musicians, children, teens, and seniors are present, to make this Holy, six-hour Pilgrimage from Caracas to the Mountain of Sortes in Chivicoa, Yaracuy. Marion is checking her list and trying to organize seating for the passengers. Her family/team has finally loaded everything. Her cousin, Manuel arrives.

> **Marion:** Hola Manuel, how wonderful you could make it.
> *(She embraces him and ushers him into the loaded bus.)* Everyone, I would like you to meet my cousin, Manuel, a medium of the highest light that Venezuela has to offer. Buen Viaje everyone. Vamonos a Sortes— Arriba!!!!!

Scene 3b— The Journey in the bus

The bus radio broadcasts the famous Ruben Blades and Willie Colon *recording of the hit salsa song, "Maria Lionza."*

"En la Montana de Sortes de Yaracuy	*In the Mountain of Sortes in Yaracuy*
en Venezuela . . . Vive una diosa, en la Montana de Sortes por Yaracuy ..	*in Venezuela ……. A goddess lives in the Mountain of Sortes in Yaracuy*
Vive una diosa, una noble reina de	*A goddess lives, a noble queen, of great*

gran belleza y de gran bondad	*beauty and great generosity . . .*
Amada por la naturaleza,	*Loved by nature, illuminated by*
Illuminada de caridad.	*charity . . .*
Y sus paredes son encantamientos,	*And your walls are enchantments,*
y su techo hecho de tejas bellas	*and your ceiling made with beautiful tiles.*
la luna, sol, el cielo, y la montana son companeros	*the moon, sun, sky, and mountain are your friends*
El rio, quebrada, y flores son sus mensajeros.	*The river, hills, and flowers are your messengers*
O Salve Reina Maria Lionza— O Venezuela	*Oh, Sacred Queen Maria Lionza— O Venezuela*
Y va velando con su onza cuidando su tierra entera,	*You ride across your land on your onza, vigilant*
desde el Guarijo hasta Cumana de los Latinos	*from Guajira to Cumana Cuida el destino Caring for the destiny of the Latinos*
Vivir unidos sin Libertad	*To live united without liberty.*

CHORUS

Maria Lionza y sus milagritos un ramo flores te voy a llevar	*Maria Lionza, for your miracles a bouquet of flowers I will bring you.*

**Un ramo de flores de rosas
blancas por la pureza de tu
bondad,** *white for the purity of your goodness*
**Maria Lionza y sus milagritos
un ramo flores te voy a llevar
Por toda la gente hasta los serritos
que hay en Caracas protegera.**

(transcribed and translated from cassette tape)

The six-hour bus ride southeast to Yaracuy becomes a full-blown musical salsa dance and sing-along number that reflects the Afro-Native spirit energy of a busload of hopeful and happy pilgrims, ready as ever for a mystical experience. The 'Ascension' is reflected in the evolution of their city behavior, all the way from Caracas to the foot of the mountain where a mystical presence definitely takes over. They know they are about to climb the mountain of Maria Lionza. It is 3 am in the 'madrugada'(dawn) when they arrive and disembark from their dream states to greet the "Altar Mayor."

Above the stage is a catwalk throne where the real Maria Lionza, the Negro Felipe, and Chief Guaicaipuro sit monitoring the rituals below like a control tower.

Scene 4 — The Mountain of Sortes
— Chivicoa, Venezuela

4a. The Altar Mayor— (Main Altar)

This is an important stop before one cross the bridge over the Yaracuy River to enter the sacred grounds of the Mountain of Sortes, a national park 6 hours from Caracas, set aside for pilgrims by the government of Venezuela. The Altar Mayor consists of three major shrine "rooms" to Maria Lionza, her Trinity, the Court of the Indigenous natives, and Dr. Jose Gregorio.

These three-sided, open-air altars are charged with dancing candle flames and fragrant flowers, where people smoke their first tobacco to call spirit, and make their offerings, promises, and requests. Marion organizes her team to hold hands as she crosses herself and prays on behalf of the group.

Marion: In the name of God, the Father, the son, and the holy ghost .... I call upon Maria Lionza, el Negro Felipe, Guaicaipuro, and all her courts: the Indians, the Africans, the Doctors, the Don Juanes of Nature, and all Cosmic forces of the Universal Mother and Father. Penetrate into each of our living cells so that each instant your love will fill us with illumination, understanding and peace. We thank you for this new day, our daily bread, and for all our benefactors. We pray for the peace of the world, for each one of us here today. We pray for shoeless children, for the hunger of the entire world, for our senior citizens, for invalids, for the sick, for those full of egoism or hate, grudges or desperation, that a ray of your light enters them to believe in Universal love. We pray for those who have lost their faith, for those who have been persecuted by justice, for prisoners just or unjust. We pray for disoriented and corrupt youth. We ask that you bring our government to a level of democracy that honestly serves our people, to organize our schools, and give light to our professors and scientists, to elevate our social services, to protect and reform our institutions with knowledge and wisdom. We ask these blessings for all who guide humanity. Madre— help us pray for our enemies, protect them, inundate them with love. Dispel us of all bad thoughts, of all arrogance, of all pride, of all stinginess, violence, and impatience. Help us to be generous, humane, and permit our spirits to regenerate the beauty of nature. We pray for all our ancestors, brothers and sisters, and children in the flesh and in spirit. Give the mediums the strength and the protection to fulfill the needs of those with us now. Allow us to be touched by your generosity and healing powers as we enter your sacred land.[7]

Everybody finishes their personal prayers, and before they make their way across the bridge in the early morning darkness, Marion invokes Don Juan del Rio Yaracuy for permission to cross.

Marion: En el nombre de Dios, etc., con la bendicion de su Reina Maria Lionza, pedimos permiso para nosotros, pelegrinos humildes, para cruzar su rio sagrado, Señor Don Juan de las Aguas. Buscamos la pureza de su Rio Yaracuy para limpiarnos, curarnos, y accelerar nuestra evolucion espiritual. Por favor, bendigan nosotros con su poder y gracia, Señor Don Juan de las Aguas.

(In the name of God, etc., and with the blessings of your Queen Maria Lionza, we ask permission for us humble pilgrims to cross your sacred river, Don Juan of the Waters. We seek the purity of your river Yaracuy to clean us, cure us and to accelerate our spiritual evolution. Please bless us with your power and grace.)

Scene 4b— The Ascension of the Pilgrims

They begin to sing.

Caminante pelegrinos	**Walking Pilgrims**
"Encontrastes el camino de la pena y la verdad	*You found your way in pain and in truth*
No le temas, no le temas el destino que te espera	*Don't be frightened of the destiny waiting for you*
es de bondad 2X	*It is of goodness*
Este caminito verde que va subiendo hacia monte	*This green path that winds up the Mountain*
Este camino de Sortes que esta encima del cerro	*This path of Sortes above the hill*
Es el altar de la Diosa, de la Reina Caquetia	*Is the altar of the Goddess, the Caquetia queen,*
Patrona de las cosechas, de dulce nombre, Maria	*Patron of the crops, and of the sweet name, Maria*

Llega la noche	*The night arrives*
la luna espera	*The moon waits*
las mariposas que van llegando	*The butterflies are arriving*
ensenando pelegrinos y caminitos	*Showing the pilgrims the paths of Sortes*
de Sortes	

Continuing with another song:

Por la Noche Fresca	*By the fresh (beautiful) evening*
y la luna clara	*and the clear moon,*
que juegan el rio	*the river plays*
y con el aroma de tus lindas flores	*and with the aroma of your pretty dewy*
llena del rocillo	*flowers*
Voy hacer el barco de cosas floridas	*I will make a boat of flowered things for*
para ti mi Reina	*you my Queen Goddess of the waters, of the fertile land*
duena de los rios 2X	*owner of the rivers . . . .*
Por los caminitos, la que va cruzando tus lares,	*By the paths, those who go crossing your Bridges*
Son las mariposas que vuelan en tus altares,	*The butterflies fly over your altars*
Yo reze mi canto cerca la agua hasta arriba	*I recite my song near the water all the way up*
que llega, que anda camino a las serranias . . ."	*the path of the hills that winds and arrives.*

(transcribed from cassette tape)

They begin the long climb up the mountain singing to call Maria and the spirits, passing the portals of other groups of pilgrims, whose flaming altars, and passionate songs and drumming chants illuminate the way. The ambiance is mysterious and dream-like. Patients are ritually laid out, encircled by candles (velados), in front of their elaborately dressed altar., Some sleep, others sing, drum, and shout out "fuerza" to bring down the next spirit's performance.

It is a veritable Disneyland of passion, mystery, magic, and initiation as the young and old backpack in the dark, up the narrow river path to the summit of the holy mountain where Maria Lionza's Palace of the Coronation[8], or "Escalera" (staircase) waits for them. In blue dream light they ascend to the rhythm of the drum, energized by the enlightenment that awaits them above.

Scene 4c— The Queen Mother's Altar on the mountain peak

Upon arriving at the Queen's royal summit portal, everyone drops their packs, and falls to them knees in front of the stone "palace" altar and prays.

Marion: (*requesting permission through a conjured Tabaco*):

"Oh, miraculous Queen Maria Lionza. You who have sacrificed your splendid beauty for the love of Christ, without taking advantage of the pleasures that you have over the earth…. The powers that Christ gave you…. the infinite power to cure the sick, to come to the help of the people, to speak for them and console her followers on Earth. I pray on my knees and with an infinite devotion that you bless us with permission to work in this your sacred sanctuary, for our good and for your glory. Amen."[9]

They begin to sing, and Marion continues to invoke spirit with her tobacco.

"En la Montana de Sorte, en Yaracuy	*On the moutain of Sortes in Yaracuy*
hay una Diosa encantada en la noche tropical, desconcertante	*there is an enchanting goddess in the disconcerting tropical night*
y hermosa sobre una danta cabalga	*and so beautiful mounted on her danta.*
Es Maria Lionza, la que cuida las Culturas…	*It is Maria Lionza, she who cares for the culture*
duena de los animales, de los arboles y el agua, los pajaros y los nidos, la que enlucera el camino,	*Matron of the animals, trees, and the waters, the birds and their nests, she who illuminates the road*

la que afina las guitarras.	*She who tunes the guitars.*
Es Maria Lionza de cabellos negro, y ojos claros	*It is Maria Lionza with black hair, and clear eyes*
eres muy rica en tesoro y en gran amor que derramas/	*rich in treasure, and great love that she spills—*
Te traere un ramo de rosas y canto de la sabana	*I bring you roses, and song of the land*
si tu me haces un milagro	*if you will make me a miracle.*
En la montana de Sorte	*In the mountain of Sorte, the divinity*
la divinidad del bosque	*of the woods*
tiene su reno y morada, Maria Lionza, Maria Lionza	*has her reign and residence, ML, ML*
Diosa nuestra madre y reina	*Our Mother Goddess*
Queen la diosa Venezolana.	*Goddess of Venezuela*
Maria Lionza, a ti el Indio perseguido	*ML, for you the persecuted Indian*
buscando su libertad lucho con fe y te invocaba	*looking for liberty, fought with faith, & invoked you*
Nunca olvides a tu gente el pueblo de Venezuela	*Never forget your people, your village of Venezuela*
que con gran fervor te clama.	*Who cry out for you with great fervor.*
Maria Lionza tus hijos aun Sufrimos	*ML, even though your children suffer*
te pedimos nuevas fuerzas para continuar luchando	*we ask you for renewed strength to continue the fight*
que tu patria un dia sea libre	*So that one day your country will be free*

y que tu suelo sagrado no lo pisoteen extranos."	*And that your sacred ground is not trampled by strangers anymore.*

By Cristobal Jimenez— Llanero composer[10]

As they sing, Marion examines the tabaco, presents it to the pilgrims triumphantly. The ashes are white and fluffy. She gives the 'go' signal, and the pilgrims begin to build the altar with statues of the spirits of many pantheons who work under the protection of Maria Lionza. Candles are lit, offerings are made, liquor is spritzed over the altar, tabacos are conjured, and everyone makes their way to the river to purge, purify, and bathe ("despojos")[11].

Scene 4d— River Purification

In the river Marion and her "bancos" (assistants) smoke conjured tabacos around all the initiates with prayer for purification. A single drummer keeps the magical beat, and the river purge turns into a sacred mystical purification ritual. Candles are lit on the river rocks. A special drink is passed around which causes people to vomit, and purge. They are given a piece of special blue soap to scrub down with, and then toss downstream over the left shoulder. The water is cool, pure, and invigorating, surrounded by the majesty of natural jungle life, complete with tropical flowers, monkeys and birds and the magical presence of Maria Lionza and her huge pantheon of spirit helpers. Specially prepared herbal "banos" are administered on the banks of the river. The initiates shiver with the frigid purity of the early morning baptism. Multicolored beaded protector necklaces, knotted prayer belts, stars and crosses (including the Cruz de Caravacas) are all purified in the bath and river water, as well as smudged.

— On the catwalk above there is a conference amongst the Three Powers, and they agree to send Guaicaipuro down first. It is not long before Marion's cousin, Manuel falls into trance standing in the water. He begins to shout and spin his arms madly splashing water everywhere. It is indeed, the great warrior and Cacique, Guaicaipuro

Marion: Bienvenido hermano, adelante!!!

Guacaipuro: Buenas tardes mi gente!! Listo trabajar!! Take me to the altar . . . (Good afternoon my people! I am ready to work!)

Scene 5 — The Descent of the Spirit
— Tongues of Fire and the work of the Pentacostal Brujos (witchdoctors)—

4e— Maria's Altar

We return to the Queen's land altar where 'arepas con huevos' (cornmeal eggburgers) are being cooked over a "fogata" (fire). As the lights come up, we also hear the mysterious sound of the cicadas (locusts)12 in the trees. Marion has put finishing touches on the altar. The pilgrims are seated in a semi- circle in front of the altar. The work paraphernalia is ready to go holy water, dozens of different color candles, bottles of rum, anise, aquardiente, red wine, flowers, cigars arranged in the form of a cross, various offerings— food, fruit, herbs, incense, perfumes, agua de colonia, Nazarene crosses, knifes, pins, pieces of iron and magnets, feathered headdresses for the Indians, ribbons, walking sticks, hats, skirts, dresses, earrings, scepters, capes, crowns. Guaicaipuro (Manuel) is marking the four corners with his knife. The bancos follow him. He walks like a prehistoric man with what we might think is an angry expression on his face. He (Guaicaipuro) draws designs with white baby powder on the earth to create a star formation in front of the altar for the next stage of the "mystery" called **Velaciones or Velados**. *Nine people are directed by Guaicaipuro (Manuel) to lay down inside this design forming the spokes of a wheel with their bodies (heads in the center), while bancos and assistants surround their individual bodies with small, different colored candles. Guaicaipuro looks over all of this activity with great care and dignity. From the catwalk, Maria Lionza and el Negro watch ceremoniously. Guaicipuro (Manuel) is given a handful of tobaccos which he holds up high to conjure:*

> **Guacaipuro:** Fuerza de la tierra, el viento, el fuego, y la agua, con Dios Poderoso— Por favor que esta hoja de tabaco, mi hacha sagrada, reciba la luz magnetica necesaria para ver la verdad, conocer el mal y combatirlo.
>
> (Strength of the earth, wind, fire, and water, with God Almighty— make this leaf of tobacco, my sacred tobacco, receive the magnetic light necessary to see the truth, to know evil, and to combat it.)

The assistants (bancos) begin to puff sacred tobacco smoke over the bodies of the "meditating" initiates. Things begin to happen, when several people begin to go into trance simultaneously. This will be portrayed as a musical holographic dream/drama of descending spirits. Keep in mind that the following vignettes will crisscross in a three-ring circus manner, where the dialogues are sequential, but the stage is teeming with multiple spiritual encounters.

Guacaipuro: Buena noche todo. Guaicaipuro come here to help you move your future. We watch you, and we protect you from evil.

Guaicaipuro walks around the circle of bodies observing the initiates and his cigar— looking up, taking swigs of cocuy. He stops in front of a young mestizo (African-Latino).

5A. SCENE WITH GUACAIPURO AND MARTIN

Guacaipuro: You are Cero's son, Martin, and I come to take drinking devil out of you. *(Martin begins to tremble on the ground, and his father Cero approaches, with a coca cola bottle filled with a special elixir including the urine of a macho turtle. Guaicaipuro goes through an advanced transmutiation)* En el nombre de Dios Poderoso, I call upon the Seven African Powers[13] to help me exorcise the demon that drives this man to the bottle— I call upon all great Venezuelan warriors to protect this man once we take away the dark parasite spirit who is sucking his blood.

Martin begins to shake like crazy and leave his body, and the bancos lift him into a standing position. He takes on the body language of a monster who speaks in tongues and confronts Guaicaipuro who waltzes around him like an animal ready to fight. The wrestling match begins, and Guaicaipuro soon has the possessed Martin straddled across his shoulders, spinning him around as he shouts a war cry. He drops Martin onto the ground, who then regains his own consciousness.

Guaicaipuro: Bring me the jarabe (syrup)!

Martin opens his eyes and Guaicaipuro takes him in his arms like a baby.

Martin: Where am I?

Guacaipuro: I am Guaicaipuro, and we have healed you. But there is one more thing. Repeat after me I promise to drink this jarabe in front of the altar of our Holy Father and Mother and all my African and Indian ancestorsand promise never to touch a drop of alcohol again in my life . . . .

Martin repeats the promises one by one and drinks the jarabe as all the disciples and initiates watch. It is clearly distasteful, and he tries to reject it, but Guaicaipuro is firm. They watch Martin go through an exorcistic madness for 10 minutes upon swallowing the jarabe. On the catwalk above, Maria Lionza rises with vigilant concern, and el Negro gets ready to descend.

Guacaipuro: Good........ Now *(He picks up a bottle of whiskey, takes a swig and pours it into Martin's mouth).........* you will drink this!!!

Martin: Please, I can't!!! This is crazy!! What are you doing?

Cero: Martin, have faith in spirit!

He forces Martin to drink pure rum alcohol which makes him really sick and throw up— Guaicaipuro takes him in his arms again and looks him close in the eyes saying

Guacaipuro: You must feel the pain. Drink this now!!!! You will never drink again for the love of yourself and your family. You understand this and you will serve the Great Spirit.

Everybody: Amen que se sea!!! *(Cero is weeping with joy. Guaicaipuro returns to the catwalk and Manuel returns to his body.*

5B. SCENE WITH ROSITA, NEGRO FELIPE, & INDIA ROSA

Meanwhile, El Negro Felipe has entered Marion's body, and he is working on Rosita's pregnancy, cutting up melons and papayas which he mashes all over her pregnant belly, activating the concoction with doses of rum, which he intermittently sips.

El Negro speaks with a special stutter which is often confused for singing, but probably comes from his rum habit.

Felipe (Marion as): Oh, mi hija! You are so young and so precious, and your boy will be fine and healthy. The India Rosa will be here soon to bless you and your baby, but I am here to "quitar la pava". (get rid of the bad)

Rosita: Oh, Gracias hermano. My mother thanks you, my father, my baby thanks you how can I repay you?

Felipe: Listen to me hija. The father of this baby has another woman who is driving him crazy, and she has sent brujeria to you. But your protector, la India Rosa, has been with you always. We will sweeten your spirit, and pacify all negativity, we will make your spirit beautiful, and I will personally liberate you from the chains of this unevolved boyfriend of yours.

Rosita is shocked and upset by this information. Negro Felipe puts his hand on Rosita's belly and prays. Upstairs on the catwalk, Maria Lionza 'makes a spiritual call.'

Maria Lionza (as herself): At this time, I call upon the India Rosa to descend and help this innocent creature and her baby in their moment of need. I ask this in the name of the father, the mother, and the holy ghost.

Felipe: En este momento, en el nombre de Dios, el hijo, y el espiritu santo, Yo, el Negro Felipe, pido de mi hermana la reina Maria Lionza para ayudarme quitar la pava de esta mujer innocente. Alejele del padre de este nino para que ella puede olvidarle y abrir sus caminos para el bienestar del nino y la familia. (In this moment, in the name of the father, the son and the holy ghost, I ask my sister, the queen Maria Lionza, to help me remove the darkness from this innocent woman. Distance her from this baby's father so that she can forget him and open her roads for the well-being of the child and the family)

Marion's daughter, Sophia, has gone into trance with la India Rosa and approaches Rosita and el Negro Felipe, who makes a final blessing over Rosita and puts her under the care of la India Rosa. (El Negro has a love affair in spirit with the India Rosa.) Sophia has taken on spirit.

India Rosa (Sophia): Estoy aqui mi hija. Todo esta bien. Maria Lionza sent me to reassure you of my vigilance.

Rosita: I just feel so much better to hear your voice. Thank you, Rosa. Please tell me about my baby.

India Rosa (Sophia): You must understand that your baby was traumatized when you were struck, and in order to make the birth easy, we must strengthen your uterus with the yucca (yam) elixir, which has been prepared for you.

Marion returns to her body from Negro Felipe and fetches the special syrup. Then the India Rosa blesses it.

India Rosa: Learn this special yam recipe and drink this often mi hija, and I promise you an easy delivery in September. As for the father and his girlfriend .you should be thankful. She is gaining a problem you are losing..... *(Pause)* Do you hear me, Rosita? Do you understand me????

Rosita: Yes India, I feel like a fool. Thank you for waking me up.

India Rosa: You are young, you are beautiful and intelligent, with a loving Mother. You have a good heart, and I will always be there to take care of you and your baby. Better me than some cheating cabron! I bless you and ask you to keep roses by your bed to remember me. Te bendigo hija mia.

5C. SCENE WITH HUGO CHAVEZ and SIMON BOLIVAR

Maria *(from the catwalk):* Yes Simon, we hear you, and by all means, your moment has come to speak to Hugo Chavez. He awaits you passionately, as he does the liberation of our country. I trust your counsel will be the best Venezuela can offer.

Manuel has transformed into Simon Bolivar who descends coughing, which indicates that his appearance reflects the end of his incarnation when he had tuberculosis. He is blindly searching for Hugo Chavez, and Marion comes to his aid.

Marion: Bienvenido Libertador, we are honored by your presence and beg your blessing.

Bolivar (Manuel as): Gracias hermana por ayudar me a tierra. (Thank you, sister, for grounding me.) I bless this company of Venezuelans with every drop of the blood I once possessed, when I tell you that your Patria is on the brink of major revolution. I have been called by my Queen, Maria Lionza for the Commandante of the Fuerzas Armadas, Señor Hugo Chavez, to discuss the matter. I can wait no longer to be in his company.

Chavez: Commandante Hugo Chavez Frias at your service

Sir! *(Shouting and rising from his lying position.)*

Bolivar: Where is he! Take me to him!!

They embrace and weep, as everyone gathers round. Chavez gathers himself and prays on bended knee to Simon Bolivar:

Chavez: "Oh Great Liberator, Simon Bolivar, who came to this land guided by Divine Light and the Great Power of God and Divine Providence with which you liberated five nations" …. I thank the Queen Mother Maria Lionza, for this opportunity to meet you at last.

Bolivar: The pleasure is mine indeed. Where can we talk?

Chavez: Oh padre, mio, where have you been? The country is lost with these selfish leaders. Maybe now there is hope for the people. I don't know where to begin . . . everything is so dirty, dark, greedy, and corrupt . . . No electricity, no water, the schools are always on strike. I'm sick from it.

Bolivar: *(coughing)* Listen to me! You must take care of yourself, for your strength and clarity will determine the success of this golpe (coup). The situation is more serious than you know. They are transferring public funds to Swiss banks through the President's cocaine mafia: your telephone system is about to take a major crash; garbage collection in Caracas is three weeks overdue; and the children are rioting in the schools. This is MY country they are screwing around with— MY people!!! And it must stop!!

Chavez: Gracias a Dios, I know now that I am not alone. I salute you Commandante. You renew my frustrated heart and soul.

Bolivar: Oh no........This is Venezuela we are talking about, were the Trinity of the races will always reign. I spent too many years fighting for this flag, for these people, to watch my country fall back into the hands of greedy, unorganized Castillian opportunists. You must take over the state house in Caracas, abduct Carlos Andres Perez, track the stolen funds, kick his mistress out of the country, announce a military takeover, and have a press conference. I will help you.

Chavez: That exact plan, minus the extrication of Carlos Andres' mistress, has been waiting only for your command sir, for I have studied your work, and I do not treat the strategy of war lightly.

Maria: *(From the catwalk)* No, the mistress has to go, she is clearly disrespecting the wife of the President, even if the President is corrupt, we will not let her corrupt the office.

Bolivar: Maria Lionza says the mistress's glamour clearly outshines her virtue, and she is sabotaging Venezuela's families.

Chavez: Understood, sir.

Bolivar: I'm proud of you Chavez. Light me a candle with a glass of red wine and talk (pray) to me. Vaya con Dios entonces— Te bendigo. No esperes un momento mas. Adios mi hijo. (Then, go with God— You have my blessings— Do not wait another moment. Goodby my son)

Chavez: Venezuela thanks you. My children and their grandchildren thank you. (*He bows respectfully*).

Maria Lionza throws two white roses to Chavez and Bolivar from the catwalk.

Maria: Know that I love you both dearly, and despite the blood on your hands, I deeply respect your courage.

Marion: I believe that the great cacique Tamanaco wants to speak.

Maria: (*From the catwalk*) Tamanaco, yes, be our guest. Your words are welcome at all times.
The young drummer, Rafael, suddenly begins to convulse, grabbing his throat. He rocks back and forth, and then dissolves into the posture of a Chief Tamanaco.

Marion: Sr. Chavez, there is more. Wait. *(addressing her assistants)* It's Tamanaco, get his feathers and the cocuy.

Tamanaco slowly gets situated in the young drummer's body He grabs his throat painfully, because he died from decapitation, and speaks.

Tamanaco: Good afternoon todos. El Cacqique Tamanaco esta aqui. Bring me my hacha and Sr. Chavez.

Chavez: Here I am brother. *Marion gives Rafael/Tamanaco his cigar/*

Tamanaco: *(Embracing him with tears in his eyes, almost speechless)* We are all watching you, all of your ancestor caciques who died for you, all of the Africans who worked the agriculture and mining in this country, all of us who struggled for liberation. And none of us like watching this lucha, after so many died in vain so long ago. Hombre . . . we are surely behind you in spirit— warriors for the truth and justice we all desire and deserve for Venezuela. Take my hand and go with the power I transmit to you from the bows and arrows of a hundred Venezuelan Chiefs. Reclaim the order of our land, once and for all. Te bendigo, mi hijo Adios y vaya con Dios!

Chavez: Gracias Tamanaco. I am honored and overflowing with your 'fuerza.' *(Fuerza is the alchemical energy of strength, kundalini, prana, chi)* I will light you many green candles.

Chavez exits.

* * *

5D. SCENE with the GRINGA CECILIA and TAMANACO

The gringa, Cecilia has been curled up watching all this with dropped jaw wonder and amazement. Tamanaco approaches her and looks straight through her.

Tamanaco: This must be the Gringa. *(He examines her) Poco* suerte en amor![14] (Little luck in love) What are you doing on this land, blond one?

Gringa: My father died of cancer, and I'm interested in the way you people make medicine and spiritual healing.

Tamanaco: We have the 'mapurite.' Do you know this?

Gringa: I'm hoping to learn more about it today.

Tamanaco: The Doctor will come to explain that. I must tell you. Your father, Joseph, loves you . . .. he hears your prayers, and he will always support you because he believes in the goodness of your heart. For this I have been sent along with him to be your protector. He asks me to watch over you.

Gringa: My father, the republican said that? I don't know what to say. I think I'm speechless for the first time in my life. Of course, I appreciate your concern and could probably use a few holy ghosts with all the crazy things I've been through.

Tamanaco: I will protect you, and although you have not had the opportunity for true love in your life, I can tell you that the universe will send you three daughters someday, they are part indio, but they are not from these shores. I will help you find them.
They will love you like no man has ever loved you. I will protect you, and you will find happiness in your own homeland.

Gringa: You know, difficult as that is for me to understand, I really want to believe you and thank you for caring about me. You have to remember that the closest thing I have to this is Startrek on TV. *(She breaks down)* And I don't know why I'm not married. *(more tears)* Please tell my father, Joseph, I miss him so much. so so much. He was a good man, and he died a painful death to cancer. And I'll just say hello to my grandfather Florentino Diaz, while I'm at it. Hola Abuelo! *(she waves at the sky)* Te quiero mucho! I love and miss you both very much!!

Tamanaco: Cecilia. These men are watching over you, in a world where not many men could keep up with you. I will watch over you from this day on. Mi Gringa bella, the Doctor Jose Gregorio is calling, and I must go. Get yourself a green and brown necklace and I will bless it for you. Te bendigo mi hija. I will always protect you, wherever you are on the earth. We will speak again.

Gringa: OK! Bye .... that's nice. Thank you so much. Is there some place I can reach you by phone maybe? Would you like to get together next week? And you wouldn't happen to know where I can find Maria Lionza, because you just can't call anybody up on the phone around here.

Marion: Cecilia, listen to me.......Hello?

Gringa: Hello?

Marion: Let me try to explain. You see, the way this works is..... Tamanaco will be your protector, from now until forever. This is a moment you will never forget, even if you never make direct contact with him again. He will always be your protector. If you call him spiritually, he will be there, just like your father, your grandfather, or anyone with whom you have had a relationship. These people live in spirit, and they hear your prayers.
However, you can't call them on the phone. You understand that right?

Gringa: Yes, of course. I guess, the artist in me got carried away into some virtual holographic idea for a moment. Never mind... I'm fine Marion.

Marion: Are you really? Sometimes Americans have problems with this work.

Gringa: Are you kidding? This is the best theater I have ever seen in my life!

Marion: This isn't theater Cecilia... this is real. Now... Doctor Jose Gregorio Hernandez[15] will speak to you about the cancer plant after he does this spiritual operation. I'm going to do the oracion and call him. Do you think you can handle this?

Gringa: I wouldn't miss it for the world...

Maria: *(From the catwalk)* Ok get ready Doctor!

Marion lights up a cigar and prays over a middle-aged woman, Anita Gonzalez.

5E. SCENE - Dr. JOSE GREGORIO and ANITA GONZALEZ

Marion: "Oh unique spirit of God without beginning without end. God of the sky, Creator of the Universe, and from whose ocean I am only a drop. I invoke in your name, Dr. Jose Gregorio Hernandez to cure this suffering pilgrim, Anita Gonzalez, in the name of the Father, the Son, and the Holy Ghost. I ask that your spiritual generosity and desire to help the needy, penetrates into this creature who desires to be healthy again— Anita Gonzalez. Inspire us with your divine power, knowledge, vigor, vitality, and ability to heal. Fortify the life energy and peace in the mind of this your creature Anita Gonzalez. We pray to you, Doctor Jose Gregorio Hernandez, that you flow over this creature, Anita Gonzalez and all who suffer, with the power of love and mercy, giving us strength to resist and conquer evil." Please come to us now in the hour of our need.[16]

Manuel is already prepared— dressed in white coat and gloves. He effortlessly takes on the Doctor with a gentle jolt, and prepares to operate without anesthesia, on Anita's cancerous tumor in her breast.

Doctor (Manuel): Doctor Jose Gregorios Hernandez present to serve you. Good afternoon.

Group: Good afternoon, Doctor.

Doctor: Good afternoon, Anita.

Anita: Good afternoon, Doctor. Thank you for helping me.

Doctor: I heard your prayers. How could I not come? I am here to give you a chance to fulfill your destiny in this life. You have a husband . . . . grandchildren . . . . a fabulous garden, neighbors, and a library that needs you. There are still many missions for you to complete in your life, and we need you . . . and above all . . . remember. You are in the hands of God right now. As long as it will take you to recite a Padre Nuestro and tres Ave Marias is as long as this operation will take. OK? Are you ready?

She closes her eyes and recites

Padre nuestro, que estas en los cielos.
Santificado sea tu nombre
Venga a nosotros Tu reino
hagase tu voluntad aqui en la tierra
como en el cielo
El pan nuestro de cada dia Danoslo hoy
Perdona nuestras deudas, asi como snosotros
perdonamos a nuestros desudores,
y no nos dejer caer en tentacion
mas libranos de todo mal. Amen

3X— AVE MARIA

Dios te Salve Maria
Llena eres de gracia
El Señor es contigo
Bendita tu eres
Entre todas las mujeres
Y bendito sea el Fruto de tu vientre, Jesus
Santa Maria, Madre de Dios
Ruega Por nosotros, pecadores
ahoroa y en la hora
de nuestra muerte. Amen

The Doctor has indeed extracted something from Anita's breast in the time it took to say three Hail Mary's and a Padre Nuestro. He is examining it in a glass of water, while Marion holds cotton over the open wound.

    Doctor: I cannot tell if any of the malignancy escaped, in which case, just to be sure . . . you must drink the Mapurite Infusion'.

    Anita: How do I make that?

Gringa: Excuse me Doctor, but I have travelled over 3,000 miles to ask you that very same question, and to steal some of your time regarding this very recipe.

Doctor: Very well, Gringa .... You can write it down for two, while I patch her up. Here are the ingredients, as the mapurite is powerful, but needs certain catalysts which activate the antioxidant processes that dissolve malignant tumors and clean the blood. These combinations have been passed on to me through the spirits of Amazonian Indigenous Shamans over the years who say they have been advised by the divas of the spirit world. Wherever it comes from, the list has proven effective over my years of practice. I repeat a special jarabe, of which mapurite is the largest ingredient.... exists, and has proven to dissolve cancerous tumors and to irradicate malignancy from the blood.

Gringa: I'm ready Doctor. *She has a pencil and paper and writes.*

Doctor: OK— Besides Mapurite (relative of our Pokeweed which grows in Caribbean – scientific name Petiveria Aliacael), we have Mastuerza (Mullein), Salbia (aloe vera), Savila (sage), Sangre de Drago (dragons blood bark), Bachaco Oriental (red ant saliva), kananga water, holy water, Yin Ting, Sandria (watermelon), mentol de la India, Manteca de Raya, Manteca de un obillo negro de besugo toro (The meat of a black spot on a male sea bream fish.) *(This exact recipe was dictated to me by Jose Gregorio in spirit).* You mix it up, without heating it, and drink it seven times a day.

Gringa: Doctor, is it possible for someone who is suffering at the terminal stages of cancer to be cured with this concoction?

Doctor: Absolutely. Once the virus is arrested, it can no longer consume remaining tissue, which will automatically rebuild if it has not been completely damaged. The Medical Spiritual court is in great agreement on this ancient recipe and has healed many hopeless cases with this treatment. We highly recommend it.

Gringa: Thank you Doctor, I'm sorry I didn't meet you before my father died. He would have been very impressed with your philosophies.

Doctor: I have talked with your father several times. Why do you think I am here now to meet you? You may share this recipe with your American Doctors. I'm not sure how seriously they will take it, but I will talk with you more on the subject if you wish. I must go now. Good afternoon.

Marion begins to pray to la Reina statue alone:

Marion: "I implore the sublime influence of the Queen Maria Lionza as my protectress by the grace that God has granted her to me. To you, my powerful Queen, I deliver all my needs so that you bless me with the power and protection that will allow me to liberate all evil and to provide happiness to my patients, and that the light of God will guide me and my thoughts always. I am your admirer, my Queen, for your strength, your knowledge and your great benevolence; I ask in the name of God to irradiate my body with your holy fluidity to distance all bad thoughts," ambushes, or black magic. I seek to heal in your name, with your fuerza, and your love."[17]

Veruska takes the Gringa aside.

Veruska: Cecilia, I will help you with the remedy, because I know a little about this plant. It grows in many tropical places by different names and is a very toxic plant which must be used wisely. My aunt did cure herself of breast cancer with tea made from this "mapurite." *(Mapurite is also the word for skunk and the plant has this smell)* It's technical name is "petiveria alliacael" and I will help you follow up on this, because it should be formally researched.

Gringa: Oh, thank you Veruska. This has all been so magical, and confusing for me. But something tells me, that perhaps this plant could be used not only for cancer, but for la sida (aids) as well. I have a feeling about that . . .

5F. SCENE WITH VERUSKA

Up on the catwalk, Maria is getting ready to descend. The pilgrims become distracted by Veruska, who begins to shake, rattle, and roll, and before long she is in trance, bursting with melodic strains of her voice filing the mountain with the familiar Catholic melody of Ave Maria. The assistants rush around looking for her cape, scepter, crown, and red wine and by the last note, everything is ready.

Marion: La Reina wants to come into Veruska .... Fuerza!! Fuerza!!! Adelante diosa/reina . . ..

Maria Lionza(Veruska): Buenas Tardes mis discipulos, como estan hoy?

Manuel: We are clearly delighted to be in your audience Holy Queen.

Maria Lionza (Veruska): I am pleased to be hosting such a diverse tribe of initiates this weekend. Welcome to my palace. Do you see the natural wealth in which I live like a Queen? Can you understand why I prefer this to the civilization that destroys itself in the name of progress? Here we have preserved a doorway for you all to enter into the other world through the animas of nature and the pure vibrations of spirit. The more unconnected man becomes to Nature the more insensitive he will become to his fellow men, and the system will implode from there. This is why you are so drawn to this pilgrimage- to the mountain where you can purify and liberate your spirits from the anguish of the city. Let us all bathe together in the beauty of God's glorious sunlight.

"By sending forth your Spirit, the faithful shall be created, and you shall renew the face of the earth . . .. Holy Spirit, you fill the hearts of the faithful, and kindle in them the fire of your love" (Pentecost Alleluia[18])

Cecilia: Maria, is it really true that there were origins in the Amazon of other mother-cult societies?

Maria (Veruska): Oh yes, my grandfather found goddess figurines in the gold-mining caves of el Tocuyo, Estado Lara, where the famous San

Juans, or Don Juanes of the nature spirits live. I used to play with them when I was a child.

Cecilia: I'd like to know more about that Señora.

Maria: OK, pour me some more wine. There are many Goddess stories from our ancestry. In Estado Guarico in a cave called Batatal is a female serpent with passionate eyes, who is sometimes related to the Candomble fire serpent Mboi-tata. The Chibcha recognize a universal mother goddess, Nabusa, relating especially with wild animals, trees, and rivers, similar to my practice. There were feminine deities relating to fertitlity like Bachue, the Earth Mother divinity of vegetation and protectress of the Muisca women. The Tucuna and Jivaros Indians believe in Nungui, a feminine goddess of fertility. The Incas venerated Pachamama, who still receives offerings from Peruvian farmers.[19]
Yemaya is also connected to aquatic deities as she is the Brasilian/ Yoruban Ocean Mother who provides similar maternal blessings. Then don't forget of course the Virgin of Coromoto, who has also appeared to my father and insisted that he get baptized. They mix us up sometimes, but I have become a mythical combination of the Virgin Mary and Yara. Yara is my true god mother, half anaconda snake, half blue-eyed human. The legend insists she seduced a young Indian into her subterranean sexual waters, whose location in Yaracuy, is not far from where I was born. This very site was clearly of ancient indigenous matrilineal culture based on all the goddess queens who I channeled there.[20] And not far from there, in Nirgua, my first parish and shrine were built in 1653 after my death, to preserve my divine legacy to the spirit of Nature and all Venezuelans. It was called "Nuestra Señora Maria de la Onza de Prado de Talavera de Nivar."

Cecilia: We would be very interested to hear more about your life as an Indian princess Maria . . . Like, were you ever in love?

Anita: Señora . . . Did you really ride that "onza" animal naked?

Rosa: What kind of supernatural powers did you have when you were alive, Maria? Could you really communicate with animals?

Cecilia: How did you die? Do you miss being in a body?

Anita: Will you ever reincarnate again?

Cecilia: You can use my uterus if you want.

Rosa: Or mine too .... if it could be an immaculate conception!

Maria: I don't believe many people have asked these questions. May I have some wine please? Perhaps you would like to take a trip to my last session in 1653— August 15th— to my house in Nirgua.

Cecilia: You mean like the time tunnel?

Maria: I mean a past life that you and Veruska had with me . . . . when I died.

Cecilia: Yes, take us there!

Maria: Musicos! Toquen los tambores por favor! (Musicians! Play the drums please!) I suggest you just get on my butterfly, and we'll fly your back. Just close your eyes. Put your mind blank . . .. and let's go . . .

Maria begins to shake. They begin to transport to another dimension. Veruska and Cecilia will shift out of their bodies to another place, where they will occupy different bodies, from a different incarnation. The sudden sound of the "cicadas" begins to vibrate from the trees. This sound permeates the journey. The real Maria descends from the catwalk.

SCENE 6 — Time tunnel choreography

The transition will be made through a musical journey, constantly accompanied by the mysterious vibratory sound of the cicada's wings. Maria Lionza has disappeared from her catwalk throne, and el Negro and Guaicaipuro remain. The choreography is a collage of images, sensations, flashbacks, and dreamlike experiences that reflect past scenes from Act I...... We see: Yara, the Virgin del Prado de la Talavera, pregnant Princess Anna Carolina and Cacqiue Guare, Don Juan y Doña Herminia De la Talavera being served by la Negra Hamurapi, Queen Isabella and King Ferdinand, Colombus, the Conquista battles between soldiers and Indians, African slaves, and Maria Lionza holding Tamanaco in her arms. This hypnotic collage of flashbacks creates a swirling spiral energy to occur on stage, taking us through time. The light finally fades on Maria & Tamanaco.

Scene 7— The Assumption— Maria Lionza's final day in Nirgua —August 15, 1653 (About 20 miles from Sortes)

This rewind of turbulence shifts the scene to a mystical fairy land, an indoor/outdoor jungle altar, high on a rain forest mountain, next to a natural spring and reservoir. When the lights come up, we feel like we have arrived in an overgrown paradise. Marion's present-day team appears as pre-incarnated Caquetios tribal members preparing the temple altar, flashed back to a Shangri- la existence deep in the rainforest. These Caquetios Indians have escaped the domination of the Spanish ruling class in the Seventeenth Century, under the protection of Maria on her sacred land. The scene opens as Maria enters as an old woman (as the same actress on the catwalk), mounted on the back of her danta/ onza/ tapir. She painfully dismounts. The sound of the cicadas' fades.

Maria Lionza: Oh, I'm just getting too old for this. Where are the sisters? Jazmin, Yarita, help me! Oh, Goddess mia. My mother warned me about this hermit life in my better years. Thank Goddess for you my sweet onza— my namesake— my flying angel. Too bad you can't cook. Anything has to be better than those two young nuns that gave up monastery life to live with me. They are great fun ... But they can't even boil water. And now they've discovered those goodlooking boys!! I'll never eat again ...

(Cecilia as) Jazmin and (Veruska as) Yarita arrive with two handsome Indian young men, all carrying baskets laden with fruits, vegetables, and herbs.

Jazmin (Gringa as): Maria, where have you been? We expected you yesterday!

Yarita (Veruska as): We were so worried about you.

Jazmin: It's a miracle you made it. Let us help you. You look exhausted.

Yarita: How was the Virgin of Coromoto? Did you see her?

Maria: Yes, I saw her, it's Mary all right— the only difference is that she hasn't aged a day since I last saw her on my first hour of birth sixty-three years ago. There are certain advantages to living in spirit girls. I don't know how they do it, but I'm going to find out. Her skin just seems to get younger.

Jazmin: Maybe that's because she's a virgin.

Maria: Excuse me Jazmin, but unfortunately, I still qualify for the same status . . . Oh well, they did build her a beautiful statue, right there where I was born in the river— 63 years ago. So, any visitors while I was gone?

Yarita: There are several dozen pilgrims waiting for you tonight . . . . they are at the foot of the mountain, and I said I would light a fire if you were willing to hold court

Maria: Of course we're holding court. Light the fire. What's for dinner? And where's my snake? Have you been feeding her the barley?

Yarita: Yes Maria, she's fine, and look how much she misses you. *(she takes the snake from her perch on a tree branch)* I'm going to check on our new cooks. I have no idea what they are making.

Maria: Make sure there's no meat Yarita!!

Jazmin: Maria, look what we found in the river this time— all these little clay goddess figurines.

Maria: I have dozens of those. I told you that this is a sacred, pre-historic mother goddess site which sources the Guanare river, which also connects with the Yaracuy and my moutain of Sortes in Chivicoa to the southwest. You are the only white person who knows about this place Jazmin, and it's only because you were a nun that I trust you, and that's the way I want to keep it.

Jazmin: What about that Spanish soldier, who was in love with you? Wasn't he a white man?

Maria: Fernando.... yes... he wanted me........ a Spanish count, with stars in his eyes for property in Venezuela by marrying into my mother's bloodline. The greed comes with the blue blood. Yes, I was in love, but I knew the sacrifice would sabotage my spiritual destiny and Venezuela's. He bribed my sister one day to lead him to my home in Sortes. But he was ambushed and killed by local Indians who knew that no Europeans were permitted on my sacred land.[21] I wept for him for weeks. I was so unhappy. I had written him in Spain telling him to forget me, that I had chosen another path, but his ambition drove him blindly, to his demise. Somehow, I don't believe it was love. From that day on I knew I would always be a virgin, dedicated to Jesus Christ, Father Sky and Mother Earth, and all her children. Loving and preserving endangered flora, fauna, and humanity is the most important thing I can do for Venezuela. On this sacred land I have studied plants and their remedies, the stars, the cycles of the moon, the habits of insects— I talk to birds and fish, monkeys, and my onzas, to my Don Juans and the spirits of the trees and the rivers. I am a happy woman, and I still can heal people. My old nursemaid, la Negra Hamurapi's great grandchildren are around me, and I watch the tribe who farms my land multiply. Except for the atrocities and pain of my Father's people, I have been blessed by divine providence with a rich metaphysical life, and a glorious natural paradise for a home. And look at this, such royal service before my very eyes.

Yarita has returned with a bottle of red wine, which always puts a twinkle in Maria's eye.

Yarita: How would you like to be remembered Maria, when we write about you in books? *(pouring her a glass)*

Maria: Well, let's see... I spent most of my life trying to help the native people and African slaves to escape the oppression of my mother's people. There were many years when they didn't trust me, but I was dedicated to creating sacred land where ancient traditions could be preserved. I did not last long in civilized society, so I can't claim much of a ladyship. But I shall always claim a spiritual connection to this country, along with Guaicaipuro, Yaracuy, Tamanaco, Yaguarin, and all the Caciques of the resistance. I include el Negro Felipe as well and the liberated slaves, la Negra Francisca, la Negra Tomasa, la Negra Matea, el Negro Primero, el Negro Miguel. And what about Jose Gregorio? I hope Rome finally gets around to beatifying him some day. What a saint! I do love him dearly. These souls and so many more have enlightened our rich Venezuelan culture through the "Tres Potencias" Trinity and our precious belief in racial peace and equality.

Maria drinks her wine.

Yarita: I think you may be talking about future spirits mi Reina.

Maria: You know at the moment my soul seems to be flying through several incarnations.

Yarita and Jazmin look at each other like they are not sure what is happening.

Jazmin: I am going to wait to light the torch to signal the pilgrims Maria, until after you've been given permission. Are you ready?

Maria: Am I ever ready?

Yarita: Here are your tobacos. Let's see. *She hands Maria a few tobacos to conjure.*

Maria makes the sign of the cross with the tobacos and begins to pray.

Maria: En el nombre de Dios Poderoso, el hijo, y el espiritu Santo, deme la fuerza, la proteccion, y la sabiduria transportar esta noche fina abajo las estrellas en esta paradiso mio, para estar disponible para los desfortunados y enfermos. Te pido en el nombre de la Virgin Maria y todo sus poderes.

(In the name of, etc., give me the strength, protection, and knowledge to transport this evening below the stars in this paradise of mine, to be available to the unfortunate and sick. I ask in the name of the Virgin Mary and all her powers.)

Maria smokes the tobacco and everybody can tell that the roads are only partially open. There is a dark warning in the cigar ashes providing enough indication to cancel the session, but Maria really wants to work and celebrate. Up on the catwalk, el Negro and Guaicaipuro look concerned.

The Mysteries of Maria Lionza

Yarita: What does it mean Maria?

Maria: It's not dangerous.

Jazmin: But Maria, you are tired from the trip. Let's make it tomorrow for the pilgrims.

Maria: Nonsense, I'm fine. Light the torch and fill my glass.

Jazmin reluctantly goes to light the torch and ring the bell, and Yarita begins to smoke a tabaco with Maria. Jazmin returns, and pours herself a glass of wine, and lights up a conjured cigar. Some of the other local natives join them, making offerings to the altar. Some of the Afro/Latino men begin to play the tambores. Women join Maria in the smoking circle, spitting into the clay pots, and murmuring prayers.

Jazmin: This sure beat monastery life any day!

El Negro addresses Guaicaipuro up on the catwalk.

El Negro: Something is not right.

Guaicaipuro: You must go down now, maybe you can clear her heart.
Maria begins to rattle and sway, taking deep breaths and dropping her cigar. Jazmin and Yarita back her up and cry over and over, until she finally goes into trance, bringing down el Negro Felipe into her body.

Yarita & Jazmin: Fuerza para la materia, proteccion, luz, y evolution!!

Felipe: Buenas Noches todos. What a beautiful evening you have arranged here for us tonight. Unfortunately, I am really in the mood to party with Maria, but I can tell that she is not strong enough to hold court this evening.

Jazmin: Oh no . . ..

Felipe: Mis hijas, she is very sick. Her time has come. I will bless the altar and standby should you need me.

Yarita: Oh Negro, I suspect it's her heart.

Jazmin: I knew she shouldn't have made that trip alone to Guare.

Negro: Guaicaipuro has something to tell you and then we must call off the session.

Jazmin: What's wrong? What's going on?

Yarita begins to shake, and Guaicaipuro descends into her body.

Jazmin: We've got to call Maria down to earth; she can't take this fuerza.

Guacaipuro: Wait a minute. I must tell you that we are making a path for Maria, to deliver her to the angels and archangels. She is almost ready to go. El Negro and I will take care of her. We have been waiting for her. Now it is time. Make her as comfortable as possible . . . . She is about to make the Assumption. Bring her down into her body now so she can pass over consciously.

Jazmin: *(Panicking)* Oh no Dios mio!! OK... I call Maria Lionza to the earth. Bring this creature to the earth. Now, please, in the name of God Almighty. A Tierra!!! Por Favor!! A Tierra!

Maria is weak and has difficulty coming back this time. Yarita returns to her body and Guaicaipuro leaves. The locals have made her a bed of leaves in front of the altar, and they gently lay her down. The energy required to bring down spirit has jolted her heart.

Jazmin: Please talk to us Maria . . . where are you? Get me some holy water.

Yarita: Please speak, Maria . . . It's Yarita and Jazmin, sus hijas!! Wake up Maria!! Chicos, toquen los tambores por favor!!

The boys start to play the drums, and Maria barely revives.

Maria: Well girls, I guess this is it. We've had some pretty miraculous experiences together out here in the jungle. My only regret is that you didn't learn how to cook better. Can I have my wine please?

Jazmin: Don't make jokes at a time like this Maria! Please don't leave us.

Maria: I will always be with you. You can always find me, because I've taught you all the prayers myself. I must continue my work in spirit now. Bring me my snake and my onza and let me rise. *(Jazmin gets the snake, Yarita brings in the onza, and Maria insists upon mounting the onza with her snake around her neck, lying on her belly)* I can see el Negro and Guaicaipuro waiting for me, and all the angels. Yes, this will be a grand reunion. Jazmin, I want you to ask one of those Friars to paint a picture of el Negro, Guaicaipuro and myself and call it Los Tres Poderosos. This will be the Trinity that you remember us by. You can hang it over the fireplace. This will really make me happy.

Yarita: *Jazmin and Yarita are weeping.* Please Maria, this is crazy. Just rest, you will be fine in the morning.

Maria: No, open the door. I must go now, my sisters. I can smell the roses, I can hear the music, and I see the light .... and I love you. Always say the rosary for me .... I will be there for you always. *The onza walks her outside and then ... leaps into the air, flying towards heaven) Jazmin and Yarita are speechless reaching after her with their rosaries. Music pours out of the sky which lights up majestically upon her Assumption, and butterflies seem to come from everywhere.* **Angels appear** *singing a short libretto:*

**"May you be blessed my daughter by God Most
High, beyond all women on earth. (Judith 13:23)
The trust you have shown shall not pass from the
memories of men but shall ever remind them of
the power of the mother Goddess. (Judith 13:25)
Glory be to the Father, and to the Son and to the holy
mother. As it was in the beginning, is now, and ever shall be
. World without end. Amen"**[22]

BLACKOUT

Scene 8 — The Coronation— October 12, 1995
— La Montana de Sortes—
Dia de la Raza and Maria Lionza's Birthday
A Celebration of Love and Wisdom

Scene 8a— Fiesta spirit at the Altar Mayor on the mountain of Sortes.

A fully dressed statue of Maria Lionza in pure white is presented in the altar mayor (without her crown). October 12, Maria Lionza's Birthday and The Day of the Races, is one of the year's biggest fiestas on the mountain of Sortes in Venezuela. The three powers sit above on the catwalk with great dignity. Salsa music is playing live in front of the Riverside entrance near the Altar Mayor. People are praying, making promises and offerings, lighting candles, and smoking tabacos. Others are dancing in the river, cooking over fires, and children play. There is fire on the dance floor in front of the Altar Mayor where three couples are dancing skillfully. They spin, lift, twist, pretzel, dip, and step off the ground in an exciting, opening salsa choreography. Devotees don't seem to be disturbed by this 'rumba' because it is El Dia de la Raza, when the magic of all the races mixes to celebrate Venezuela and its miraculous hybrid culture.

When the song ends, there is a fanfare which brings out the moving shrine and statue of Maria Lionza, which will then be carried all the way up to her grotto at the top of the mountain, followed by 'pelegrinos con promesas' (pilgrims with promises). They will accompany the Holy Queen to the Coronation. Three mediums are dressed as el Negro Felipe (Manuel), Maria Lionza (Veruska), and el Cacique Guaicaipuro (Marion), and they will lead the procession. **The pilgrims begin to sing** *as they cross the bridge and walk in solemn procession to celebrate her birthday high atop her Mountain of Sortes at her Royal Portal and the "Palace of Coronation."*

Tribute to the Reina

"Eres la misma ternura	*You have the same tenderness,*
Eres quietude y cancion	*The same quietness and song*
Eres esperanza y amor	*You are hope and love*
Porque eres la luz que brilla	*Because you are the light that makes*
en los ojos	*the eyes shine*

de un fulano que espera tu bendicione.	*Of a guy waiting for your blessing*
Porque te abre cada mano para recibir	*Because you open each hand to receive*
tu esplendor que ilumine esperanzas,	*Your splendor which brightens hopes*
y ammare su corazon	*and anchors the heart . . . .*
Te porte cosas bellas con este canto	*I bring you beautiful things with this Song*
Cosas que se oyen al ritmo de estrellas en quebradas	*Things that hear the star's rhythms in the hills*
de aguas alegres y cristalinas	*of happy and crystalline waters.*
Dichosas y cantarinas—	*Sayings and songs that come from the jungle*
se va metiendo en la selva	
en este paradiso de Yaracuy	*Of this Yaracuyan paradise.*
Del corral de mis ensuenos eres tu mi portadora	*From the corral of my daydreams, you are the carrier*
trabajando por nuestras madres	*working for our mothers . . . .*
mano de mi mandador	*hand of my maker . . .*
Eres la soga tendida que va enlazando luceros	*You are the rope that connects the bright lights,*
Eres la lampara prendida que luminan mis senderos	*You are the lamp that illuminates my paths . . . .*
Senderos que tu trillaste	*Paths, that you plowed . . . .*
Los senderos de mis vida	*Paths of my life.*

CHORUS

En la Montana Maria Lionza, en sus alturas	*In ML's Mountain, in her high altars*
Eres su Reina, de sus cosechas, de sus montanas de su splendor/	*is the queen of your crops and your abundant mountains*
Mysterios encanto que va siguiendo empostaduras	*Mysterious enchantment that follows*
Cosas que murmura el ritmo del rio en un dulce canto	*the overgrown things that murmur the rhythm of the sweet singing river.*

REPEAT Chorus

End: En la Montana llena de paz, coges de amor y ternura." 2X	*En the mountain filled with peace, one gets love and tenderness 2X*

(transcribed and translated from cassette tape)

Scene 8b— Soliloquy

The company exits the stage.
A solo pilgrim (who played the poet street prophet in the beginning) lights a small candle in front of a small bust of Maria which sits on a rock on the path. He prays with his bottle of rum:

> **Poet/Prophet:** "Who are you, Maria? Where did your accent come from? Are you maybe the girl that was coveted by the adventurous men who fled from the Criolle King and made her home in nature's earth? Are you the Queen of the water? . . . the one from the clouds and mysteries that another people loved, from a farther riverbank? I know nothing of legends . . . My love just loves you purely— you are the grace of the people— After the Immaculate, you are the one. I know this from the beginning of time. You are my Queen."

(transcribed from poetry on cassette)

The Mysteries of Maria Lionza

8c— Palace of the Coronation

The lights come up, and we are in front of Maria's Royal Altar at the summit of the mountain. The company enters and places the statue of Maria in the grotto altar. They all stand in front of the statue, and each recites a different line of the following poem:

"Maria—You are the one who perfumes the night,
who nurtures the crops,
who tunes the guitar ...
You give moonlight to the lemon trees
and make the rivers flow ...
You who gives water, and humidifies the lips of the thirsty ...
You who gives strength to men ...
You who makes the wheat grow from the ground ...
You who sweetens the breast of women so that the babies can
feel maternal tenderness with their milk ...
I have felt you like a lover on my chest,
I have lived in your blood, and slept in your bones ...
My eyes have learned from your enchantments in the hills ...

Your beautiful green hills, Maria, are surrounded by dreams ...
There can only be heard the voice of silence,
spelling marvels to the beat of the wind.
When I arrived at your portal,

How beautiful you appeared to me
You dress with fragrances that lift my soul ...

How strange your green eyes ...
What a river of light emerges from your body ...
What words emerge from your lips, so wet with feelings ...
The glow of the ring at your waist ...
Such flowers in your hair ...
Never in my years of maturity have I seen beauty so perfect ...
You are the queen of the fertile mountains and the robust trees,
of enchanted and perfumed flowers,

reminding us of your spiritual beauty.
Mother of millions of believers in our villages,
growing in influence every day …
So great and eternal like the natural power of the star king
You materialize as the mother of the seeds …
Queen of the mountainous parks,
of the fertile jungles,
of the black beaches and the singing waters.
Mother Goddess of the aboriginal skies, come down to us now …
We are waiting for you to manifest the beauty of nature in your
physical presence once again on this your sacred birthday
— Our Dia de la Raza!"

(transcribed and translated from poetry on cassette tape)

The three mediums stand in front of the altar holding hands. The tambores begin. The wind is blowing, and the 'materia' (mediums) are collecting fuerza from the miraculous vortex in which they stand. Shortly all three of them transport in a splendidly synchronistic moment of mystery.

El Negro (Manuel): Buenas Noches todos. Me alegre estar aqui para honorar la Reina esta noche, porque, como siempre, este ritual es como un festival de amor. And I still put rum second to love! (Good evening everybody. I'm happy to be here to honor the Queen this evening, because, as always, this ritual is like a festival of love.)

Guacaipuro (Marion): Y yo tambien tengo el argullo de estar parte de nuestra celebracion de la Trinidad de las Razas con la Madre como nuestra Reina. She has taught me to have patience with white people over the years. And I also am proud to be part of this celebration of the three races with the Mother as our Queen.

Maria (Veruska): Buenas noches todos. Maria Lionza bendice a todos los presentes en el nombre del Padre … yo ofrezco proteccion espiritual para todos. Pido a todos orar "como homenaje a las fuerzas de la Naturaleza, el aire, el agua, la tierra y el fuego, elevando la oracion hasta el Padre Creador del Universo que les permitia tener viento como un coro eterno." (Good evening, everybody. Maria Lionza blesses everybody present in the name of the Father and offers spiritual protection for all. I ask that you all pray, in honor of the forces of Nature, the air, the water, the earth, and the fire; elevating the prayer to the Father, Creator of the Universe, allowing the wind to sound like an eternal chorus.)

Negro: "Who is this arising like the dawn, fair as the moon, resplendent as the sun?" (Song 6:10)

Guacaipuro: "Like the rainbow gleaming against brilliant clouds, like blossoms in the days of spring." (Ecclesiastes 50: 7,8)

Maria: *She sings*

"I am the rose of Sharon,	
I am the lily of the valleys."	
"My throne is in a pillar of clouds,	(Song 2:1)
and for eternity I shall remain."	
"Approach me, you who desire me,	(Eccles 24:4, 9)
and take your fill of my fruits."	
I am like a vine putting out graceful shoots,	(Eccles 24:19)
my blossoms are sweeter than honey. "And	(Eccles 24: 17,20)
now my children listen to me;	
listen to instruction and learn to be wise."	(Prov 8: 32,33)
"Happy are those who keep my ways,	
who day after day, watch at my gates." "For	
those who find me find life,	(Prov 8: 34, 35)
and win favor from the Lord."[23]	(Prov 8: 36)

Negro Felipe and Guacaipuro ceremoniously lift the crown and hold it above Maria Lionza's (Veruska) head. They recite:

Felipe: Oh God, Divine Almighty Power of Heaven, Crown of the Faithful

"Bless this crown, we beseech thee, and so sanctify our servant, Maria Lionza upon whose head this day you do place it, for a sign of royal majesty, that she may be filled by your abundant grace, with all queenly virtues, through God, Amen."[24]

Guacaipuro: "God (Father sky) crowns you with a halo of glory and righteousness, that having a right faith and abundant fruit of good works, you may obtain the crown of an everlasting kingdom, By the gift of (the ancient Mother Goddess,) whose kingdom endures forever." (Taken from the formal Coronation of Queen Elizabeth II by the Archbishop of Canterbury and slightly rearranged to serve my purposes.)

The crown is placed. The crowd applauds.

Negro Felipe: We honor you Maria Lionza because we feel your love, we need your love, and we never want to be far from your love.

Guacaipuro: Maria, until eternity you are Venezuela's Queen/ Angel, for the halo of your love can only be celebrated with such a Royal Crown for a true Queen of Heaven and Earth.

Maria: It is from my heart that I bless each of you tonight for celebrating El Dia de la Raza with me on my birthday, in a true spirit of sincere humanitarian love. Oh, my dear children, Could the mystery be, that our blood all runs together deep in the veins of Mother Earth, and from her same womb we all come and go? I ask you this in the spirit of peace. Yes . . . we are all brothers and sisters, and I will gladly lay my blessing down on anyone who dedicates themselves to that world family. So, fill my glass, and show me a real Coronation party!!!!

Felipe: Feliz Cumpleanos mi hermana! Care for some rum?

Maria: Negro! Five hundred years, and you still can't remember my drink! You are the rum drinker!

Guaicaipuro: Ah yes, mi Reina....... *(pouring Maria a glass of red wine)*
He remembers your birthday, and that's good for Venezuela.

Happy Dia de la Raza!!

There is a reprise of Ruben Blades salsa song about the Montana de Sortes; and once again there is a multi-level fiesta/ritual that becomes the song and dance FINALE of the Mysteries of Maria. Some dance, some pray, some talk to the spirits, others drink, most are looking for happiness, and they all sing as passionately as they can on this Holy Birthday of the (mixed) Races. As the new moon reveals itself, the poet/prophet returns for his final delivery holding a candle. He stands in the foreground to the side and recites-

Poet/prophet:

**"Sortes, your plants are moved by the seasons . . .
Down the rocks of the Yaracuy, slide the memories of the water . . .
That's how I reconstruct the Mysteries of Maria in my heart,
along with the whispering wind,
which always flies through the air, like a spiritual gust of eternity ....."**

(transcribed and translated from poetry on cassette tape)

THE END

BIBLIOGRAPHY

The Mysteries of Maria Lionza

Acts 1 & 2

Ashton, Joan, Mother of All Nations, Harper and Rowe, SF, 1989

Berecht, Fatima, Editor, Taino, Pre-Columbian Art and Culture from The Carribean, The Monacelli Press, Inc. NY 1997

Blanco, Celia, Manual EsotericoU, Representaciones Loga, Miranda, Venezuela, 1988

Carroll, Michael, P., The Cult of the Virgin Mary, Princeton University Press, 1986

Christian, William A., Local Religion in Sixteenth Century Spain, Princeton University Press, 1981

Cunneen, Sally, In Search of Mary, Ballentine Books, N.Y., 1996

Durham, Michael S., Miracles of Mary, Harpers, SF, 1995

Fox, Mathew, Editor, Hildegard of Bingen's Book of DivineWorks, Bear & Co. Santa Fe, N. Mexico, 1987

Hebert, Albert, The Tears of Mary and Fatima, Why? - Albert Hebert S.M.; Paulina, La, 1983

Marsland, William and Amy, Venezuela Through Its History, Thomas Crowell Co., N.Y., 1954

Mervin, Sabrina & Prunhuber, Carol, Women-Around the World and Through the Ages, Atomium Books, Wilmington, DE, 1990

Moreno, Santiago de Jesus Rodriguez, Biografia y Origen de su Majestad Reina Maria Lionza, Editorial Los Llanos, San Juan de los Morrows, Guarico, Venezuela, 1979

Moron, Guilliermo, A History of Venezuela, Roy Publishers, NY, 1963

Oviedo y Banos, Don Jose, The Conquest and Settlement of Venezuela,

University of California Press, Berkley/La/London, 1987

Perottet, Tony, Editor, Venezuela, APA Publications, Singapore, 1994

Pollak-Eltz, Maria Lionza, Mito y Culto Venezolano, Universidad Catolica Andres Bello, Caracas, 1985

Salazar, Homero, Yara; El Libro Del Siglo: La Historia de Maria Lionza, Editorial El Aragueno, CA, 1988

Tavard, George, The Thousand Faces of the Virgin Mary, The Liturgical Press, Collegeville, Minn., 1996

Warner, Maria, Alone of All Her Sex, Vintage Books, NY, 1983

Weber, Christian Lore, Circle of Mysteries, Yes International Publishers, St. Paul, Minn. 1995

Wilbert, Johannes, Editor, Encyclopedia of World Cultures, South America, Vol. VII, GK Hall and Co., Boston, Mass.

BIBLIOGRAPHY

The Mysteries of Maria Lionza

ACT 3

Alvarez, Manuel Diaz, El Medico de Los Pobres— Dr. Jose Gregorio Hernandez, Ediciones Paulinas, Caracas, Venezuela, 1991

Blanco, Celia, Manuel Esoterico, Representaciones Loga, C.A., Miranda Venezuela, 1988

Castellanos, Iris, Maisanta— En Caballo de Hierro, Fuentes Editores, Caracas, 1992

Maria Lionza y Su Corte Celestial, LibroOferta, Caracas, Venezuela, 1990

McMahon, Rev. Msgr John A, Censor Librorum, Scriptural Rosary, Christianica Center, Chicago, 1966

Montoya, Roberto Hernandez, The Cult of Venus in Venezuela, http://www.

analitica.com/bitblio/rhernand/venus-i.htm

Moreno, Santiago de Jesus Rodriguez, <u>Biografia y Origen de su Majestad Reina Maria Lionza</u>, Editorial Los Llanos, Guarico, Venezuela, 1979

Pollak-Eltz, Angelina, <u>Maria Lionza, Mito y Culto Venezolano,</u> Universidad Catolica Andres Bello, Caracas, Venezuela, 1985 Rivero, Armando, <u>Maria Lionza— La Diosa del Amor y de la Fortuna</u>, Producciones David-River, Caracas, Venezuela.

Salazar, Homero, <u>Yara, El Libro del Siglo, La Historia de Maria Lionza</u>, Editorial El Aragueno, C.A., 1988

Simpson, George Eaton, <u>Black Religions in the New World</u>, Columbia University Press, New York, 1978

ENDNOTES

The Mysteries of Maria Lionza

Acts 1 & 2

1. Wilbert, J., Encyclopedia of World Cultures, Vol 7, pg. 340
2. Yara is a Pre-Columbian Goddess of the Waters from the Tupari culture who is half woman and half anaconda/snake, who lives in the underworld and brings benevolence, fertility, and healing to tribal members through the shaman. She represents the ancient "Earth Mother" who actually is half animal.
3. Parintins.com-Toadas: Caprichoso 98: Canto daYara
4. NOVA Online/Warriors of the Amazon/The Last Shaman (4)
5. Bercht, Fatima, Taino, Pre-Columbian Art and Culture from the Caribbean, pg 41
6. World Religions, SA Indians, pg 1021
7. Tamanaco was a great Venezuelan Indian Chief in the 16th century. He is a poetic anachronism in this context because I am featuring him because he is my personal protector who, among many, lost his life for his people.
8. Christian, W., Local Religion in 16th Century Spain, pg 91 & 111— I have tracked down this hermitage, outside of Toledo, Spain where the principal character of this story, Maria Lionza, draws lineage, based on her mother and father's same name— (The Virgin) del Prado de la Talavera de la Reina.
9. precitool.com.mx/talavera.htm— (translation from Spanish) "At the end of the 13th century the Arabs introduced to Spain, through Majorca, a special white, antique ceramic glaze with beautiful ornate designs, which became famous near Toledo in the Cathedral work, and later was brought around 1550 to America by the Dominican monks of Talavera de la Reina.
10. Christian, W., pg. 113
11. catholicchurch.org/iglesia/maria/cantos.htm

12 Christian, pg 100. The water at this particular shrine had curative properties and came from an underground sulphur hot springs below the hermitage which arrived with an apparition of the virign in the 16th century.

13 Adams, Henry, Mont Saint Michel and Chartres,

14 Christian, pg 82 "The poor or the powerless have the visions, and the eventual imposition of their truth upon the town authorities is a sure way of showing that Mary or the saint comes to serve everybody; that the bond set up between the saint and the town is also a direct bond between the saint and each person of the town, beginning with the powerless."

15 Hoye, Daniel, Monsignor, Household Blessings and Prayers, pg 362

16 www.udayton.edu/mary/resources/engseven.html

17 Herbert, A., The Tears of Mar y-and Fatima Why?, pg 32

18 Moreno, Chapter One—This book is a channeled account, from Maria Lionza herself of her life story. It also conflates with the stories she personally told me of her Mother and Father.

19 Warner, pg 262

20 Fox, Mathew, Hildegard of Bingen's Book of Divine Works, pg 379

21 Marsland, Venezuela Through It's Histor y, pg 55— "The encomendero won the right to the services of the Indians in exchange for certain benefits he was supposed to provide. According to the laws, he had to protect the Indians from injustice, make them live in villages and observe civilized social mores governing family life. He was ordered to instruct them in the Christian religion, organize domestic government under the authority of the Indian chief, direct their work and destroy all savage habits and inclinations."
   **European Voyages of Exploration: Latin America— www.acs. ucalgary. ca/HIST/tutor/ervoya/Latin.html"
   The leader and main investor of an expedition would have the title of "captain" and was invariably an important encomendro; a member or former member of a colonial municipal council, a senior settler in the area, a wealthy man, or a nobleman."

22 The Yaracuy River in Barquisimetro, Venezuela is where Maria Lionza's Sacred National Reserve is for the practice of her cult in present day.

23 Marsland, pg 54—The European smallpox wiped out two thirds of the indigenous population. "When the plague began to diminish in 1581, the decimated indians ceased to give the Spaniards serious trouble."

24 There are different legends about Maria Lionza's parents, but all agree that whichever parent was Indian, knew that the tribe would reject the child because of "clear eyes".

25 There was a serious drought in Venezuela in the early 1590's along with the plague, which increased the arrival of African slaves to do work in the fields that the Indians could not do.

26 Moreno, pg 14— La Negra Haimarupi was the actual Black nursemaid of Princess Carolina, and Maria Lionza who arrived around the same time as the family did in the 1570s and had been thoroughly indoctrinated into the Catholic Church.

27 Songs to Mary/Bride of God;Anima Mariae http://cgi.geocities.com/Athens

28 Marian Titles in the Popular Religiosity of Latin America; www.udayton.edu/ mary/resources/engseven.

29 Cuneen, S., In Search of Mar y, pg 61

30 Advocaciones Marianas—Venezuela; aciprensa.com/advvenez.htm—(translated from Spanish) "The 7 of October 1944, Pope Pio XII declared the Virgin of Coromoto the Patron of the Republic of Venezuela and her coronation was celebrated in 1952, three centuries after her apparition.

31 Cuneen, pg 275

32 http://catholic.net/RCC/Indices/Inspirations/mass-parallel.txt—Ordinary of the Tridentine Mass— 1962Mervin, Sabrina and Prunhuber, Carol, Women Around the World And Through the Ages— pg 199

33 http://lcweb2.loc.gov/cgi-bin/query/r?frd/cstdy:@field(DOCID+es0017)— SPAIN:The Golden Age "Once Islamic Spain had ceased to exist, attention turned to the internal threat posed by hundreds of thousands of Muslims living in the recently incorporated Granada. 'Spanish society drove itself', historian J.H. Elliot writes, 'on a ruthless,

ultimately self-defeating quest for an unattainable purity."

34 http://encarta.msn.com/index/conciseindex/5b/o5b68000.ht m — Torquemada,Tomas de

35 http://www.acs.ucalgary.ca/HIST/tutor/ervoya/columbus.html— European Voyages of Exploration

36 Bercht, F., pg 171

37 http://www.elmbavenez-us.org/cultural/fiestas.html— "This is a carnivalesque celebration, in which devils with many horns and different human or animal faces parade around the town to arrive at the main church. These devils are paying penance, and the amount of horns show the many sins they are paying for. Just in the same way as this celebration took place in 16th century Spain, so it was taken to its colonies."

38 http://www.uhhp.com/h9.html— King Ferdinand's letter to the Arawak/Taino (letter was reprinted in one of Bartoleme de las Casas)

39 Moron, G., A Histor y of Venezuela, pg 35— Fray Bartolome de las Casas (1474-1566) was a Spanish missionary and historian known as the Apostle of the Indians who was the first to criticize the oppression of Native Americans by their European conquerors. He gained royal permission to colonise the whole Venezuelan coast with farmers brought from Castille, and by means of peaceful persuasion he hoped to convert and pacify the natives. The task was to protect the Indians from slavery and other ill-treatment. But the monastery was wiped out by the Indians in 1520.

40 Blanco, C., pg 489— Padre Nectorio Maria was another famous Spanish Franciscan monk who wrote about Indigenous Venezuela

41 http://cgi.geocities.com/Athens/Acropolis/5743/marysong.html

42 Oviedo y Banos— Chapter VII

43 Ibid, pg 227

44 Blanco, C., pg 119— El Negro Felipe was an Afro-Cuban slave who followed in the footsteps of Negro Miguel around 1550 as a liberator. He forms part of the trinity of Maria Lionza, and graces every Espiritista altar in Venezuela with his healing presence.

45 Oviedo y Banos, pg 226— Tapia was a soldier whose historical claim to fame as an associate of Pedro Alonzo, was to seize an abandoned Indian baby lying on a beach, and grasping her by the foot he submerged and drowned her in the waters saying "I baptize you in the name of the Father, the Son, and the Holy Spirit."

46 Ibid, pg 200

47 Lyrics come from personally recorded tambor sessions in the jungle pueblo where I lived (Birongo, Ven)

48 Cuneen, pg 148

49 Oviedo y Banos, pg 227

50 Tavard, pg 161

51 Carroll, M.— Carrol makes a lot of psychological analysis about the "machismo" complex from Spain and Italy. What I have gleamed from the Spanish Conquista machismo is that so many strong Indians and Slaves who resisted domination who were murdered, left a lot of submissive male genes around to be submissive to the crown and the white European male with all his organized control issues.

ENDNOTES

The Mysteries of Maria Lionza

Act 3

1 Rivero, pg 42 (A standard prayer to Maria Lionza)

2 'Mapurite' means skunk in Spanish and is one of many vernacular names used for this tropical miracle plant, formally called 'Petiverea Alliacael.' I followed three people who were using this plant as a cure for cancer in Venezuela and became convinced that it worked.

3 Castellanos, Iris, Maisanta, en caballo de hierro, pg 17— discusses Hugo Chavez Frias, as the commander in Chief of the Armed Forces, also great grandson of Pedro Perez Delgado, or "Maisanta", El ultimo hombre a caballo", who opposed

Juan Vicente Gomez in the late twenties.

4   Ibid, pg 6

5   Robeto Hernandez Montoya, The cult of Venus in Venezuela, pg 2— http://www.analitica.com/bitblio/rhernand/venus-i.htm

6   Ibid, pg 1

7   La Reina Maria Lionza y Su Corte Celestial, pg 43

8   Pollak-Eltz, Angelina, pg 71— "Los peregrinos prosiguen su camino y llegan al primer portal, donde depositan ofrendas y encienden algunas velas. Desde aqui empieza la subida; antes de llegar al Palacio de la Coronacion, hay que llevar a cabo el mismo ritual en cada portal. Llegados a la "escalera" (otro nombre del Palacio de la Coronacion) preparan el campanento y luego rinden homenaje a la Reina."

9   La Reina Maria Lionza y Su Corte Celestial, pg 45

10 Rivero, pg 53

11 A "Despojo" is a brujeria term for banishing darkness from a person, place, or thing. This can be done with special baths that are concocted (with ammonia as a main ingredient), gunpowder rings, house cleaning, special candle trabajos, or anything that distances and banishes the negativity hindering some process.

12 The cicadas have a mysterious sound in summer, and is considered a romantic sign since the male creates this sound for the female by vibrating two flaps in his throat. This sound is considered auspicious for spiritual work in Venezuela. The ancient Greeks also highly appreciated the love song of the 5 eyed cicada.

13 Simpson, George, pg 164-65 "This cult originated in the mountains of Sortes and in the state of Yaracuy during the colonial period in an area where African, American Indian, and European cultural elements were intermingled. In its original form, it was based on veneration of natural forces and on the spirits which inhabitied rivers, caverns, and the forest .
    ... In recent years, the migration of Cuban and Trinidadians to Venezuela hs introduced a number of African spirits, and in particular the SEVEN AFRICAN POWERS. This includes, Obtala, Orula, Yemaya, Oshun,

Ogun, Chango, Elegua. The cult of Maria Lionza does not approve of Santerian animal sacrifice on her sacred land, and there is conflict in this arena.

14 TAMANACO, the great Indian Chief of Venezuela lived in the mid 1500s. I met him in spirit in the back room of a Perfumeria in Catia in 1991. He was the first Venezuelan spirit with whom I'd ever conversed in this practice, and he immediately offered to be my protector. He has manifested himself to me physically during the writing of this project. As part of the Corte India, one lights a green candle to invoke him.

15 Alvarez, Manuel Diaz, El Medico De Los Pobres— Dr. Jose Gregorio Hernandez was the "Doctor of the Poor People" and lived during the turn of the century. He died tragically in a car accident in 1919. I actually interviewed him on videotape regarding the recipe for the cancer cure. Also, on videotape I have this very operation which is mentioned in the script. He worked on people for free, during his life, and in spirit. He is known all over Latin America for his altruism and is supposed to be beatified some day in Rome.

16 Blanco, Celia, pg. 484 (translated from the Spanish)

17 Ibid, pg. 103

18 Scriptural Rosary, pg. 71

19 Pollak-Eltz, pg. 28

20 Ibid, pg. 31

21 Moreno, Santiago, pg. 26-30

22 Scriptural Rosary, pg. 75

23 Ibid, pg. 78-79

24 "The Coronation of her majesty Queen Elizabeth II, June 1953"— http://www.oremus.org/liturgy/coronation/cor1953b.html

Cecilia Anne Gruessing, M.A.

The Mysteries of INANNA

A Mythical Goddess Play

Cecilia Gruessing - 1999

The Mysteries of Inanna

Cecilia Anne Gruessing, M.A.

INTRODUCTION

In an effort to research Goddess "origins", I have chosen Inanna because she represents so many firsts in history's mythological line up of subsequent Goddesses. Her legacy is profoundly rendered in poems, hymns, and the Epic of Gilgamesh dating back to 2500BC in Sumeria, with homo sapiens most early recorded history reflecting a nature-based society. This was clearly a transition from matristic to patriarchal culture at that time. Sumerian archaeology shows evidence of a Mother Goddess cult as far back as 4000BC.

Inanna provided the origins for Ishtar, Astarte, Aphrodite, Athena, Artemis, Isis, and many others as the multi-dimensional Queen of Heaven and Earth (and Venus & the moon); Goddess of War, The Almighty Priestess of love, sex, and fertility; Goddess of Wisdom and oracles, Queen of death and rebirth; Protectress of plants, animals, and the wonders of the earth, and countless other glorious titles. No other Neolithic Goddess society offers the ancient historical recorded legacy that Inanna leaves.

Ironically, we do not see the customary characteristics of wife and mother in Inanna's character, and this uniqueness makes her archetypal journey an unusual and lonely one, perhaps reflecting the persona of some buried ancestral sisters of liberation sublimating their powers within Inanna's manipulated mythology. Subsequent derivations of her archetype have carried on this struggle to this day in search of emotional, spiritual, and physical liberation.

In the form of a musical drama, I have designed the "Mysteries of Inanna" as a labyrinthic journey of her legendary descent to the underworld, past the seven planetary Gods and their gates. At each level she must give up a symbolic piece of her clothing representing her knowledge and powers. I have correlated ancient and modern character flavors of planetary archetypes as the 7 gatekeeper Gods of the Heavens and threshold guardians that Inanna must interact with on her journey below, in search of her destiny. The ascent of her mythological character development has been artistically woven inside her descent, by reconstructing her lost qualities after having sacrificed those powers to the jealous male gods.

I use footnotes to document the ancient sources of dramatic events, as well as several feminist and scholarly analysis of Inanna. Most importantly, I have created MY OWN metaphoric interpretation of the myths and hymns in an updated version of the myth, yet still maintaining much of the translation of the original text from the cuneiform tablets as dialogue.

Inanna's ascent through written literature in the early Sumerian cuneiform tablets (from 3,000 BC, but only recently translated late 1990s) clearly indicates women's historical struggle through her Goddess archetype, to maintain natural order, despite the distortion by the male authors of the day. Enheduanna (A famous Babylonian temple priestess poet) offers a much clearer report of Inanna's leadership qualities, presenting a legitimate warrior, queen, and lover.

I have taken the liberty to completely reverse the significance of several of the incongruities I have found in her mythology. Where, for instance, Sylvia Perera (Descent of the Goddess) takes the information as fact, and reorganizes it psychologically to accommodate the masculine authorship (Dumuzzi's power), I flat out deny some of the authentic literature because it just doesn't reflect feminine and Neolithic Goddess morality. I believe that women's contact with mother earth and her crops, gave her a very important role in decision making.

I believe that Inanna was a natural woman, who followed her instincts, and wanted to be free and undominated by anything or anyone. She had compassion for her people, and understood the ways of agriculture, knowing that good crops and harvest meant survival for her people. She understood the seasons and the heavens, coming from Venus, with the star of Venus as her emblem. She was not subservient to unfair law, and always fought for freedom.

For instance, I disagree completely with the construction of her dark Underworld queen sister, Ereshkigal as a vampire witch. This character suits the male fear of a femme fatal-crone-gorgon-harpie. I believe that Inanna and Ereshkigal accept their dual duties to the Earth, and discover their sisterhood through the descent myth, which subsequently becomes a positive ritual empowering the fertility of the planet. It is an excarnation ritual, and a way to discover and confront one's dark side, where creativity is inseminated.

Miss Inanna Hussein initiates my story of Inanna in a modern-day setting, with her perspective as "Miss Universe" representing Iraq. She must relinquish her crown because of philosophical disagreements she has with her uncle Hussein, who is dictator of Iraq. 5,000 years after the original Inanna story, Sumeria has become a major world hot bed of feminine oppression and patriarchy. The oracle of the Mysteries of Inanna will call her and take her through the descent initiation. Her ego, and all of the nurturing social laws which identify her, are ceremoniously stripped away. All titles, all glory, all knowledge, voice, life force, love, fertility, and joy are removed, and Inanna is left to die during the 3 days of the dark of the moon, hung upon a peg. Upon her return, she discovers that all she wants is male-female egalitarian love and cooperation in a society whose obsessions with power obliterate those desires.

The last introductory revelation I would like to point out about this research deals with the stars, and their religious significance to this project.

If the constellation Taurus was in the sky around 3000 BC, then the Gemini twins had to precede that date, exactly during the documented discovery of Neolithic Mother-Goddess cults throughout world history. Besides the wide fertile, matristic hips of figurines found in pre-historic locations, archaeology has also shown us primitive partner images of women holding hands throughout her archaeological findings. These are clearly twin images. Could this starry umbrella have dictated the behavior of society at that time, in the form of a matrilineal and egalitarian lifestyle for women? Inanna's character leaves us with that persona of femininity.

**I want to thank my teachers, Mara Keller, a feminist scholar, and Joan Marler, editor of The Civilization of the Goddess, for bringing the work of MARIA GIMBUTAS to my attention and offering my artist/ playwright/ thespian consciousness the opportunity to translate history with an "ARCHAEO-MYTHOLOGICAL-ARTISTIC" perspective. I hope you enjoy the work.

Ceil Gruessing, San Francisco, Winter '99

The Mysteries of Inanna

TABLE OF CONTENTS SCENES, SETTING, AND CHARACTER BREAKDOWN

The setting of this play calls for two limbo time zones. One is a modern-day consulate party, and the other is an imaginary set of gates marked by a labyrinth floor plan of 7 spirals. The upstage altar which constantly remains on the stage requires a huge statue of Inanna standing on a lioness and a table area for food and religious regalia. This sculpture is initially veiled. Somehow a moon waxes and wanes during the course of the show. And in the corner, is the ever- present Hullupu tree (date palm) artistically enveloping a wooden, throne seat.

1. **SCENE 1**— PERSIAN NEW YEAR
   — Modern day gala— Iraqi Embassy .... *page 140*

2. **SCENE 2**— Gate one— SATURN
   — King Kronos— Removal of the crown .... *page 147*

3. **SCENE 3**— Gate two— JUPITER (Enki)
   —WISDOM— the earring .... *page 148*

4. **SCENE 4**— Gate three— MARS (Mt. Ebeh)
   — EXPRESSION/JUDGEMENT— the necklace .... *page 151*

5. **SCENE 5**— Gate four— HELIOS (Sun)
   — PROPOSALS/PROSPERITY — the breastplate .... *page 154*

6. **SCENE 6**— Gate five—VENUS
   — BEAUTY RITUALS— the zodiac girdle .... *page 156*

7. **SCENE 7**— Gatesix— MERCURY(Dumuzi)

— SACRED MARRIAGE —The sceptor .... *page 158*
8. **SCENE 8**— Gate seven— MOON—The Hullupu Tree
— GENESIS— bracelet & rings .... *page 161*
9. **SCENE 9**— THE CENTER RING— ERESHKIGAL
— DEATH/REBIRTH .... *page 164*
10. **SCENE 10**— THE RETURN OF INANNA
— Death of the King .... *page 166*
11. **SCENE 11**— BACK TO PERSIAN NEW YEAR
—The Reunion .... *page 168*

CHARACTERS

- **Inanna** Hussein— Middle Eastern Woman/singer-dancer (25-35)
- **Company of female priestesses**— four hermaphrodites at gala/ and at the Venus temple
- **Company of International guests**, including disguised Planetary Gods
- **Mrs. Geshtinanna**— Iraqi Ambassador's wife
- **Reporter**— played by Ereshkigal actress
- **Kings Kronos**— Saturn— Older man
- **Jupiter**— Middle aged man
- **Mars**— Young African/Latino
- **Helios**— Businessman (50-60)
- **Mercury**— Strong young man (25-35)
- **Snake**— Middle Eastern male dancer
- **Anzu Bird**— Asian female dancer
- **Lilith**— Large, Black blues singer-40
- **Ereshkigal**— Blond German woman (35-45)

The Mysteries of Inanna

SCENE I— PERSIAN NEW YEAR
— Modern day gala— Iraqi Embassy

Our story begins with this very bourgeois, old world royal banquet-gala, congregated in the Iraqi embassy in Washington, DC for a traditional Persian New Years Celebration. A veiled statue stands in a central altar/food area.

Royal dignitaries from all over the world congregate to witness the unveiling of this statue commemorating the ancient Goddess Inanna. The media informs us that we are waiting for the procession or, special entrance of Miss Universe - Inanna Hussein, with her entourage and ceremonial goodbye to the crown. Tonight, she will honor her country's already defunct respect for her crown by formally stepping down from the throne and her responsibility to Iraq's political platforms on the world stage.

Presents are heads of state, dignitaries, and distant royalty quietly chatting with other guests, who will later (in different costumes) perform the judgmental roles of the planetary Gods in her sequential descent to the underworld. The women wear veils.[1]

We are in the ballroom of the Iraq Embassy setting up for the gala. A News Media team of journalists presents the following scene in the foreground as their correspondent speaks to the camera.

Reporter: This evening, we bring you news of Inanna Hussein. She is the guest of honor for the Persian/American New Year's Celebration at the Iraqi consulate in the USA. Not only is she this year's departing Miss Universe from Iraq, but she is also under exile in the USA as refugee royalty. The deep irony is that she is the black sheep niece of Sadam Hussein. Inanna has been staying at the consulate in Washington DC with high security around her very limited excursions into the American public eye. She condemns the violent tactics of her Uncle Sadam Hussein's dictatorship. At midnight this spring equinox, Inanna, will relinquish all her blood rights to the Queenship of her royal inheritance, and walk her Miss Universe title for the last time in exile from her motherland. Her father, Sadam's brother, died several years ago mysteriously. She is the oldest heir in the King's family, despite the insignificance of matrilineal nepotism in the traditional Islamic royalty system.

Inanna, however, has achieved international focus as the Miss Universe, 1999, with a clearly passionate position of non- violence delivered from the voice, and soul of an exceptionally "goddess- like", inspired and beautiful young woman of the new millennium.

Scene 1a— Introductions

Mrs. Geshtinanna who is the wife of the Iraqi ambassador welcomes the guests—

Mrs. Geshtinanna: Good evening and Happy New Year to all of you. Thank you for coming. We celebrate tonight an emotional testimony to endings and beginnings. Not only do we honor the end of the great reign of our Miss Iraq as Miss Universe, but also, we gather to express our solidarity for our homeland so far away, and yet so close to our hearts. Our beloved country Iraq has been through so much pain, destruction, and crisis, that we must take refuge in the resilience of personal truths that can be buried deep within our soul histories to find hope for the future. Iraq holds archaeological secrets of Ancient Sumeria, one of the oldest civilizations in the world. And the land has also been ravaged by war for centuries and millennia, destroying all of these secrets along with the lives of innocent Iraqi civilians. Sooner or later there are individuals whose truths ring out like epiphanies, and they must take action to stop all war.

Our departing Ms. Universe, Inanna Hussein, stood in front of the whole world as the young Iraqi contestant for Miss Universe, and dedicated her life to condemn violence and war from any point of view. She is dedicated to promoting peace between her country and the rest of the world at the risk of her life. This was her mission as the namesake of "Inanna", the great Mesopotamian Goddess whose origins precede history, yet whose legacies are clearly motivating her daily life. She differs from the prehistoric Inanna in one very important way.

She is a warrior who does not kill, who fights for justice with heart rather than sword. And she will continue this peace work despite stepping down tonight.

The Mysteries of Inanna

Reporter: Will the press have a chance to ask her questions?

Mrs. Geshtinanna: Unfortunately, she is preparing for her performance which is about to begin . . ..

Inanna exits from behind a curtain with a bathrobe over her costume, wearing a burka, only revealing her eyes.

Inanna: Of course, sir. I would be delighted to answer any questions.

Reporter: Can you tell us something about your past?

Inanna: I grew up in Iraq during all of the unrest with Sadam Hussein's dictatorship. My parents enrolled me in a British private school and then I went to Barnard College in the US where I studied international relations and worked as an activist for peace. When I took first place in the pageant and began to travel and visit high schools all over the world, I spoke about world peace and the role that young people must play in that endeavor.

Reporter: And how does your uncle feel about your philosophy?

Inanna: Unfortunately, because of the political differences that I have with my Uncle Sadam Hussein, I am now in exile from my country. For this reason, I must step down from my role as Ms. Universe as a representative of Iraq. This is not easy for me, as I love my family, and my country.

This comment produces a huge buzz amongst the reporters, and she is taken off stage.

Reporters: Where will you live? Who will you work for? What about your family?

Mrs. Geshtinanna: *stepping in as Inanna goes backstage.* As Inanna's longtime friend, I wish to honor her work as a pacifist thinker and leader whose focus has been children and the future. Tonight, we will formally witness her last act as Ms. Universe. With great regret I have prepared the floor for her final performance, and with great honor and hope do I

send her on her journey. Ladies and Gentlemen, the Queen Inanna will
lead us in her final royal celebration of our blessed Nowruz (NewYear). We will
also unveil a modern sculpture depicting the Goddess Inanna. It is larger than life,
cut in lapis lazuli, and depicts Inanna, naked, standing on a wild lioness, wearing her
famous regalia of many powers. Ladies and Gentlemen… Please welcome
Inanna and her last appearance as Ms. Universe.

Scene 1b— The opening number - setting the mood

The music begins, the statue is unveiled, and a completely unexpected group of troubadours and clowns enter, with the clothing of opposite sexes on half their bodies, female on the left/ male on the right. Some men are dressed up carnival style; Priestesses carry double axes and swords.[2]

With the entrance of Inanna, dressed in her seven ceremonial garments of queenship,[3] her priestesses sprinkle her throne, which is flanked by lions, with red rose petals[4]. Her seductive regalia corresponds to the seven kundalini chakras and is broken down in various versions of the story in different ways.

She wears a crown, scepter/rod, ear pendants, necklace, breast plate, hip girdle, and a garment of ladyship (breechcloth, and bracelets on her wrists and ankles). Her presence is spellbinding, her beauty, even veiled, breathtaking. The sincerity of her eyes, her fearlessness, her sensitivity, her dignity, strength and fire are riveting. There is numinous light around this woman, Inanna, Miss Universe, with her crown[5] and other important royal garments representing the symbols of her ancient inherited knowledge and power (called the "mees"). The cameras cannot get enough of her. INANNA begins to sing Arabian Jazz style:[6]

THE EXCELLENT BEGINNING
By Mohammed Taqui Bahar

**"Tis spring, flowers full and happiness in the green grass vine
The Great Wild Bull dances in the sky[7]**

**All the blossoms are blooming except mine
lose not heart free spirit on New Year's**

Day I heard from the lips of a lily today.

Do not sing the seven shams this New Year's Eve
I beg thee complaint, curse, corruption, cacophony,
clumsiness, chaos, and cruelty
The seven symbols— serene greenery, scented hyacinth and
sweet apple, senged, samanu, salway and song spell.
Send the seven symbols to the table of a lover
Throw the seven shams to the door of an ill-wisher.
Tis New Year's Eve, rid the heart of darkness
Eventually this black night will turn to light
Carry out the New Year tradition and Goddess willing
Bring back the feeling with our ritual.

CHOREOGRAPHY— During this dramatic, Middle Eastern, contemporary, hip hop, belly dance sound. the company members decorate the altar with:

The ceremonial cloth (sofreh-ye haft-sinn) is spread on the altar floor.
Coins are tossed on the cloth for prosperity and wealth
A basket of painted eggs for fertility
A Seville orange floating in a bowl of water is the Earth floating in space.
A goldfish in a bowl represents life and the end of the Pisces astral year.
Rose water— cleansing
Incense pot to burn Rue
Hyacinth and or Narcissus flowers
Candles— Enlightenment and Happiness (children)
Mirror - for the reflection of the Creation.[8]

Inanna prays during this ritual preparation, for her people-

Inanna: I pray "to the star twin ancestors [9] of many winters back, to the love of mother earth and father sky, for the suffering of the innocent, for the clarity of the blind, to the future of all children on earth, for the humility of the proud, for the total annihilation of weaponry, and the building of bonds between cultures, nations, and religions. I call upon the soul of the ancient ancestors who lived on my beloved land seven thousand years ago, before Mohammed, before the oil, before the Shahs, before the Kings. Oh Sumeria - Ancient Mesopotamia - the Tigris and Euphrates River valley- hot, tropical, lush, and flowing with love, food and life!!![10] Queen Inanna, I call you!!

Once more the dancers enter bringing seven sacred dishes - each beginning with the letter S, sinn, and each representing the seven angelic heralds of life — rebirth, health, happiness, prosperity, joy, patience, and beauty.

Sabzeh— wheat or lentil sprouts— rebirth
Samanu— sweet, creamy pudding made with wheat sprouts
Sib— apples for health and beauty
Senjed— the sweet, dried fruits of the lotus tree for love
Seer— garlic for medicine
Somaq- sumac berries, sunrise, and Good over Evil [11]

The lights change, the torches are lit, and Inanna dances with her expatriate priestesses who carry tambourines, kettle drums, and trumpets.[12] *It is a dance of reverence and then seduction, calling, and swirling ecstasy, during which Inanna dances in circles to the furious beat of drums. She whips her veils around one by one, juggling them, tossing them, wrapping them around men in the audience as the femme fatale Salome.*[13] *At each circle she sheds one of seven veils*[14] *until suddenly everything freezes in cold blue light. There is a reality shift.*

KING KRONOS enters with great majestic strides and stands behind Inanna

Kronos: Inanna, it is time for us to talk. Come with me.

Inanna: With all due respect King Kronos, I'd like to make one more phone call before removing my crown.

Kronos: Your dark sister Ereshkigal knows you are coming. Saturn is conjunct with your sun; it is time to descend. Meet me at the gate of the first spiral. Make it fast.[15]

Kronos hands her a phone and watches.

Inanna: Hello, Ninshubar, ...darling, what's wrong? Why are you crying? Yes, I know we're on the news. Listen to me, Ninshubar, pull it together . . . .

OK . . . I'm leaving shortly as the sun crosses the equator. "I'm going to the mountains, to the wilderness to pray."[16] If I don't return within 3 days,

bang the drum, tear out your hair, scream and yell, and send out the eunichs, for surely, I will need your loyalty dear sukkal, if this should pass. Is that clear Ninshubar? Good. I'll see you next week.
..Happy NewYear, my dearest friend.

The phone suddenly flies out of her hand, bells chime. She begins to sing libretto style as she reluctantly and savagely tangos with Kronos.

Inanna: Song/Prayer/Lament

**I wish to open myself to receive the potent forces dormant
in the underworld.
I sacrifice myself to gain new power and
knowledge, and I surrender to the unknown,
to be broken down,
and reformed,
in search of my true essence.**[17]
**I must go down to meet my own instinctual
beginnings, even if I go down fighting—
to find the face of the Great Goddess,
and her original strength.
Oh dear Sophia, Lady Alchemy
help me understand the judgment of the 7 planetary
gods,**[18]**as this untamed lion submits ever so
reluctantly.**

There is a sadness to the exquisite dignity and humility with which Inanna bravely takes her last walk with her horned crown. And the labyrinthic journey[19] *from the center of the spiral down, begins. There is music as she dances a spiral floor plan ending with a gate where Kronos stands as Saturn, dressed in a hooded robe with a scythe like the reaper.*

The music stops, he opens the gate, and gestures for her to sit on a chair near a table holding a burning candle. The mood is sinister, and Inanna is definitely uncomfortable.

SCENE II— GATE ONE - Saturn, King Kronos

Kronos: (*pacing back and forth reading from his cell phone*) Let us begin with your great achievements through many incarnations: Goddess Inanna, Queen of Heaven and Earth, Priestess of Love and Fertility, Venus— Light of the World, Morning and Evening Star, First Daughter of the Moon, Loud Thundering Storm, Goddess of War, Righteous Judge, Forgiver of Sins, Holy Shepherdess, Hierodule of Heaven, Opener of the Womb, Keeper of the Storehouse, Framer of All Decrees, the Amazement of the Land.[20]

Inanna: Why King Kronos, I'm so flattered that you've been watching me and my work all these years.

Kronos: How could one miss. Even Jupiter is jealous of your thunder. But my dear, you confuse the genders. These cultic practices where dancers wear outfits that are half man, half woman are dangerous. You presume to be a hero, loving warfare and seeking lovers— you turn men into women and women into men!

Heaven and Earth must be separate, as men and women are.[21]

Inanna: Yes Kronos— I am free, Queen of the Stars and I move through the heavens unencumbered, and that confuses you— I am undomesticated— the ultimate femme fatal, with the power to call fear and attraction. (*she growls*)

Kronos: Your restlessness, and lack of patience upsets progress, causing unnecessary storms. Perhaps you need to be grounded after ruling from such a distance, and let the future take its course.

Inanna: You can be sure that I have never had anything but the planets best intentions in mind. After all, the great God of Wisdom (Enki) did give me the higher powers of the enduring crown, and lasting ladyship if you recall.[22] And by the by........I am no longer going into battle, I now reject violence and war, and I will gladly erase the title of Goddess of War from all of my credits as of now.

Kronos: *(Dismissing her)* Nevertheless, *I* am the Black Sun,[23] and the ultimate law. It's all over Inanna. You must surrender your crown. Your sister is waiting for you below.

Inanna: I cannot give up this crown, I earned it and I wear it for hundreds of Goddesses throughout time.

Kronos: Your sister needs the crown.

Inanna: Who is my sister?

Kronos: Ereshkigal, your other side, who is the dark snake Queen of the Underworld., she wants your crown so she can fly as the birds do, to and from the heavens. You will soon see how your functions are interwoven.[24] Do not challenge the ways of the Underworld. They are divinely inspired, and you must honor your dark sister and negotiate your differences.

Inanna: "Is there a god who can vie with me? Enlil gave me heaven and earth. I, the Queen of Heaven am I! He has given me Lordship, Queenship. He has given me battle and combat. He has given me the Flood and the Tempest. He has placed heaven as a crown upon my head. He has tied the earth as a sandal at my foot. He has fastened the holy garment of the 'mees' about my body and gave me the holy scepter."[25]

Music begins.

Kronos: Give me your crown Inanna and go on to the next gate.

Inanna: How cold and irreverent you are mighty Saturn. Oh, Great Mother, remember me in your prayers.

She reluctantly removes her crown and hands it to him; thunder and lightning fill the skies, she is humiliated and runs into her next cycle in the labyrinth pattern.

SCENE III— GATE TWO— Jupiter/ Zeus - as Enki

The music subsides to rolling thunder and Inanna arrives at a second gate, behind which sits Jupiter, large, muscular with a belly, scantily clad in a loin cloth with a full beard, his legs perched up on a table laden with food and wine. The music has shifted to a hypnotizing drumbeat.

Jupiter: Come in Inanna, I've been looking forward to this for a long time . . . Do you hear me? I am Jupiter.......... Zeus???

He is eyeballing her feather and diamond earrings.

Inanna: I know who you are… and why do you want, my earrings?? They would look good on you. Don't bother shaving, you'll look like a fruit tree.

Jupiter snatches an earring off her ear; she contains her surprise and regroups.

Jupiter: Can I offer you a glass of wine? *He pours two glasses.*

Inanna: *(taking **his** glass)* Is it wine or poison?

Jupiter: You underestimate my hospitality.

Inanna: What do you want from me? I don't like it here.
He gets close, making her uneasy, trying to snatch her other earring.

Jupiter: I want the earrings . . .. the "mees"......your secret power of hearing!![26]

Inanna: You can't have them. *She enrages him standing defiantly.*

Jupiter: Yes, I can, and I will. "You're not worthy. You're not qualified. You don't have the right credentials. Who do you think you are?"[27]

Inanna: *Inanna moves him away from her face.* You........ sit!!! I am a woman, and again I will recite my rights dear King, so that you understand. (*This becomes a dance around Jupiter's chair*) I choose my own lovers; I bestow the rites of shepherdship; I give life to the lamb whose meat nourishes your fat belly; and most important, my philosophy of nature and life is much more understanding for the planet than your childish philandering and pillaging. *He moves in on her.* You are embarrassing. And please don't try any of that shapeshifting on me

Jupiter: Your great achievements, all the things you do to prove your value, the emblems of your position, mean nothing down here. Give me the "mees"[28] They are the communication keys to travelling the universe, and I want them back.

Inanna: You bestowed them upon me.

Jupiter: You stole them so you could operate your own boat of heaven (*spaceship*).

Inanna: You were drunk, showing off, and you gave them to me, and I make use of this knowledge and power for my people. For I have listened and learned well, how to use the gifts of the gods.

Jupiter: You don't even know where "the mees" come from.

Inanna: You take me for a fool. The "mees" enabled our people, the Annunakis, to have technology to travel from the planet Niburu, before the flood, to establish a civilization in Sumeria, Ancient Iraq. These powers are mine too. And I must use them for the good of the people. Not like you.[29]

Jupiter: *He takes her in his arms.* Why don't you want to have a child with me? He would be more powerful than all my others.

Inanna: Because my destiny, is not as a wife, and mother.

Jupiter: Then just teach me some of your Goddess skills, and I will be your consort, your student, Inanna. I must have you. I don't know how you escaped me last time. *As he tries to kiss her, he grabs the other earring.* Ah yes, sweet victory!

Inanna: Finish the bottle alone, and take your selfish thunderbolt elsewhere, and know.....that only he who applies natural logic and knowledge for the benefit of humanity can truly possess these powers as psychic power. My soul cannot be violated, enslaved, silenced, impregnated, or eliminated. Good evening, Jupiter, I believe more threshold guardians await. Enjoy my earrings, maybe you'll learn to listen to the birds.

Inanna fixes her hair, finishes her wine[30], and bows before strutting out like a queen, on her next circular path. There is more drumming.

SCENE IV— GATE THREE — Mars/Aries, as Mount Ebeh

A feverish Venezuelan rhythm is introduced to accompany the tambor drumming, which is being played live by Mars, a black man dressed in red warrior, African regalia. He plays upon a tilted log with two batons called a Tiki-tiki.

Inanna arrives at the gate and enters focused like a samurai on Mars as he plays. She dances around his drum and altar fire. She gets in his face until finally he must dance the tambor with her. They don't touch, but become dangerously close, ducking, turning away, bucking like rams, challenging each other's hip movements, and dexterity of feet. He is singing to her in African style, and she answers back in repetition. They take torches and duel. Suddenly she goes into trance as if possessed by an oracle.[31]

Inanna: *(channeling – singing)* "When I stand in the front line of battle, I am the leader of all the lands When I stand at the opening of the battle, I am the quiver ready to hand. When I stand in the midst of the battle, I am the heart of the battle, the arm of the warriors. When I begin moving at the end of the battle, I am an evilly rising flood. When I follow in the wake of the battle, I am the woman inspiring the weak. Get Going— Close in on the Enemy!"[32] My Lions are hungry!!

Mars: *(singing)* "Lady of blazing dominion, clad in dread, riding on fire-red power. Inanna/holding a pure lance. Terror folds in her robes. Flood-storm hurricane adorned. She bolts out in battle— plants a standing shield on the ground. Great Lady Inanna, battle planner, foe smasher. You rain arrows on enemies, set strength against foreigners. Lion roar across heaven - on earth bodies struck - flesh cut wild bull - hooves planted - battle ready against foe fiery lion - the upstart and rebel— you persuade with your gall.[33] (Enheduanna)

Inanna's warrior spirit continues to emerge, and the music stops— they stare at one another)[34]

The Mysteries of Inanna

Mars: So glad you got my invitation .... I believe we have some unfinished business.

Inanna: We did our "festival of manhood" battle dance[35] for the year, OK? As far as our previous disagreements, history knows that you lost, I killed you, I struck your heart with sorrow, and now you must cooperate with the eco-systems of the land. What other agenda could there possibly be?

Mars: I want to possess the powers of that double strand Lapis Lazuli necklace that happens to be holding your neck together. I suspect you may be completely unaware of the properties carried in this sacred piece of jewelry.

Inanna: Not only do I understand the "mees" and their powers, but I've applied them towards your own defeat. *(Pointing to beads on the necklace)* This necklace is one of the "mees" for battle strategy, this bead is for weapons, this for straightforwardness, the destruction of cities, fear, terror, strife, victory, craft of the smith, the art of woodworking, metalworking, judgment, and decisions. Clearly, I prefer to abandon aggression, but I must know that justice will prevail.

Mars: Oh, Sweet Lioness, when will you realize that you are becoming outnumbered? And Enlil (male Sumerian Gods) will not raise their swords to me. Progress marches on and nature will be tamed as seen fit.

Inanna: So Big Strong Ebeh Mountain Mars .... you insist upon rebelling from natural law, erupting and upsetting the balances of nature for your own spiritual freedom. How can you separate energy from matter, and not realize your arrogance in ignoring the cycles of nature? This is my domain, and you deliberately disobeyed me.[36] Fury grabs my throat . . .

Mars: Silence woman!! The necklace now belongs to Mars. Give it to me, or I shall take it by force.[37]

Inanna: "You thick hided elephant - I will twist your trunk. You oversized bull - I will wrench your neck, grab your thick horns, throw you in the dust, stomp you with my hatred, grind my knees in your neck ... till tears wet your face and sorrow grips your heart."[38]

Mars: Put it this way, beautiful warrior— We can dance around the fire all night, or you can cooperate. *He takes her arm, they wrestle, and he steals the necklace.* And give up your aggression!

Inanna then shifts consciousness and falls out of the warrior trance.

Inanna: May the bleak bird of heartbreak nest in your shadows.

A sharp pain is suddenly cast upon Inanna. Holding her throat, she runs around in a frenzy until she gathers herself, and begins to sing a mad woman's Lament falling to the floor)

"Me the woman he has filled with dismay . . .

Has filled me, the queen of heaven, with consternation . . .

I, the woman who circles the land— tell me where my house is,

Tell me, where is the city in which I may live?

I, who am your daughter, the hicrodulc, who am your bridesmaid— Tell me where my house is . . .

The bird has its nesting place, but I— my young are dispersed.

The fish lies in calm waters, but I— my resting place exists not.

The dog kneels at the threshold, but I— I have no threshold."[39]

Mars: But remember this Inanna you yourself in your last incarnation declared that you would renounce all violence and war in the name of peace. And finally, you must relinquish this wrath just give up the warrior Inanna

...right here right now put your strength to other purposes and leave the fighting to the men.

Inanna is stunned, proudly confused. During the song, Inanna dances another rotation with frustration and approaches the next gate— a pole with a rolled-up reed mat— the symbol for her storehouse door and her vulva.[40]

SCENE V— GATE FOUR— The Sun— Helios— Proposals

Inanna is cold and lonely, clutching her heart.

Inanna: Good Goddess, in Heaven, could this be my storehouse? This is my door, my symbol. Where am I really? Where are the baskets of grain, the corn, the fruits and meat— the beer and the bread??[41] What happened to all my prosperity?

Slowly a golden light heats the storehouse, illuminating a long conference table and two chairs. Helios enters with a golf club, dressed in a conservative yellow suit with a green tie. He throws a file on the table and walks around the table and begins to putt as he speaks.

Helios: Good morning, Inanna, let me get right to the point.

Here we have seasonal deficit, precipitated by your descent, causing considerable stunts in agricultural production, land infertility, and drought.[42] We are seeking a prosperous New Year, and we are not happy about the empty storehouse either. So, as part of your descent we must now discuss the enactment of a final sacred marriage between us before you transfer your powers of fertility to another Goddess.

Inanna: So, despite your ironically frigid overtures, now you see how important my talent is for transforming matter into divine sustenance. However, you are obviously thinking about replacing me. Too bad you aren't as interested in my heart, for then the Sacred Marriage would mean so much more than the mere acquisition of my fertile storehouse and her secrets.

Helios: We must work together— you are nothing without my heat. Divine matter requires heaven and earth, like the sun and the moon, to cooperate. The alchemy of the Sacred Marriage "rescues the hidden, feminine aspect of God from imprisonment in matter (the black earth) by his opus, and reunites her with the manifest masculine deity"[43]

Inanna: How many Kings and Gods have I already married to fertilize the people's storehouse?[44] My temple was a menstrual hut before it held the fruits of the earth.[45] How audacious of you to think you understand the ways of the womb. The women who have worked in my temples recording the inventory started writing these "Amargi" tablets around 3500 BC. And Amargi means "freedom and return to the women."[46] (Stone 41)

She takes the golf club from him and begins to putt herself.

Dear Helios, I do not need to be rescued. I make myself beautiful so that your attraction will bring abundance and prosperity to the land. Fortunately, MY heart belongs to Mother Earth and her children. Or we would all starve.

Helios: Sweet Inanna, forgive my disrespect. Now I will try chivalry. I have forgotten the law.[47]

"May the Lord whom you do call to your heart, the king as your beloved husband…., enjoy long days at your lap so sweet, give him a reign goodly and glorious, Give him the throne of kingship on an enduring foundation. Give him the people-directing scepter, the staff and the shepherd's crook. Give him an enduring crown, a radiant diadem on his head from where the sun rises to where the sun sets…. From the land of the Hulappa tree to the land of the cedar. Overall Sumer and Akkad give him the staff and the crook. May he exercise the shepherdship of the black-haired people wherever they dwell. As the farmer may he make productive the fields. As the shepherd may he multiply the sheepfolds."[48]

Inanna: Thank you, Helios. I hear your prayers and now, I wonder what part of me do you wish to remove.

Helios: I have always given you my unconditional heat and light. I pray not only for your full storehouse, but for your lonely heart, who no one seems able to satisfy. Give me the breast plate which covers your beautiful abundant bosom, which in turn shelters that fragile fluctuating center we call the Goddess heart, and I will protect you. You are my most precious star and moon. Please give me your promise of eternal love and I will always empower your fields with sunlight and abundance.[49]

Inanna: The Great powers of Inanna cannot ever be replaced. If I return from this journey, I will see you again. Take my breastplate and know that you must use it to call compassion into the divine marriage between father sky and mother earth. Goodbye Helios. To you I sacrifice my heart. Please keep it warm.

Inanna gives Helios her breastplate and begins to walk proud and half naked onto her next spiral down.

SCENE VI— GATE FIVE — VENUS — Inanna's Goddess Rituals

CHOREOGRAPHY

Inanna continues her journey along the fifth spiral, holding her scepter high, and we hear the sound of birds, in wind whistled trees. She comes to a rose-vine covered gate and enters. She finds herself inside exquisite gardens, surrounded by a forest of cypresses, filled with roses, jasmine, verbena, and their scents. It is dusk, with a new moon in the darkening sky, and the clear brilliance of the star Venus, emerging with the sunset. Footpaths lead into tiny ponds with floating water lilies and exotic fish, to bird covered gazebos and kiosks of luscious fruits. Inanna sees a temple and hears the music of middle eastern belly dancing music. She approaches and the smell of frankincense incense takes over. She remembers this place. There is the date palm tree near the temple. There are her beautiful, veiled priestesses, her sacred prostitutes, her vestal virgins, dancing entranced, inside the lushly adorned temple of love. She rushes to the door.

> ***"As she moves through the open temple doors she begins to dance to the music of the flute, tambourine and cymbals. Her gestures, her facial expressions and the movements of her supple body all speak to the welcoming of passion. There is no false modesty regarding her body, and as she dances, the contours of her feminine form are revealed under an almost transparent saffron robe. Her movements are graceful, as she is well aware of her beauty. She is full of love, and as she dances her passion grows. In her ecstasy she forgets all restraint and gives herself to the deity."*** [50]

Inanna's priestesses are happy to see her, and she breathes joy once again. They lead her off to the baths. Musicians are playing in the corner. Here the priestesses remove Inanna's zodiac girdle of 12 stones, place it on the altar, and they all perform ablutions— washing their faces, feet, hands, and arms up to the elbows, before praying. They veil their faces and lay a rug on the floor. They begin by pressing the open palms of their hands over face and eyes, shutting out all evil. They bow to the four directions, bending, kneeling, touching their forehead to the ground, and resting back on the heels while they sing in prayer. Here continues a series of cosmetic mystery rituals. After bathing Inanna with a loofa and pumice stone, the women ladle perfumed water over one another and henna their hair, hands, and feet. Some of them stamp floral designs into their skin. Inanna's beautiful black hair is washed with egg yolks, oiled and scented. They manicure her nails and body. Her eyes are painted with black kohl, guarding against the evil eye. They whiten their skin with almond and jasmine paste, paint their faces. The women mix and trade their magical scents with one another. Cloves and ginger are rubbed on their bodies as aphrodisiacs.[51] *(fn Croutier pg 80)*

Then Inanna is led into a ceremonial salon where she must remove and relinquish her zodiac girdle. Then she is directed to rest upon the altar (same as the Iraqi embassy altar). The priestesses feed her and dance for her around a sacred fire with embers of sandalwood, frankincense and myrrh, occasionally swirling over the fire, arranging their clothing as a tent to capture the fumes. Snakes and birds are everywhere along with Inanna's pet lions. Roses are sacrificed to the altar.[52] *There is sexual joy, bliss, and sisterly comfort among the women.*[53] *Inanna stands, and begins to* sing and dance *as the company accompanies her on her next spiral path. She is preparing to perform the Sacred Marriage, and her processional choreography is powerful, mystical and erotic.*

As the drums increase in volume, Inanna approaches the next gate dancing. There stands her most famous consort Dumuzzi (Mercury), on the other side of a rodeo gate, dressed like a cowboy with hat, boots and spurs, jeans, tight white shirt, lasso and of course— muscle bulging everywhere. Here is the original Marlboro rodeo man (horned bull), in contemporary comic perspective. One can feel the chemistry between this culture clashing "bride and groom". She enters.

SCENE VII— GATE SIX— Mercury (as Dumuzzi)
— The Sacred Marriage

Dumuzzi pulls a rose out of his cowboy hat and speaks with a southern accent. He gives her the rose and offers to take her scepter.

Inanna: *She pulls back.* I don't know you.

Dumuzzi: Yes, you do. I am Hermes Dumuzzi, the cowboy. We've met before.

Inanna: No, you're not the one. I want the farmer.

Dumuzzi: But I can provide for you beyond your wildest dreams.

Inanna: No, you are a wanderer I can feel it.

Dumuzzi: Your brother, your father, and your mother have already endorsed our marriage. Give me a chance. I'm a good cowboy.

Inanna is becoming amused and allows him to seduce her.
The following dialogue is taken from Samuel Kramer's translation of Ancient Sumerian texts ***"The Sacred Marriage Rite".***

Inanna: Is that so? Very well— talk to me.

Dumuzzi: "You bathed for the wild bull
For the cowboy Dumuzzi, you have bathed
You perfumed your sides with ointments,
And you have adorned yourself irresistibly
With amber you have coated your mouth
With kohl, you have painted your eyes

When the lord, lying by holy Inanna, the cowboy Dumuzzi
shaped your loins with his fair hands
with milk and cream he filled your lap
He stroked your pubic hair and watered your womb,
when on your vulva his hands he laid,

He smoothed your black boat with cream,
when like his narrow boat, he brought life to it,
when on the bed he caressed her,
Then will she caress him, a sweet fate already decreed for him,
She will caress his loins, the cowboy of all the lands,
Inanna will decree a sweet fate for him.[54]

During the following dialogue, Inanna and Dumuzzi will dance and play catch with her scepter, until he keeps it. She is becoming entranced by the cowboy and is transformed by his seduction and southern drawl. Finally, she falls into complete trance......

Inanna: "My sacred vulva, the horn—The Boat of Heaven, is full of eagerness like the young moon. My untilled land lies fallow.

Dumuzzi: Great Lady, the king will plow your vulva.
I, Dumuzzi the King will plow your vulva.

Inanna: Then plow my vulva, man of my heart! Plow my vulva!!

Dumuzzi: At the king's lap stood the rising cedar.

Inanna: He is the one my womb loves best

Dumuzzi: O Lady, your breast is your field. Your broad field pours out plants and grain. Water and bread flow from on high for your servant. Pour it out for me Inanna. I will drink all you offer."[55]

They dance together, then disconnect.

Inanna: Tonight I, the queen, am shining bright and dancing, singing praises of this evening....He meets me— My lord Dumuzi meets me. He puts his hand into my hand. He presses his neck close against mine. My high priest is ready for the holy loins; My lord Dumuzzi is ready for the holy loins. The plants and the herbs in his field are ripe. Oh Dumuzi! Your fullness is my delight!!

Dumuzzi arrives performing these movements inches from her body. He takes the scepter and keeps it ... She crumbles near the altar. He lifts her up and they dance.

Dumuzi: *Continues to dance during the dialogue.*

She called for it, she called for it— she called for the bed!
She called for the bed that rejoices the heart. She called for the bed that sweetens the loins. She called for the bed of kingship. She called for the bed of queenship. Inanna called for the bed.[56]

Let the bed that rejoices the heart be prepared Let the bed that sweetens the loins be prepared Let the bed of kingship be prepared

Let the royal bed be prepared.

All taken from "The Sacred Marriage Rite" translations of Samuel Kramer.

CHOREOGRAPHY

Inanna courageously removes the large breechcloth wrapped around her hips, the magical "Garment of Ladyship". Inanna spreads the bridal sheet across the bed.

Inanna: The bed is ready! The bed is waiting!![57] Let us go.

The sound of water, rain, rolling thunder, and the ocean builds as Inanna and Dumuzzi wrap up in the sheet, and dance with it as the sacred marriage connection, over, under and around each other. The rain becomes a river and the current takes them.

SCENE VIII— GATE SEVEN
—The Moon— Genesis & The Huluppu Tree

The sound of rain and rushing water increases. Inanna is overtaken by the water and grabs on to a floating tree. The ANZA bird thunders in (played by an Asian woman), with eagle wings, with a lion's head, and a griffin's body. The waters soon subside, and Inanna lies on the shore. The Anza Bird awakens her with nudges and roars.

ANZA Bird: "Mighty, majestic, and radiant Inanna, you shine brilliantly in the evening, . . . you brighten the day at dawn you stand in the heavens like the sun and the moon .... your wonders are known both above and below .... to the greatness of the holy priestess of heaven....to you, Inanna, I sing!"[58] Comeback Inanna. May the wings of your soul return to us now!

Inanna: *(awakening)* Where am I now?

Anza: You are at the last gate of the moon, where you were originally born from the great primordial mother waters. Here is your hatchet.

She hands Inanna a butterfly shaped ax.

Inanna: This belongs to me.

Anza: Yes, when you lived under the twin stars, before the bull. When women tilled the land and made love not war. This was your tool and your symbol— The interface of the phallus and the winged dove of peace.

Inanna: I want to go back there, to the Motherland in the stars. I really do not want to fight!

Anza: You must honor this Huluppu tree (date palm)[59] for saving your life and realize that it is dying. This tree is your bridge between the worlds and has been the spiritual source of your throne and queenship.

Inanna: Oh, dear sweet date tree, forgive me. With great joy and gratitude let me take you to my garden. Let me support your life as you have supported mine.

She plants it, in a vessel[60] and begins to dance around it with the Anza bird. Inanna is happy to be here in her garden, under the shade of the date palm, with her lion bird friend, and has regressed to her childhood innocence playing in the tree. She gives the Anza bird the gold ring on her finger, and then perches in the tree happily.[61]

A Snake (a Latin male) dances in and coils himself around the tree. Night falls and the full moon reveals itself. He and Inanna dance a playful pas de deux revealing the respect that the snake elicits from Inanna as well as the protection he offers her, coiling around her belly.

Snake: We dance well together. I see you are learning the moves of the underworld.

Inanna: Yes. It is a different beat. And what do you want my dear serpent?

Snake: There doesn't seem to be much left. (*Inanna is naked*) SSSSSSsssssssssssooo. How about thissssss?

He lifts up her leg, wrapping himself around her and points to the gold ring anklet on her left foot.

Inanna: And what message do you bring me from the underworld?

Snake: I was sent by the mother to enlighten and protect you. This is my mission. I have wrapped myself around your royal scepter, around your eggs. I have ordained your prophetic wisdom with the eternal oracular connection I represent. As I shed my outer skin, you shed your inner skin, and so we are immortal. We have been siblings for thousands of years, and I am your closest ally.[62]

Inanna: Very well. I give you my ankle ring, and my power of the dance. I must go— I have many rivers to cross… below the Earth.

She gives him the gold ring on her left ankle, and he rests his head in the nape of her neck. She pulls away.

Off stage we hear the lunar wailing, minor keyed, bluesy, African American voice of LILITH, a large and shapely black woman dressed like a Black Madonna.[63] This character is the ultimate Black Mother. She enters with a basket of apples, singing, and happy to see

Inanna and her friends. She cradles Inanna in her arms against her big, beautiful nurturing body. Lilith, as the dark moon goddess, teaches her that we are all aspects of the moon.

> **Lilith:** Come here baby, and rest on my bosom. Your father has brought you home. You're on the doorstep of a great catharsis. And you are still so beautiful and radiant. You are both the full glorious horned moon mother, and the scorpion who destroys and laments the waning of the vanishing moon. I will give you all my lunar mysteries Inanna. The secret revolves around the unconditional germination of the love seed. Watching life grow is our joy, and so we learn to turn love into magic, with mother nature instructing us, with the touch of our hands, the movement of our bodies, the food we grow, the songs of our hearts, and the fertility of our wombs. Come let us dance—give me your gold bracelet and I will teach you the mysteries of love, before you face your sister. I must have your bracelets to germinate the seeds…to activate life!

Inanna removes her bracelet, and she becomes weak. The following dance is a profound testimony of mother/daughter/sister love between Lilith and Inanna, as Lilith energizes her again. They dance with the tree, embracing it, swinging from it, picking its fruit. All of the lunar moods of women appear love, pain, radiance, compassion, thunder, seduction, joy, generosity, kindness, defiance, fertility, and complete uninhibited desire. The snake and the bird intermingle with the choreography until they are all interwoven, and Lilith lifts Inanna over her head with her strength.

Suddenly we hear the sounds of trumpets. King Kronos with his scythe, Jupiter/Zeus with his thunderbolt, Mars with his battle ax, Helios with his golf club, and Dumuzzi with his machete enter stealthily, angrily, like soldiers, watching this scene of love like voyeurs, vicariously excited and moved to aggression, by the sex, love and territory that is not theirs. After rotating the tree like animals ready to pounce and impale their victims, they begin to swing and chop at the tree, scattering the love, destroying the life of the tree, interrupting the natural rhythm of nature, until they mold it and shape it into a "proper" throne for Inanna, where a "proper" queen should sit in the "proper" service of her people. They kill Lilith, the snake, and the Anzu bird.

Inanna is left weeping on her date tree throne, and the Great Dark Queen Ereshkigal enters, carried by, the Annunaki creatures, who are her underground, extra-terrestrial helpers.

The Mysteries of Inanna

SCENE IX— Queen Ereshkigal and The Execution

Queen Ereshkigal is pregnant, tired, and dressed in black. She moans a lyrical, minor key dirge. She is wearing Inanna's horned crown. Inanna is frightened and clings to her throne. Ereshkigal struts over to Inanna.

Ereshkigal: These are the consequences when you've got something the boys want. Imagine how important you must be, to have all those Gods running for you with their sticks flailing. I'm sorry it's been so rough. Let me help you.

Inanna: First tell me how we are sisters?

Ereshkigal: I decompose and regenerate all of the life force that you nurture and inspire in the upperworld. We are a team, and we have been married to the same wild bull . . .. only now ..he will die.

Inanna: My Wild Bull Dumuzzi is waiting for me above.

Ereshkigal: He won't be for long, for as he desires you, he also desires your power and must be initiated as well into the laws of the Goddess. And what we are about to do is exactly in tune with the equinox, and infinitely more important to the planet than Dumuzzi's designs for power.

Inanna: And what might that be?

Ereshkigal: I need to see the sun again. We must merge and regenerate. Your descent journey has been systematic dismemberment of your body and soul powers. And we need to take the alchemy one more step.

Inanna: So here I am naked before you .... Dear Sister. What reconciliation could be left after all.........I have surrendered everything and still survived…...

Ereshkigal: *Angrily* While you are up there making things grow,

I am down here dealing with last year's vegetation. My business is decomposing, reconstructing, and transformation. It's a dirty business and somebody has to do it. But I need a break. And time is running out.

Inanna: OK, OK!! So, what must we do— let's go! This is a one-way ticket to hell and I'm not about to die in limbo. What do I do?

Ereshkigal ties a small bone cube necklace with eyes on each surface around Inanna's neck, (see Wolkstein, pg. 60)

Ereshkigal: Stare into my eyes. Follow me— dance with me. Let me inside your soul— permit me to pass on the "mees" to this child inside of me. Thank you for your sacrifices, Inanna. They do not go unnoticed. Hold me, hold the baby. Forgive me for my harshness. I am so very heavy with pregnancy and unhappiness from the darkness. You must help me give her Goddess soul, a rebirth with the blessings of both worlds. The gods had to take away your precious knowledge to mix it with the soil to feed the new souls. My sweet sister, who I love and cherish so much, send me your precious love light from Venus, and my dark Moon light will illuminate our temples with divine mysterious life and together we will renew the earth.

Suddenly all the sacrificial "mees" that were taken away from Inanna appear strung up across the stage on a rope. (The crown, the earrings, the necklace, the breast plate, garment of ladyship, the scepter, the ring, the ankle bracelet, and her wrist bracelet.)

Inanna: What is happening to you now. You're huge, you are bursting with life. What can I do for you?

Ereshkigal: We must say goodbye now. For through our homogenized death this new soul of ours will be born— a new Inanna. Stare at my eyes. Hold my belly. This is it. Say Goodbye Inanna.

Inanna: But I can't, I'm not ready.........*(she screams)* Ninshubar! Help!!! Bang the Drum— Ninshubar! *(she struggles)*

Ereshkigal: Forgive me, my sister but for the last part of the initiation I must hang you on a wooden cross to die for three days, while the moon disappears. Dark and cruel as this appears, we cannot give life to the future, without sacrificing our lives. History will impale and dismember many heroes for years to come, courtesy of the patriarch.[64]

Inanna: Please don't do this Ereshkigal— I cannot bear it.

Ereshkigal, with a mighty groan, lifts Inanna and hooks her onto a branch of the hullupu tree over her throne. This suddenly causes her water to break. Ereshkigal goes into labor. Inanna dies on the peg. The sound of drums returns. Ereshkigal screams and moans. Two genderless little scorpion fairy creatures (the galla) appear who seem to help her through her labor. After much circular movement, Ereshkigal gives birth to a new adult Inanna, young, beautiful, this time blond (wig). She is even more commanding, more alluring in her beautiful dress.

Ereshkigal: Oh Inanna, you are still so beautiful ....now I am truly part of you. But beware, you cannot stay in the Upperworld unless you send down a replacement sacrifice, for these are the laws of universal balance. Send me your lover, Dumuzzi.

Inanna, redressed in white, retraces her steps on the spiral labyrinth, accompanied by her two scorpion fairy friends sent by Ninshubar and the drums. This sequence of circling clockwise is eventually met by Dumuzzi sitting on her throne in his gallant white cowboy attire, pretending to ride a bull.

SCENE X- DUMUZZI DESCENDS for THE CIRCLE OF LIFE

Dumuzzi sings: "Since the Lady Inanna descended to the land of No-Return, the bull does not spring upon the cow, the ass does not bow over the jenny. The man no more bows over the woman in the street. The man sleeps in his chamber. The woman sleeps alone." (Enheduanna)[65] And the land is dry.

He sees Inanna.

Dumuzzi: Finally, you're back. We have all missed you so much Inanna. The land and the people have been barren in your absence.

Inanna: Who are you and why are you sitting on my throne? *(confused)*

Dumuzzi: Don't you remember me? I have taken over the royal duties in the absence of my Queen Inanna.

Inanna: I have returned and still hold the title of the Queen Inanna. And I am not so easily disposed of. Now you must make the journey of the New Year's traditional descent of the old king to make way for the queen's new consort. My scorpions will accompany you.

CHOREOGRAPHY

She transfers "The Eye of Death" necklace to Dumuzzi. Clearly, she is disappointed, confused, and angry and Dumuzzi continues to woo her. They dance together, repeating former dance steps… and she remembers.

Dumuzzi: I am your lover; I am your king. Please don't make me go down there. How can you not remember our love?

He dances with her, kisses her, and Inanna breaks down .and shifts consciousness.

Inanna: Yes, of course, …….. now I do remember our Sacred Marriage, and the vows we committed to the land. I have just returned and learned the laws of the underworld which bind our souls to a never-ending cycle of death and rebirth. I will see you again. With only these brief moments of reunion, after the equinox between the seasons, will the twilight renew our love.

I know that your heart is filled with tears[66], but if you are to be a truly great king, you too must journey to the Great Unknown, to provide for the fertility of the land and the soul. *(She gives him his Shepherd's crook, and takes the scepter back)*

Dumuzzi: I will look forward to our reunions on the equinox. Will you sing for me when I'm gone?

Inanna: I will wait for you knowing that at the end of my desire is your sweet love. I kiss you now in anticipation of the next cycle of fertility. *They kiss and she recites.*

"Your right hand you have placed on my vulva
Your left stroked my head,
You have touched your mouth to mine,
you have pressed my lips to your head
That is why… *she pauses, pulling away*
you are ill fated."[67]
And must go. I will see you in six months.

He circles counterclockwise down the labyrinth with the two scorpions, as Inanna sadly dances around her throne singing:

Inanna sings: "Gone is my husband, my sweet husband. Gone is my love, my sweet love. The wild bull lives no more. The shepherd, the wild bull lives no more. Dumuzzi, the wild bull, lives no more." When he slumbers the sheep and lambs' slumber also. When he slumbers, the she-goat and kids slumber also."[68]

Inanna falls asleep on the throne. BLACKOUT
The male/female entourage from the opening of the show returns for the gala with a dancing entrance for the segue into……

SCENE XI— RETURN TO 1999— THE PERSIAN NEW YEAR

We return to the New Year Gala at the Iraqi Embassy. The crown sits on top of the lapis lazuli sculpture of Inanna riding a lioness. All of the guests are now dancing a production number with Inanna's hermaphrodite (male/female costumed) entourage.

There is applause as Inanna enters in a beautiful modern ball gown. She is swept away to a private area by Mrs. Geshtinanna, as the performance has clearly upset her ability to address the crowd.

Inanna: Please forgive my distraction Madame, my mind has been elsewhere. This has all been so difficult for me, but I must thank you for your support and hospitality.

Mrs. Geshtinanna: Your performance was beautiful, terribly sad and moving, and brilliantly danced. I do believe in you Inanna. We must find a way to protect your voice. You will always be an Iraqi, a Sumerian, and we will continue to fight for peace. I must go now to relieve my brother from his long day of watching my children. He very much wants to meet you. I will send him at once. Goodbye Inanna.[69]

Geshtinanna leaves and Inanna goes to touch the wild lapis lazuli lioness sculpture which supports her effigy. Her friends ask her to dance, and she graciously declines disguising her sadness elegantly. The music changes from party to sentimental. The lights change, mounting a pool of light around Inanna and her sculpture. The guests leave as a tall, dark, and elegant man in white enters the room (Dumuzzi with a cowboy hat). Geshtinanna points him in the direction of Inanna. He removes his hat and places it on the bull's horns.

Dumuzzi: Have we met before?

Inanna: I'm not sure.

Dumuzzi: You are the Queen, and I am your King, at your service. Let's dance and I will remind you.

They waltz around the sculpture together to dramatic music, and the lights fade.

THE END

BIBLIOGRAPHY

The Mysteries of Inanna

Apostolos-Cappadona, Diane; Dance as Religious Studies, Crossroad Publishing Co. NewYork, N.Y., 1993

Baring, Anne & Cashford, Jules, The Myth of the Goddess, Arkana-Penguin, London, 1991

Batmanglij, Najmieh, New Food of Life — Ancient Persian and Modern Iranian Cooking and Ceremonies— Mage Publishers, Washington, D.C., 1986

Bolen, Jean Shinoda, Goddesses in Every Woman, Harper & Rowe, NY 1984

Bolen, Jean Shinoda, Gods in Every Man, Harper & Rowe, NY, 1989

Caldicott, Moyr— Myths of the Sacred Tree— Destiny Books, Rochester, Vermont 1993

Casey, Rita Anne, Inanna & Enki in Sumer (Phd. Dissertation CIIS), 1998

Croutier, Alev, Harem-The World Behind the Veil, Abbeville Press, NY, 1989

Cumont, Franz, Astrology & Religion Among the Greeks & Romans, Kessinger Pub. Co., Montana, 1912

Dante, The Inferno; The Great books Foundation, Chicago, 1954

Dexter, Mirriam Robbins, Whence the Goddesses, Pergamon Press, Elmsford NY, 1990

Eistler, Riane, The Chalice and the Blade, Harper & Rowe, SF, 1987

Forest, Steven, The Inner Sky, ACS Publications, San Diego, Ca. 1988

Fiore, Sylvestro, Voices from the Clay— Uiversity of Oklahoma, 1965

Gadon, Elinor, The Once and Future Goddess, Harper & Rowe, SF, 1989

Grahn, Judy, Blood, Bread and Roses, Beacon Press, Boston, 1993

George, Demetra, Mysteries of the Dark Moon, Harper, SF, 1992

Harding, Ester, Woman's Mysteries, Harper and Rowe, SF, 1971

Hall, Manly P, The Secret Teachings of All Ages, Philosophical research Society, Inc, Los Angeles, 1977

Jaskolski, Helmut, The Labyrinth- Symbol of Fear, Rebirth, Liberation, Shambhala, 1997

Kensky-Tikva Frymer, In the Wake of the Goddessses, Free Press, 1992

Kinsley, David, The Goddesses' Mirror, State University of New York Press, Albany, 1989

Kluger, Rivkah Scharf, The Archetypal Significance of Gilgamesh, Daimon Underlag, Einsiedeln, Switzerland, 1991

Kramer, Samuel Noah, From the Poetry of Sumer, University of California Press, Berkeley, 1979

Kramer, SN, History Begins At Sumer, Doubleday Anchor Books, Garden City, NY, 1959

Kramer, SN, The Sumerians, University of Chicago Press, Chicago, 1972

Kramer, SN, The Sacred Marriage Rite, Indiana University Press, Bloomington, Ind, 1969

Leadbeater, CW, The Chakras, The Theosophical Publishing House, Wheaton, Ill, 1927

Lerner, Gerda, The Creation of the Patriarch, Oxford University Press, NY, 1986

Murdock, Maureen, The Heroine's Journey, Shambahala, Boston, 1990

Macetti, Maunela Dunn, The Song of Eve, Fireside, Simon
& Schuster, Inc., Ny, 1990

Myss, Caroline, Phd., Anatomy of the Spirit, Three Rivers Press, NY, 1996

Mathews, Caitlin, Sophia, Goddess of Wisdom, Mandala, London, 1991

Newmann, Erich, The Great Mother— Princeton University Press, 1955

Perera, Sylvia Brinton, Descent to the Goddess, Inner City Books, Toronto, 1981

Corbett-Qualls, Nancy, The Sacred Prostitute, Inner Coity Books, Toronto, 1988

Redmond, Layne, When Drummers Were Women, Three Rivers press, NY, 1997

Rogers, Robert William, Cuneiform Parallels to the Old Testament, Abingdon Press, NY, 1912

Ruether, Rosemary Radford, Womanguides: Reading Toward a Feminist Theology, Beacon Press, Boston, 1985

Sandras, NK, translator, Poems of Heaven and Hell from Ancient Mesopotamia, Penguin books, Middlesex, England, 1971

Santarcangel, P., Le Livre Des Labyrinthes, Gallimard, Vallechi Editore, Firenze, Italy, 1967

Sitchin, Zecharia – The Twelth Planet, 1976

Starhawk, Truth or Dare, Harper & Rowe, SF, 1987

Stone, Merlin, Ancient Mirrors of Womanhood, Beacon Press, Boston, 1979

Stone, Merlin, When God Was A Woman, HBJ Publishers, San Diego, 1976

Walker, Barbara, The Woman's Dictionary of Symbols & Sacred Objects, Harper & Rowe, SF, 1988

Warner, Marina, Alone of All Her Sex, Vintage books, Random House, NY, 1976

Whitmont, Edward, Return of the Goddess, Arkana, London, 1983

Wolkstein, Diane and Samuel Kramer, Inanna— Queen of Heaven and Earth, Harper & Rowe, NY, 1983

ENDNOTES

The Mysteries of Inanna

1. Mathews, pg. 180 "She must go veiled because she is ashamed of her wrong doing . . ."
2. Grahn, pg 202
3. The seven garments of queenship were called the "mes", which were the powers that enabled Inanna to operate her spaceship.
4. Grahn (202/233)
5. Redmond pg 77 "She wore the lunar horned crown of ten formed with seven superimposed pairs of horns. These horns show her as the ancient cow goddess.
6. Bahar, pg 88
7. Around 3000 BC at the time of the Epic of Gilgamesh, the constellation Taurus was in the sky.
8. Bahar pg 389
9. During the Neolithic period, the constellation of the twins, Gemini was overhead, which may account to the sisterhood and mother daughter images that come out of that period.
10. Fiore pg 12-14— During the Hassunah (5th millenium BC), the Halaf (middle 5th BC), and the Ubaid (end of 5[the] BC) Female clay figurines were found all over Sumeria indicating the life of a Mother-Goddess cult.
11. Bahar pg 387
12. Redmond, pg 78— "The primary instruments used in Mesopotamia were frame drums, larger drums, lyres, harps, cymbals, sistrums, and flutes of metal and reed."
13. Adams, pg 103— "Salome becomes the archetypal image of woman as the evil and destructive force whose sexuality, if not her very existence, threatened the lives of men with her dance of the seven veils."

14 Mascotti, pg.134—Herod, wanting to show his daughter's beauty at a feast, asks her to perform the Dance of the Seven Veils to please him, after which she asks for the head of St. John the Baptist.

15 Cashford, 184—The temple represented the bond of heaven and earth, like the tree pillar, and the ziggurat was a temple whose pathways were external, a stairway mounting in a spiral from stage to stage, the megalithic way of approach to the divine state.

16 Casey, pg 262

17 Perera, pg 53

18 Ruether pg 218-19— "Likewise in Babylonian culture, the cultivation of astronomy led to speculation of the stars and planets as the dwelling place of the Gods. Human souls were also seen as originating there and becoming incarnate through a process in which they descended to earth through the gates of the seven planetary systems."

19 Jaskolki pg 45—The Labyrinth is a uterus drawn out long, seven times convoluted. People of the Enlightenment conceived of it as a birth canal which the child must find it's way out of to be born. The Labyrinth, therefore is a spiritual entry into the world, a symbol of emancipation and self-realization.

20 Cashford, pg 176

21 Kensky, pg 29

22 Kramer, History Begins at Sumer, pg 99

23 Walker, pg 4

24 Dexter, pg 20

25 Kramer, Poetry of Sumeria, pg 96

26 Casey, pg 120

27 Starhawk, pg 114

28 The "mes" are principals of knowledge and law which Enki gave to Inanna.

29 Zitchin, Zecharia – The 12th Planet

30 Neuman, pg 287— "Among the Sumerians, Inanna was the Celestial Mother Goddess of the wine. She is not only the queen of the ennobled fruit of the

soil, but also of the spirit matter of transformation that is embodied in the wine. The transformative character of the Feminine rises from the natural to the spiritual plane."

31 Stone, pg 210— In Mesopotamia at the oracular shrines the priestesses were understood to be in direct communication with the deity who possessed the wisdom of the Universe. Those who believed in prophetic revelation, did not believe in pre-destined fate— they believed they could act upon their destiny.

32 Kinsley, pg 133

33 Casey for Enheduanna, pg 236

34 Starhawk, pg 96— "Sacred Possession serves many functions. It is an ecstatic state, and ecstasy reminds us that the sacred is immanent. When the great powers are moving through us they also bring knowledge, abilities, healing, that go beyond our ordinary limitations."

35 Kensky, pg 66 -"Inanna was the very spirit of battle. Warfare, "the festival of manhood", was "Inanna's Dance", a theme that was repeated throughout Mesopotamian history. Mars was also known as a dancer.

36 Casey, pg 243

37 Starhawk, pg 177— "The King controls speech as well as action. War is always accompanied by censorship." Here we are addressing the throat chakra, the necklace, and Inanna's voice.

38 Casey, pg 141

39 Perera, pg 19

40 Cashford, pg 194

41 Grahn, pg 114— "The earliest recipes of beermaking are Sumerian, and are under the auspices of the Goddess. Metaformic elements surface continually in the process of beermaking.The barley sprouting was guarded by dogs, and the recipe of bread, wine, and honey was a warm red color."

42 Corbett, pg 33— "When Inanna makes her descent to the underworld, no passion is felt on the earth; sterility overcomes the land."

43 (Mathews/Von Franz pg 261)

44 Kensky, pg 59— For a review of the Kings with whom Inanna performed the

Sacred Marriage.

45 Grahn pg 247

46 Stone, pg 41

47 Stone, pg 137—The priestess Inanna brings her lover to her own house and

48 she makes him king by allowing him to enjoy long days at her holy lap.

49 Kramer, Poetry of Sumer, pg 80-81

50 Kramer—The Sacred Marriage, pg 62

51 Corbett, pg 22

52 Croutier, pg 84

53 Grahn pg 233

54 Kensky, pg 48

55 Corbett pg.24 and Wolkstein pg 44 (a mix)

56 Wolkstein pg 37,39

57 Casey pg 220

58 Wolkstein, pg 41-42

59 Kinsley, pg 113

60 Wolkstein pg 7-9

61 Ibid pg 196 "Before Inanna in the field is a date palm within a vessel, the focus of ritual libations."

62 Ibid pg 180/194

63 Stone, pg 199— "The evidence of this Sumerian tablet points to an original serpent goddess as the interpreter of dreams of the unrevealed future. Several sculptures unearthed from Sumer, which date from about 4000 BC, portray a female figure with the head of a snake."

64 Birnbaum pgs. 108, 153, 167-68

65 Grahn pg 256— "In the Christian descent myth, the bleeding Son was hung on a peg-tree cross, to die for three lunar days before a glorious resurrection, just as Inanna had before him." She was the first.

66 Wolkstein, pg 162

67 Ibid

68 Kramer, Poetry of Sumer pg. 81-82
69 Cashford, pg 222
70 Wolkstein pg 74-79 In the myth, Geshtinanna was Dumuzi's sister who mourns his descent, and replaces him in the Underworld.

The Mysteries of Inanna

Cecilia Anne Gruessing, M.A.

St. Sara la Kali

Queen of the Gypsies

A Musical Pilgrimage

Ceil Gruessing,   Spring 1999

The pilgrimage of the Gypsy Roma to France May 23-25
The journey of the Tres Marias… Led by Sara La Kali

Cecilia Anne Gruessing, M.A.

INTRODUCTION

St. Sara la Kali, Queen of the Gypsies

Jai Ma Kali Ma Jai Ma Kali Ma
Oh Queen Mother of a thousand names
Saint Sara la Kali - Black Sara
I call you and your flaming dance

You have been invoked to write this musical theater piece. My focus has been the music and dance of India and the Gypsies, the late 90's Kosovo war in Serbia, and the Hindu Goddess, Kali who the Gypsies carried with them out of NW India around 1000AD. She has driven and accompanied me over eight hours a day, for the last three weeks on this journey. The question arises:

Who is this Black Mother I have followed to the absolute edge of my identity, where all connection to life is severed by her knife?

Where the ego has no agenda and burns away in her fire? It is Kali—Queen Mother of the Darkness . . . .

Her rage envelops me as the pieces of my life fall apart.

She springs out of her sister, Durga's head, just as Athena came from Zeus. They are powerful women with missions. Kali's fury is driven by the pain she feels for all suffering. Her rage is brought upon by those who don't recognize the pain they inflict on others. She demands strength, justice, and understanding—after she breaks you down, so you can start over again.

All of the Goddess's children must dance in the flames at some point.

St. Sara la Kali Queen of the Gypsies

This project, ST. SARA LA KALI— Queen of the Gypsies, addresses firstly, my philosophy against discrimination, violence, and war. It is also an inspiring and colorful vehicle for my professional interest in the music and dance of the Gypsies, their origins in Ancient India, along with the remnants of tribal matrilineal roots, and the overwhelming synchronistic presence of the Hindu Goddess, Kali, in my life. I too, am a "gypsy of the theater". With an avid passion for Sacred Dance and Theater and 25 years as a commercial choreographer, stage director and producer, I have written this work, employing those abilities to embrace my humanity, my philosophy, my art, and my spiritual studies in the form of a musical play.

I am not the first person to be inspired by the culture of the Gypsies, or the Roma. Poets, composers, painters, and scholars have studied their mysteries for centuries. Since my recent fascination with Hindu philosophy, religion, culture and art has connected my interest in the realm of blood, music, dance, and ritual, I have written about this synchronicity in the form of a modern legend. The rich integration of music and dance that has become combined and transformed over the years of the tribal migrations, proves the tenacity of the NW Hindu nomads as a culturally hybrid race. This has been seriously documented by many scholars using linguistic paleontology to trace the similarities between the early Hindu Sanskrit and the current Romani languages.

When the Indian nobles were driven from their homes by bloody wars for supremacy, they were forced to go into hiding, which, many did by joining lower caste groups that traveled from court to court, and festival to festival, as musicians, dancers, animal trainers, entertainers, fortune tellers and magicians. The Brahman priests had labeled these people godless and stripped them of their rights. In order to escape persecution, they began to wander from land to land, disseminating the true spirit of Indian culture wherever they went. The Gypsies understand well, because of centuries spent observing many cultures— the cycle of life. The people who are in power will eventually fall, those who are the down- trodden will eventually rise— the first will be the last and the last will be first. From behind the mask of these mysterious minstrels, lies a living spiritual legacy of universal, timeless wisdom.

Protected and cherished by the Black Madonna on earth, and the Virgo Paritura (Virgin bearing child) constellation in heaven, the meek shall inherit the earth.

Thank you for inspiring the material for this integration.

Ceil Gruessing
Asian and Comparitive Studies CIIS— Spring 1999
San Francisco, Ca.

BACKGROUND AND SETTING

It is May 1999, and we are in the Balkans, a historical battleground. The Kalderone family of Roma Gypsies have sought refuge on a Kosovo Albanian farmers land, in exile from a Belgrade Gypsy ghetto, where the Serbian Army has already begun their brutal campaign of ethnic cleansing of the gypsy Romas and the Islamic Albanians. The Roma caravan is going to France for the annual international celebration of the Gypsies in St. Maries De La Mer (May 24-26) where they will meet up with their "Kumpania" and redirect their lives.

My story is a pilgrimage on the "river of exile and migration" from the motherland of India, and 1000 nomadic years west to a barren refugee camp; inside Kali's mystical campfires of ritual initiation. The story continues with a miraculous sea voyage to the Notre Dame Church of Les Saintes Maries de la Mer and St. Sara la Kali, the Black Madonna, Gypsy Matron Saint. She has guided them all the way from India to these holy Mediterranean shores. A group of American Belly Dancers rallies to the cause of the Gypsies as Red Cross humanitarians, who also are searching for magic at the Festival of the Black Madonna in Saintes Maries de la Mer. The collective journey of all these seekers embraces the pain and loss of war, the lessons of human co-existence, and the desperate stretch humanity must make to accommodate each other in the dance of life.

The ideal set would be semi-circular in an amphitheater where fire would be permissible. The stage could be divided, to accommodate a dance studio and church sanctuary, and to create the various other outdoor environments in a more central view. Stage lighting, amplified sound for the actors and musicians, and video playback would require a screen or scrim. A water source would also be ideal for the ending, even if it involved a walk for the audience. This is obviously an epic drama, with elaborate technical design, but could realistically be produced in the ideal arena. (For the moment, I am submitting this as a work of literature whose life force must initially be triggered in the mind.)

If the reader can get beyond the frightening aspects of the Goddess Kali as she is depicted in religious imagery, there is a secret about her to behold. The subsequent connection between Sara (Tara), the goddess Kali, the Virgin Mary as the Black Madonna, and the Gypsy Rom culture give this work an even more exciting flavor. I hope you enjoy and learn from the Goddess energy in this work.

Thank you, Ceil Gruessing

KALI Hindu Goddess

St. Sara la Kali Queen of the Gypsies

CHARACTER BREAKDOWN

The Roma family— Kalderone

- **Kalima**— a swarthy, Balkan Gypsy woman in her fifties, dark-skinned and strong.
- **Kalika**— the young, dark, mysterious and beautiful 23-year-old daughter of Kalima.
- **Krishna**— the exotic, dark beloved son of Kalima, 28 ish, who plays clarinet & guitar
- **Rama**— the jovial younger brother of Kalima, 45 ish — Guitar and Fiddle
- **Sita**— wife of Rama— 45 ish— singer/dancer
- **Ganesha**— son— early twenties— plays excellent Guitar
- **Hanuman**— son— late teens— plays Fiddle
- **Durga**— sister of Kalima and Rama— 40 ish— singer/dancer
- **Rudra**— Durga's husband who married into the family; plays Accordion,
- **Bima**— their beautiful dark older daughter— 16 ish— sings/dances and plays Tambourine
- **Lakshi**— younger daughter— 12ish— sings dance and plays Tambourine

The Albanian Kosovo Dunav Family

- **Yana**— young Albanian blond mother, late twenties
- **Misha**— Yana's 6/7 year old daughter— dances
- **Shaeva**— Yana's younger brother, 30ish— blond idealistic— romantic— dances/plays guitar
- **Yashoda**— Yana and Shaeva's Albanian father— 60 ish, worn out but kind peasant-like.
- **Nanda**— the humble peasant farm mother/wife— late fifties

The American Red Angels as "The Matrikas"

- **Tsara**— educated, East Indian/American late twenties
- **Nadia**— arty Russian, Jewish, dark and candid— thirties
- **Juliette**— French/African/American student in California from Rwanda— thirties
- **Nico**— blond, loudmouth, show business California type— twenties
- **Carmen**— beautiful, exotic Latina from Venezuela— twenties
- **Su-Ling**— quirky Asian, inquisitive, intelligent— thirties
- **Sophia**— African/American news reporter, expressive, enthusiastic — thirties
- **7 Extras (4 men, 3 women) who can double up as:**
- **Father Paz**— Bi-lingual Catholic Priest— 40's Soldiers
- **Albanian Refugees**
- **Gypsies**

THE GARBA DANCE

SCENE BREAKDOWN — TABLE OF CONTENTS

ACT ONE— Ethnic Cleansing in the Balkans

Scene I— Gypsy Camp— Kosovo Village Farm, May, 1999 .... page 192

"The Rom Song"— a lament— Kalima & Ganga singers .... page 193
Gypsy Rhapsody— "Brothers & Sisters"— Kalima & Company .... page 194
Reunion between Albanians and Romanis .... page 195
Chingerdyi dance and Kalima's first prayer .... page 197

Scene II— Red Angels Dance Studio, San Francisco, Ca. -May 7 page 199

Rehearsal for French Gypsy Festival— "Garba Dance" .... page 199
News Broadcast— Crisis in Kosovo .... page 202
Message from Kali .... page 206
Belly Dance rehearsal .... page 207

Scene III— Refugee Camp— Cegrane, Macedonia .... page 207

Yana's lament .... page 207
Second Reunion with the Romani .... page 208
Shaeva and Kalika .... page 211
Back to the fire .... page 213

Scene IV— Refugee Camp—The Kali Puja—Waxing Moon .... page 215

Cleansing— "Arati" with Kalika's Song of Desire .... page 215
Invocation to Kali— Kalima, Shaeva & Company .... page 216
"Pranayama" .... page 217
Banjarra Sword Trance dance— The women .... page 219
Men's Stick Dance .... page 219
Shiva-Shakti/Kali Tantric Duet .... page 219

Scene V— Dawn— Refugee Camp— Next Day .... page 220

Arrival of the Red Angels .... page 220
Pongala Preparation .... page 223
A Romany Kris .... page 225
Shaeva and Kalika .... page 226

The Red Angels Huddle ....page 227
Company Hunger Hymn to Kali...page 229
Personal prayers ....page 230
The Matrikas (Red Angels) Garba Dance ....page 231
Sophia Reports—Take # 1 on
      Invocation & Lighting the Pongala Fires ....page 231
The Escape— Gypsy Queen Parade ....page 233

ACT TWO— The Pilgrimage

Scene I— Minstrels on the Road in a Musical "Dunyavi" Odyssey ... page 234

The EastWest parade—Waning Moon ....page 234
Sophia Reports— Gypsy Update—Take # 2 ....page 234

Scene II— Mediterranean Sea Voyage.......... .... page 235

Quest ....page 236
The Legend of St. Maries de la Mer; and St. Sara la Kali.........................page 236
Shaeva & Kalika— Part 3..page 238
The Kali Revelation ....page 239
Freedom Song—The Roma ....page 241
Storm— Sophia's Compulsive Journalism—Take # 3
      Vision of the Black Gypsy, St. Sara ....page 242

Scene III— Notre Dame de les Saintes Maries de la Mer
      May 24, 1999 .... page 244

Lowering of the Relics with Father Paz— Christian hymn ....page 244

Scene IV—The Crypt of St. Sara la Kali— an Ancient .... page 247

Black Madonna..page 247
The Prayers— the gifts— the promises ....page 247
Offerings of Flamenco dance, songs and sacrifices—
    The Red Angels "Matryka" Belly Dance w/
    Kalika— Exhibitions of Classical Indian, African,
    Middle Eastern and European Folk..page 248
Marriage Proposal— Shaeva/Kalika..page 249
Engagement Choreography: The Weeping of the
    Bride, The Henna Ceremony-Women's song
    Dance of the Virgin Tambourine...page 252

Scene V—The Procession to the Sea .... page 253

Parade of the Three Saints accompanied by
    the French Arlesiennes dancers and the Gardiens
    Horses— Chants and Affirmations ....page 253
Immersion of the Saints in the Sea— Blessing by the Archbishop.............page 253
THE FINALE— Company Cry to Kali..page 254
"I Will Carry You"— The Benediction song to Tara/Kali.......................page 255
True Gypsy Finale ....page 256

Cecilia Anne Gruessing, M.A.

UNMIK, KOSOVO | United Nations

St. Sara la Kali Queen of the Gypsies

ACT ONE

—ETHNIC CLEANSING IN THE BALKANS

Scene I— Gypsy Camp— May 1999, A village farm in Bela Crkva, Kosovo

— A grove in the meadow— The pear tree

An old beat-up van, an old Chevrolet sedan, and a large truck/camper are parked under a huge, pear tree. It is dusk and several Romany (Gypsy) families are setting up camp, making tents and unloading provisions in the light of a full moon. The women wear several layers of colorful skirts, scarves, shawls, and lots of silver jewelry. The men wear dark clothing, boots and hats. They are gypsies, and here our story begins.[1]

An older woman, KALIMA KALDERONE, begins to build an altar around the pear tree, tying red ribbons and flowers around it with the help of the women and children. They lay out fish, rice and beans, and a bottle of alcohol as offerings, and begin the "Circumambulation of the tree".[2] *The men build a fire and hang the Roma flag*[3]*(see image) on the van. Kalima removes her scarf and pins it to the tree. It is the image of the Kali Yantra.*[4]*(see image)*

She begins to sing a ceremonial lament that is echoed by the sound of her brother, RAMA's piercing melody line on the violin. He sits under the tree. She holds a red candle in her hand and sings:

Cecilia Anne Gruessing, M.A.

Scene 1 a. "The Rom Song"

Kalima:

> "In the Beginning . . .
> In the beginning was one word,
> And this word was Rom[5]
>   and this word was in the Rom
>   All that came
>   came from this word
>   came from this Rom . . .
>
> That which people know is this:
> That we are the Rom
> That we roam along the roads
> accomplishing our Tzigane[6] things
> and sleeping out of doors at night . . .
> That which people do not know . . .
>
> Land of the culture of old!
> India! Where is thy sun?
> Covered with the smoke of centuries
> We have lost thee, left thee behind!
> Countries and sovereigns were changing all around . . .
> Roads wagons and horses go by
> Through meadows sands and woodland . . .
> O history! Like in the cauldron
>
> Where peoples are cooked
> You have thrown the Tzigane family!
> You have burnt their heart in the fire . . . . . ."[7]

The haunting quality of KALIMA's voice is soon joined by SITA and DURGA, and their daughters, BIMA and LAKSHI who join her in her "ganga" song.[8] *They form a semicircle around the tree, touching shoulders, so they can listen properly to each other, echo Kalima, and connect with her mood. They sing in close intervals, and it grates on the ear as they repeat the chorus and back up Kalima with "chopping" or sobbing sounds.*

The musicians join in— violin, piano accordion, clarinet and guitar, with Balkan drums (tapan, tarabuka), plucked stringed instruments (tambura, tamburitsa, brac, bouzouki, gadulka, bass badulka), and wind instruments (frula, kaval, bagpipes, ocarina.)[9]

By now the fire is roaring and Kalima longs for her entire family (Kumpania [10]*) and expresses this in her song.*

Scene 1 b. Gypsy Rhapsody— "Brothers & Sisters"

Kalima, sings (small print) and the family answers, singing the lyrics (in capital letters).

"My Sisters ..... they had eyes dark as night,
EYES DARK AS NIGHT,
As if cut in black diamond— MY SISTERS ...

They had moon-woven hair, my sisters,
MY SISTERS ...
Glistening blue in endless mist
BLUE, BLUE, ENDLESS MIST

And teeth like wolves', my brothers— MY BROTHERS
Teeth clenched tight on their hungers— HUNGER!!

The voice they had borne, it was from the stars,
FASCINATING AND MISUNDERSTOOD ...
They had, fearsome hands, MY BROTHERS

magical hands, MY SISTERS
musical hands, MY BROTHERS
healing hands, MY SISTERS
and the world was drunk at their fingertips ...
DRUNK AT THEIR FINGERTIPS

Gone are they on all the paths, my brothers— GONE!
They were warm like fire, and fresh like the wind
FIRE AND WIND!

Let me touch your hair, your brow, your lips,
TOUCH YOUR MOON WOVEN HAIR.
Scrutinize the palms of your hands
PLEASE SHOW ME YOUR HANDS.

I'm only searching for my sisters everywhere around,
TO LIVE IS TO KNOW HOW TO LOVE
Gone they are on all the paths, my brothers
MY BROTHERS
my sisters,
MY SISTER
but in every mirror, I find you again—
I FIND YOU I FIND YOU I FIND YOU AGAIN.........

Tchalai[11]

Scene 1 c. Reunion between Albanians and Romas

Suddenly a gunshot is heard, coming from an Albanian/Kosovo farmer's son, SHAEVA with his sister, YANA, and her young daughter, MISHA. Shaeva holds a rifle on the group threateningly:

Shaeva: This is private property. What are you doing here?

Kalima: We are only here for the night. The Serbs ran us out of Belgrade last week, just like the Albanians drove us out of Kosovo in 1981[12]. Last night we paid the KLA (the Kosovo Liberation Army) our last money. We only want the shelter of your tree tonight. You know my husband, Vishnu, used to work for your father ten years ago. He took care of the horses on this farm. *She walks into the light.*

Shaeva: It's against the law to protect a Roma. You'll have to leave.

Yana: Wait Shaeva,........ we do know these people.

Kalima: I remember you Yana. You used to dance with my daughter, Kalika, when you were young.

Yana: Oh my God, Shaeva put down the gun. Don't you remember? We all used to play together. There's KRISHNA, and Kalika!! (*Kalika and Yana embrace*)

Shaeva: That's enough Yana, take Misha and go back to the house. It's not safe out here at night. The Serb police are everywhere.

Kalima: We will be gone in the morning, as we are on pilgrimage to the Gypsy Festival of Our Queen Mother Kali-Tsara in St. Marie de la Mer. We are in exile again, as you too soon will be. But we must go to France to the annual gypsy festival to regroup with our "Kumpania" and pray for our lives. This land is not safe. Please have mercy on us, and we will be gone before the sun comes up.

Yana: Oh Shaeva, I want to talk with Kalika, we must let them stay and help them this time. We cannot continue to oppress others as we are being oppressed now.

Shaeva: You lost your husband by the hands of these Serbs. We can't take any chances.

Yana: Yes, and my pain is still great. But please, these people are our friends . . . Here is an opportunity for a moment of joy despite all the darkness around us. I want to dance again with my old friend. Give me this moment of joy Shaeva . . . .

Krishna: Shaeva, remember me? We were like brothers once. Put down the gun, take my guitar, show me what you remember.

Misha: I want to dance too Mommy.

Shaeva: (*breaking down*) You know, we're all about to lose our minds here.

Kalima: Come with us, before they drive you to the camps— We have to pick up one more family, and we go directly to the border, and then west.

Yana: We cannot leave my parents. They are old, and my father will not leave the land. It was his fathers, and our great grandfather before him. They've managed to hang on to it all these years. We cannot leave.

Krishna: Then make music with us now, and we will meet again someday, when this is all over. *He offers his guitar to Shaeva who acquiesces.*

Kalika: Yana, thank you, we didn't think we would make it to the border tonight.

Yana: Oh, Kalika, for years I've thought about you and your family, but my father couldn't let me be seen with the Roma. Our life has become so restricted by the Serbs. And my husband used to work for them, until he quit, and they killed him. We've all been through hell. . . . Where is your father, Kalika?

Kalika: He died in Karaburma last winter. It was so cold Yana.[13] We all miss him so much, but at least he didn't have to go through being driven out of Belgrade.

Yana: I'm so sorry Kalima, about your husband.

Kalima: As I am sorry about your husband too. The world turns our lives in strange ways. I must pray now for all of us. You go dance with the girls, and *(to)* Shaeva ... My husband would be proud to hear you play like that!!

Scene 1d. - The Chingerdyi dance and Kalima's First Prayer

The fiddler, Rama, fires up a lively number with Eastern tones of sliding quarter notes, glissandos, and a bagpipe sound from the clarinet. Kalika pulls Yana on to the dance floor in front of the fire to dance the "chingerdyi".[14] She teaches her to clap hands, smack ankles, and scuff shoes on the hard earth in a rapid rhythmic pattern, the way the Hungarians taught them, originating with the Indian "tandava"[15]

Kalima goes to the tree and lays her red candle on an improvised altar under the Kali Yantra. She removes a small red book from her pouch and holds it to her heart, praying over the music:

Kalima: Oh, dear Queen Mother Kali, "You create and destroy everything on Earth. You can see nothing as old, because death lives in you. You give birth to all upon the earth because you yourself are life. You are the mother of every living creature and the distributor of good; you do according to your wisdom by destroying what is useless or what has lived its destined time. By your wisdom you make the earth to regenerate all that is new, and you are the benefactress of mankind."[16]
Please spare my family from this holocaust. Give us safe passage to France. Give us strength Mother Kali, and we will continue to face the wheel of life in your name. Consume our pain and we will forget past tragedies, forever seeking another road, another home.

Meanwhile, the dance has gotten wilder, and wilder— everyone is dancing madly.

Suddenly, gunshots are heard coming from the farmhouse. Shaeva grabs his gun, screams, and runs towards the house.

Rudra: It's the Serb police, they're setting the house on fire. We must pack up and go fast.

Kalima: Come with us Yana, you're not safe here.

Yana: But my parents, I cannot leave them. And Misha!! My baby MISHA!!! Where are you? Shaeva!! Help me!!! *She runs to the house.*

In less than five minutes, the campfire is extinguished, and the cars are packed, ready to leave. The Serbian soldiers are on the rampage. Misha and Lakshi, a Roma child, come running into the scene crying and looking for their mothers. The gun shots are louder. Kalika grabs Misha and Lakshi and climbs aboard the van as the gypsies pull out, leaving only the red candle burning at the foot of the pear tree. No sooner have they left than Yana has returned to the camp site, calling out, looking for Misha. She collapses, crying at the foot of the tree. Taking the candle in her hand and grasping Kalima's small red book, which was also left behind, she begins to cry hysterically.

Yana: Oh Mohammed, Great Allah if you are out there, please take care of my Misha, please protect my Misha. I pray, oh please, that they spare her

Her prayers are interrupted by the entrance of two Serbian soldiers who carry her away screaming for her baby.

Cecilia Anne Gruessing, M.A.
Scene 2— The Red Angel dance studio in San Francisco, Ca.— May 7
Scene 2a. Rehearsal of the "Garba" dance

A Tribal Indian dance[17] rehearsal is in session with six female dancers in modified traditional dress with bells on their ankles. They are: TSARA (East Indian), CARMEN (Venezuela), NADIA (Jewish Russian), SU-LING (Taiwanese), NICO (American), and JULIETTE (French African). Upstage Right is a desk and a TV. Upstage Center is an eclectic altar with the image of a Kali Yantra and a Sri Yantra, crosses and stars, along with several Goddesses including Kali, Tara, Aphrodite, Kuan Yin, Shiva, Ix-Chel, Ishtar, Mary, etc.

We hear the sound of the tabla (small drum) and a "shruti" box, (an East Indian organ type box which creates a drone sound). The girls enter and begin to sing and dance the "Garbi"[18], carrying clay pots on their heads, going round and round, bending to the right, left, and forward, stamping the feet in a rhythm of four counts, and clapping their hands in sweeping gestures. It is a devotional dance to the Mother Goddess, and they sing in "laysa" style (more lyrical than stamping).

They sing along:

> **"Come, come to Tarapith,**
> **If you want to see "Ma"**
> **Here you will get the touch of your own Mother,**
> **There is no doubt about it.**
> **Here there is no distinction of caste,**
> **Because my Ma is the mother of the Universe,**
> **We all call out "Ma, Ma"-**
> **Mother will place you all on her lap**
> **Come here and see"**
> **She wants to quench your thirst,**
> **"To give rice to the hungry,**
> **The mother is calling all her children**
> **Wherever you may be,**
> **Come, come, come here."**   Gyan Babu [19]

The dancers sit, stretch, fix their costumes, drink water.

Tsara: So how does the choreography feel girls?

Nico: Feels good to me .... I can't wait to get on the airplane.

Nadia: I'm pretty comfortable about all the dances. I just wish Sophia would get here, so we can run through all of them. But I do think we're ready for France on the 24th of May.

Juliette: Well, if it's good enough for you, then it will definitely be good enough for the gypsies in St. Maries de La Mer!!

Su-Ling: Do you think the Roma will be insulted that we come from the States with our "Gadjo" (Romani for non-gypsy) imitations of their dance roots?

Carmen: And what does Gadjo mean?

Nadia: It's like shicksa is a female non-Jew ...... Gadjo is a non-Gypsy.

Julliete: I want to get straight on these gypsy origins in India. How did they track that?

Tsara: OK ...... *(she stands, putting on her glasses, and strutting her pontification)* Research since the eighteenth century by European, Indian and Romani scholars has provided linguistic evidence that all dialects of the Romani language have common words originating from ancient Sanskrit Hindi, Punjabi, and related languages of Northern India as well as anthropological evidence showing *(she reads)* "body habits and ABO blood group distributions closely approximating those of the warrior classes of northern India."[20]

Nico: You go girl! *Cheering on her scholarship talents.*

Tsara ...... which indicates that there is now a clear consensus of opinion that the modern-day Roma of the Middle East, Europe, Asia, and the Americas originated in Northwestern India. Furthermore . . . . what makes it oh so interesting . . .

Nadia: You see what a Phd will get you?

Tsara: What makes it oh so interesting girls is that they fled their caste system!!! Their freedom, their families, and their art meant more to them than slavery. In India there have always been criminal and wandering tribes outside and beneath the caste system.[21] These people lived off of forbidden trades. Some were even nobles. There were musicians, dancers[22], metalworkers, snake charmers, fortune-tellers, peddlers. In the middle-ages they weren't considered fit to be associated with a decent Aryan. [23] And even to this day there are people in India who are considered "Untouchables". Then there were the invasions ....

Carmen: Are you going to test us on this?

Tsara: I'm hoping that you might have some sense of the mission we are on, which is to make more people aware of the rich culture from which the Roma came.

Juliette: So, when did they actually begin to leave India?

Nico: *(the doorbell rings)* Can I please be excused?

Tsara moves to the map on the wall

Tsara: One wave began in the 5th century when an Indian Jatt King gave 12,000 musicians and dancers to a Persian Monarch, Behram Gour. There were several Muslim invasions of Northern India beginning in the early 800s all the way up until Mahmud of Ghazni, who mangled Northern India after 25 years of Islamic invasions. Several tribes moved south to continue their rich religious culture, and by the 11th century, the real pioneers were moving west in caravans .... India to Persia to Armenia— and then a fork, to Syria and what would become Iraq, Turkey, in one direction, and in the other Byzantine Greece, the Balkans, and on into Western Europe and the New World. By the 15th Century the Gypsies had become part of European culture.[24]

Nadia: And so why are we so fascinated by them?

Su-Ling: Maybe because we are all running from or to somewhere, homeless, searching, trying to understand our own mysteries and cultures . . .

Nadia: trying to express ourselves to find out who we are.

Nico: Hey girls, I hate to interrupt, but Sophia is on her way up and she wants us to turn on the news. *She turns on the TV to a news program for which Sophia is on air reporting.*

Carmen: Five dollars this is about her new hairdo, and how does it look on camera. What do you bet?

Sophia *(enters harried)*: I'm sorry I'm late, I came as fast as possible.

Juliette: Where have you been Sophia? You just missed the history of India!

Carmen: Not to mention, about an hour of rehearsal.

Sophia: I'm sorry girls, but there is a war in Yugoslavia.

Nadia: OK so what is todays' breaking news of blood and guts from the sophisticated world of the American media.

Sophia: This is no time for sarcasm Nadia.

Scene 2b. The Crisis in Kosovo

Roll TV News Broadcast— Sophia as News reporter speaks on tape, showing the familiar images of refugees in holding camps in Macedonia...

Sophia: This is NATOS fifth week of bombing strategic Serb Military positions in Yugoslavia. Civilians are now being killed. Thousands of Kosovo refugees are still pouring across the Macedonian border as Serbian armies ordered by Yugoslavian President Slobodan Milosevic, are driving Muslim immigrants living in Serbia, out of their homes in a full scale. It is a violent campaign to eliminate all Albanian Muslims, Croatioan

Catholics, and Roma Gypsies from the province. Just to give you a little background— Milosevic revoked Kosovo's autonomy to immigrant residents in 1989, with violence. The struggle for power in the Balkans, throughout history and especially since the Bosnia/ Croatian War has been ceaseless, circular, and devastating. And now with the Kosovo Liberation Army revolt, and Milosevic's solution of ethnic cleansing, we are witnessing a humanitarian catastrophe and a potential continent-wide refugee problem.

For 200 years, since the Ottoman Turkish Empire lost control of the Balkan territories, Yugoslavia has been the rope in a tug of war. First, the Austro-Hungarian attempted to rule Bosnia, which sparked WW I. Then President Tito's campaign tried to re-unite Yugoslavia's disparate ethnic groups after WW II, which lead them through the Cold War.

There has been constant struggle between the Orthodox Christian Serbs, the Roman Catholic Croats, and the ethnic Muslims.

Sixty-five Kosovo Albanian men were slaughtered by Serbian police as the men stood naked in a streambed at the Bela Crkva village yesterday. One hundred and five men and boys from the Orahovac region were assembled inside a house, which Serbian police then sprayed with gunfire. Police then piled hay onto the dead and wounded, and set it afire to destroy the bodies. [25] Testimonies from refugees who are crossing the border describe merciless crimes of rape and torture against men, women, and children who are being driven from their homes as we speak. And the NATO bombing continues in an effort to bring Milosevic to the peace table with his hands tied.

Cut to Anchorman

Anchorman: And that's it for the Evening News. *(happy talk style)* Well Sophia, I understand you'll be leaving us tomorrow for a trip to Southern France to perform with your dance company at a Festival for Gypsies.

Sophia: That's right, Bob. This is an annual spring event which has been taking place since 1448 in St. Maries de la Mer where thousands of

Romani Gypsies converge to celebrate and honor their QUEEN Sara la Kali, an ancient Black Madonna, located in a cave in a church on the small island of Camargue on the Rhone River delta.[26]

Anchorman: And you'll be actually dancing there?

Sophia: Yes... with the Red Angels, of the American Dance Tribe in San Francisco, who will be joining me as I cover the story and participate in a rich cultural pilgrimage of Gypsy song and dance in the sunny French Mediterranean.

Anchorman: Well maybe we'll get a glimpse of your legs for a change in some rare dance footage.

Sophia: Didn't know I had feet, did you Bob?

Anchorman: Can't wait to see those Gypsy boots Sophia. Bon Voyage. Don't eat too much caviar!

Sophia: Goodnight Bob.

Anchorman: Goodnight Sophia, and goodnight, everyone from KTSF.

Sophia turns off the TV.

Sophia: Sorry to ruin the mood girls. *Silence*

Julliette: I am speechless— It reminds me of my Rwanda.

Nico: And we fill our time with manicures, Masters degrees, E-mail, ...

Carmen: And Monica Lewinsky.

Nadia: I have to tell you Sophie, that Happy talk thing is really pathetic . . ..

Sophia: What am I supposed to do? It's part of the job! Why do you think I dance?

Carmen: Now the whole state knows the anchorman has a crush on you.

Su-Ling: How are we supposed to go to Europe now that NATO is increasing the bombing? I mean . what if Russia gets involved? Or God forbid China??!!

Juliette: Oh now, come on girls...... we are going to France. Yugoslavia is on the other side of Europe. We've worked too hard on these choreographies, and we need to make real contact with the Roma dancers. Besides, Queen Kali is calling us. *She goes to the altar.*

Tsara: I wonder how many of the Balkan Roma will actually make it this year. You know that Skopje, Macedonia has the largest gypsy population in Europe? And they would have to go through Kosovo en route to France.

Sophia: You know, I hadn't thought of any of that.

Tsara: The Roma have been uprooted, persecuted and oppressed for centuries.

Nadia: Hitler killed 1.5 million of them right next to the Jews in WW II, and they still survived. [27]

Tsara: Sophia, I bet this war will bring more Roma on Pilgrimage to Queen Kali than ever before. *She walks over to the altar in the studio.*

Sophia: You know this is a great connection for a story. Really!

Carmen: I just don't understand the reason behind ethnic cleansing.

Nadia: Oppression, revolution, and war— That's the history of the world— the Jews, the Muslims, the witches, African Americans,

Carmen: Latinos

Su-ling: Women . . ..

Nico: It's the history of white male supremacy is what it is. If men had to carry a baby for nine months, they wouldn't want to hold weapons over other people's kids. Don't get me started on the gender thing or the sublimation of minorities.

Su-Ling: So what should we do? *Silence*

St. Sara la Kali Queen of the Gypsies

Scene 2c. Message from Kali

Tsara: *She has been standing in front of the altar lighting candles.* Kali says go to Kosovo.

Juliette: That we should go to Kosovo?

Carmen: You must be kidding!

Tsara: That the Red Angels should go dancing to Kosovo with the Pongala[28] and then make an escape Pilgrimage to the waters of the Three Saints.

Sophia: *thinking out loud,* now how could we do this?

Sue-Ling: Very cryptic indeed Tsara. The pilgrimage[29] would be to St. Maries de la Mer, but what is a Pongala?

Tsara: It's an ancient tribal Indian rice cooking ceremony that women do together to worship the Mother Goddess in the Matrilineal societies of Kerala in southern India where I come from.

Nadia: Like the "Kumbha" pots in our dance .... *thinking out loud.*

Sophia: *(ecstatically)* Why not? That's it!!!! I'll get my boss to send me to the refugee camps in Macedonia to cover the story of Kosovo gypsies on exile to St. Maries de la Mer. It's brilliant. Thank you Tsara.

Tsara: Thank Kali.

Carmen: What about us? I'm a nurse, I want to go . . . .

Julliette: I'm sure we can talk to the Red Cross about this— I will call someone tomorrow.

Sophia: That's it!! THE RED ANGLES dance for THE RED CROSS in KOSOVO! We can all go. What do you say girls?

Nadia: You know, I think we're on to something. Maybe we can really do something concrete instead of sitting here with our wet nail polish listening to bomb stories.

Nico: You mean like the old Bob Hope shows, only we'll dance for the refugees instead of the troops?

Su-Ling: Who is Bob Hope?

Nico: Never mind.

Tsara: But we must bring more Pongala supplies. Nadia, doesn't your husband work for Safeway?

Nadia: Right. Maybe he can get them to donate rice for the ceremony.

Sophia: I'll call K Mart about the other details. *She makes a note.*

Tsara: Right now, I believe that Kali wants us to dance.

Su-Ling: We definitely want to have our "Gadjo" act together.
They make a circle.

Sophia: Are we in agreement about these ladies???

Nadia: Start the music, let's do this!

Scene 2d. Belly Dance Rehearsal

They begin to rehearse a belly dance choreography, to a slow and mysterious Middle Eastern musical track. Lights change to create the very dark red mood of Kali—

FADE TO BLACK

Scene III— Refugee camp— Cegrane, Macedonia
Scene 3a. Yana's Lament

A pale blue moon lights up the cold, body stacked wasteland of a Macedonian Refugee Camp. Improvised tents, hammocks, and the debris of humanity surrounds the bodies of sleeping refugees in the early dawn light. A fire smolders where Yana and her family are camped. She is having a nightmare and Shaeva wakes up to comfort her.

Yana: *(in her sleep)*— Please don't shoot, I have money— I'll pay you!!

Shaeva: It's OK Yana, it's me. Yana! It's a nightmare!

Yana: This whole thing is a nightmare.

Shaeva: Come on, we don't want to wake Mom and Dad. They had a rough night, and Dad is really sick. I'm going to the Red Cross tent.

Yana is clearly depressed as is everyone. Moving slowly, she pulls out a small bundle from an improvised pillow and unwraps the red candle and book which she rescued from the pear tree before she was carried off by the soldiers. From her pocket she finds a small shoe of Misha's that she managed to grab at some automatic motherly moment. She improvises a small altar with these items and some rocks and photos, as she sings a lilting lament, reading from Kalima's little red book.

Yana: First my husband, now my only child… gone.
She sings.

> **"Oh Mother! My desires are unfulfilled;**
> **My hopes are ungratified.**
> **And my life is fast coming to an end,**
> **Let me call you Mother, for the last time;**
> **Come and take me in your arms.**
> **None love in this world.**
> **This world knows not how to love.**
> **My heart yearns, O Mother, to go there,**
> **Where love will fill my empty heart."**

Dr. Jadunath Sinha, Ramaprasada's Devotional songs [30]

Scene 3b. Second Reunion with the Roma— Misha found

In the distance Yana hears a violin echo her refrain. Everyone around her begins to stir and wake- up. As the sound gets louder, the morning sun rises brighter and a minstrel marching band sound develops from the sad, fiddler melody, and Yana become excited.

Nanda Dunav, *Yanas Mom*: What is that music Yana?

Yoshada Dunav, *Yana's Dad:* It's the gypsy people grandma. Can't you tell? Remember when they used to come to the village with their dancing bears? [31]

Yana: I see them now. I guess they didn't make it to the border. Oh, please Allah, let them have my Misha.

Nanda: Isn't that Misha sitting on Shaeva's shoulders?

Misha: Mommy!! *From off stage.*

Yana: Misha!!! It's really her.

She runs towards the sound of the violin which is growing louder. Suddenly we see Misha who jumps off of Shaeva's shoulders into her arms. They are followed by Kalima, Kalika, Krishna, and the rest of the Roma tribe.

Shaeva: Look who I found at the Red Cross tent.

Misha: We tried to cross the border, but they put us on a bus, and now we found you!! Oh Mommy, I missed you so much.

Yana: I prayed that you were with Kalika and not the soldiers or lost somewhere horrible. *(She holds her tightly)* Thank you Kalika, for taking care of her. I owe you, my life.

Kalika: We didn't know what to do. We tried to keep traveling west to France, but they found us last night only two miles from the border. I was in such conflict about Misha, what to do— we couldn't turn back, and I knew she was safe with us, and that we would find you again. They took our cars and put us on buses and here we are. At least we have some of our things.

Yana: I don't know whether Misha might have been better off if you had escaped with her. This is hell here Kalika— People are dying.

Kalika: All of us are homeless now, but at least we have each other.

Kalima: Stripped bare like Kali .... But we are alive, and we must be thankful.

Nanda: Kalima, you are like a vision. I am so happy to see you

They embrace. You hide your years well. I can't believe my eyes.

Kalima: You are the only Gadja woman I ever respected despite our differences. Your granddaughter has been safe with us until now that is.

Shaeva: Kalima, can you help my father? He is terribly ill, and the Red Cross line is half a kilometer long.

Kalima: Let me try. Kalika, bring me my herbs.[32] Show me your hand Yoshada.[33] *She feels his head with the other.* How is your heart?

Yoshada: No better than ten years ago. *She places a wet rag on his forehead.* Bless you Kalima and forgive me for letting your husband go ten years ago . . . he was a good man, but they would not permit gypsy employment. My hands were tied, and it know it has come to this. *He breaks down.*

Kalima: Don't speak . . . . I will give you something for your fever. [34]

The men have been building up the fire. The children are playing, fighting, and crying. People begin to line up around the fire. Everybody mixes, and there is an obvious visual weaving of colors and ethnic persuasions between the Roma and the Albanian refugees. Overall, it is still gloomy. The violin continues to be heard in the background. Krishna, Rama and Rudra begin to talk privately. Kalika and Shaeva begin to talk

Krishna: We have to get out of here make a move somehow, by tomorrow. There's only a week until the Festival in France.

Rama: It will take a miracle for us to arrive in France by May 24th.

Krishna: We have to round everybody up somehow.

Rudra: Everybody is so weak and hungry . . . I just can't imagine where the energy will come from.

Krishna: No, it should be something from within the camp, and I just haven't thought of it yet.

Rama: We can't do anything until we talk to Kalima.

Yana and the gypsy women have begun to collect food for a soup. Ganesha enters with a hedgehog. [35] *The men begin, once again to play their instruments. The mood is grey, yet strangely lifted by the arrival of the Gypsies. Kalima finishes treating Yoshada and joins her sons for a private conversation.*

Krishna: Mom, it's only a week until the festival.

Kalima: I know Krishna, and it's Tuesday. This is the night for a Kali Puja.[36]

Rudra: With all these Gadjos?

Kalima: Rudra, everybody here is desperate, and I just want the family out of here and on the road as soon as possible. We must do the puja. Where is Kalika? I need to talk to her about the ceremony. She must bathe somehow and prepare herself.

Krishna: I think she's taken a walk with Shaeva . . . . like maybe more than a walk.

Kalima: You better go find her now . . .

Krishna exits to find his sister. Kalima sets up an improvised tent with blankets, and tarps. The melancholy refrains fill the background.

Scene 3c. Aside— Shaeva and Kalika

Shaeva: I don't know where you go to be alone here.

Kalika: I feel like everyone's looking at us because I'm a Roma and you're a Gadjo.

Shaeva: Kalika, everybody is stressed out in this bloody hell, and it's all they can do to keep from going crazy. I hate those mother fucking Serbs; they killed my brother-in-law.

Kalika: Can we talk about something else?

Shaeva: Like what?

Kalika: Like........Do you remember that time when we were young when we used to play in my father's barn.

Shaeva: I remember when your father taught me how to shoe a horse.

Kalika: I don't mean that . . . .

Shaeva: I remember Kalika.

Kalika: That was the first time a boy ever kissed me. I was thirteen.

Shaeva: And I was fifteen and thank God nobody saw us. *They laugh.*

Kalika: I re-lived that kiss a thousand times. And I remember when we used to dance all of us. It was so exciting. I always wanted to dance with you. You were a good dancer.

Shaeva: And you were the best.

Kalika: You haven't seen anything yet.

Krishna enters, short of breath from looking for Kalika.

Krishna: Where have you been sister? I started to worry. This is crazy here and we really have to stick together, OK?

Shaeva: I'm sorry Krishna. We were just remembering old times.

Kalika: Is everything all, right?

Krishna: Mom wants you to dance for a puja[37] tonight. We have to find some water for you to bathe. She wants to prepare you.

Kalika: She wants to do puja here?!! In the middle of all this???

Krishna: Kalika, we need a miracle, and we are going to have a puja.

Kalika: Actually, this couldn't be a more perfect cremation ground for Kali to dance on. Where can I bathe?

Shaeva: I believe there's a small creek that runs down there near that forest. I can take you there.

Kalika: Krishna, Shaeva will take me to the river. I will return to camp right away.

Shaeva: *Krishna is hesitant.* Don't worry Krishna, I promise nothing will happen to her.

Krishna: If you don't mind… I'll go along— she's my sister and that's the way we are.

Scene 3 d. Back to the Fire—

People are eating small rations out of improvised cups made of plastic bottles. Bread is torn up and passed around. Kalima removes a small copper pot from her sack along with several worn-out plastic bags of dried flowers and herbs, powders, woods, grain and pastes. She mashes all of this together in her copper bowl, adding some local leaves and grasses to the mix, creating a special ointment which turns red when she adds vermillion.[38] The Roma girls return from the river carrying water in a big earth pot, "Kumbha", which they place near the altar. They leave a basket of red hibiscus flowers (Kali's flower) they have collected from the riverbanks. This takes place during the following dialogue while her family prepares the altar. Yana and her mother continue to cook, watching the Roma respectfully.

Yoshada: I feel much better Kalima. Thank you. Whatever you gave me completely destroyed my fever. I'm grateful for such blessings.

Kalima: Yoshada, you are not of my blood, but we have history together with our families which cannot be overlooked.

Yoshada: And now we are all gypsies. Last week I slept in my bed in the house where I have slept since the day I was born, and this week I am like you have always been, completely homeless and at the mercy of strangers. All my life I have struggled to hold onto that land.

Kalima: But we are not homeless if we believe in something.
She makes her paste.

Nanda: What do you believe in Kalima?

Kalima: I believe in the open road, I believe in my family, my Kumpania, and I believe in my goddess Kali who has guided and protected my family, and my husband's family for as long as any of us can remember. Every year we go to St. Maries, even if we have to perform along the way to pay expenses. All of my children have been conceived on the pilgrimage to see her. She is our Queen Mother, Kali-Sara, and her celebration is May 24th and 25th. We must go. I will make a ceremony for Kali tonight, and if you are strong enough to dance, we invite all of the gadjos, to help us Romas call her, our black Madonna, St. Sara La Kali!

Yana: Is she the Kali in this book? I just remembered this is yours.
Yana returns the little red book to Kalima.

Kalima: Yes, these are my real prayers. Thank you so much for saving this for me. *She hugs Yana.* Kali is frightening and wonderful, and you must be ready for her, for I know she can help us. As her destructive energy has moved NATO forces to combat Milosevic, she also can provide more creative solutions, but the transformation can be painful.

Yoshada: How can it be more tragic than this? We are ready for anything Kalima.

Misha: When will we dance again Kalima?

Kalima: We will dance tonight, but now I must find my daughter.

Kalika: *Entering with Krishna and Shaeva.* Here I am, mother, I've bathed in the creek.

Kalima: Good . . . All Roma women can come into the tent for the blessing now. And bring your bells and reliquiae.

Yana: What about Misha and me?

Kalika: Please let her come Mom. Yana's got the moves and the "rasa" (*emotional zest and fervor*) and Misha is ready to learn.

Kalima: You are Gadjo, ... but . . . Queen Kali does not see color, except for the red of blood, common to us all. We'll have to find you some bells.

Scene IV— Refugee camp, twilight— The Kali Puja

Scene 4a. The Cleansing "Arati" begins:

Krishna stands up and blows a conch shell and holds the tone for 30 seconds. The girls exit from the improvised tent wearing red, their hair is loose, and they carry candles and tree branches. The sound of their ankle bells and the swoosh of the branches is soon accompanied by the Romani drums and the percussion of improvised instruments. This is Banjara gypsy worship of Kali from India.

Kalika, dressed as the Goddess Kali, sits on the altar in front of the fire, and the dancers circle around three times. Kalima leads the chant to Kali:

"JAI MA, JAI MA, JAI KALI MAI KI JAI!!" [39]

Kalima rings a brass bell in her left hand, the chant fades and she perform the "arati", first taking a plate with five small candles on it which she waves in front of "Kali" (Kalika) with her right hand. Then Kalima fills the conch with water from the earthen pitcher (pani sankha) and waves it in front of "Kali". Next, she waves a red cloth, a red flower, and a fan (chamar).

These things symbolize the five elements— *fire, water, ether, earth and air.* [40] *A necklace of flowers, a"mala", is placed around "Kali's" neck. Kalima anoints Kalika with the special paste (arghya) and sprinkles her with water from the conch.*

Kalika sings the following devotional song during the "arati" preparation ritual.

"Mysterious Ma Kali,
Cremation grounds are your great delight,
For there you release souls from mundane experience.
I have transformed my heart into a cremation ground so you will
be attracted here to dance as flames of liberating bliss.
Oh Wisdom Goddess,
my limited desire has been consumed on
the blazing pyre of renunciation.
O Goddess of Freedom,
I am surrounded by the ashes that were my assumptions,
waiting ardently for you to come.
Please manifest in the brilliant midnight hour
of this renouncing heart.
Please dance to the intense drum of my longing upon the breast
of Absolute Reality
that appears as Shiva, Conqueror of Death,
breathless beneath your flashing feet.
The singer of this song is waiting,
eyes wide open in the wakefulness
beyond meditation."   Ramprasad[41]

INVOCATION TO KALI— Kalima, Krishna & Company

Kalima takes the water from the conch, washes out her mouth, spits it on the fire, and passes it around. Now she can begin the mantra for her mouth is clean.

Kalima: **OM KALY AI NAMAUH**
OM KALY AI NAMAUTH
GREAT BLACK MOTHER OF ALL,
GODDESS OF CREATION AND DESTRUCTION
MISTRESS OF TIME
KALI MA, WE CALL TO YOU FIRE DANCER . . .
COME AND DANCE WITH US

Krishna sings the lead, and the crowd answers Krim, Krim, Krim *after each line.*
Black hair flying— Krim, Krim, Krim
Bells on her ankles ringing— Krim, Krim, Krim
Bloody Sword is flailing
Wide Mouth is laughing
Holding severed smiling head
Handheld up dispelling fear
Handheld out offering bliss
Eyes burning with the flame
Body naked filled with stars
Necklace of skulls glowing,
Drums beating her rhythm
She dances as thunder
Jim Ryan – Professor CIIS

Everyone joins the chant after they partake of the conch water and follows Kalima as she performs "mudras" with her hands which activate the seven chakra centers in the body (Nyasa). When all have imbibed of the conch, spat, and responded with the Krim, Krim, Krim part of the mantra, Kalima rings the bell again. They all sit quietly and follow Kalima in the "pranayama".

Scene 4c. The Pranayama

Kalima: We will now purify our seven chakras breathing in with
the left nostril, and out with the right. These chakras are shaped like
wheels, and they keep the sacred spirit moving through our bodies.
The wheel is the Romani symbol for life. Breathe in, and breathe out
to make the wheels turn.
Now imagine all impurity within you rising up to the top of the head
where it meets the bright light of the mystic fire and burns away
everything dark within you. (Bhuta Shuddi) bathe in the light. Now bring the
beauty of Kali into your heart— her fire, her strength, her compassion. *The musicians begin to play softly.* When she has arrived in your heart and you feel
her heat, take the flower and blow her spirit onto the flower.

Kalima performs a special flower mudra, called the tortoise mudra, which everybody follows with their hibiscus flower and then blows into the flower. (Prana pratisha)

Kalima: Offer your flower to the goddess so that your flower will breathe life into her.

Everybody throws their flower at once towards "Kali", which causes Kalika to open her eyes and reveal her trance state. The young girls bring her humble offerings.

Kalima: Jai Ma Kali. We have called you here today on these cold cremation grounds, in the midst of our misfortune, to embody the mysteries of your wisdom, to purify our souls, and to ask for your mercy. Grant us freedom from this living hell imposed upon all of us, black, white, Albanian, Roma, Catholic, or Muslim. Liberate us from the bondage that keeps us from fulfilling our destinies. We are not ready to die by the hands of soldiers without morality. But if that be your will, do so in order to destroy the shackles of demon consciousness that bind us. We ask you to open the roads of love and creation we all long for. Show us the way, Holy Mother Queen Kali, Goddess of Destruction and Creation— to live together on this planet. We have all seen enough bloodshed. How much more must be sacrificed? Let the Romas go on to France to worship you with our brothers and sisters. And let these people go back to their homes.

Misha: *Praying with her teeny hands.* And Kali, please make those bombs stop exploding in the sky.

Yana: Hush Misha, she can't do that.

Kalika has fallen into trance as KALI,[42] and gestures suddenly towards Misha.

Kalima: The goddess hears the child.

Kali: Come to me little Misha. *Misha goes timidly to the Goddess (Kalika) and climbs in her arms. Kali blesses her with holy water and holds her high in the air.* This child will lead the dance. And I, Kali Mah will give you the strength to break the chains that hold back your freedom. And my Rom people will lead you to my shrine of the Black Madonna, so that you can live out your futures. Let the fire of the dance release you from this bondage.

Scene 4d. The Women's Banjara Sword Trance Dance

The musicians begin to play a song resembling the fiery HOLI dance of the Banjara Indians of Rajasthan[43] in which they celebrate the fertility of spring and Mother Nature. There are many complicated tones. First Kali dances with Misha. Then Kali and the women perform a trance-like sword dance. They form a running circle around Misha swinging their swords, their skirts flying as they turn, their heavy silver ornaments swinging over their bodies. Their stamping cross steps become more vigorous – four fast, two slow, four fast, two slow. The men begin to chant. KALI dances with Misha and twirls her around, then hands her off as she begins a wild crazy solo.

Scene 4e. Men's Stick Dance

The Roma men throw grain onto the fire, and begin to dance around Kali with sticks, beating them slowly, then increasing in speed until they shout with enthusiasm. Everybody is on their feet!! The women begin to sing shrilly. "As the dance gets wilder and wilder and reaches its climax, the men join hands as they stand in a circle, and the women climb up onto the men's clasped hands until a woman is standing on each man's shoulders, holding the hand of the next woman. The whole circle goes round to the accompaniment of the song— a fast moving, tremendously vibrating spectacle filled with verve and the primeval forces of a people intoxicated with the ecstasy of the love of nature."[44]

Scene 4f. Shiva— Shakti/Kali Tantric Duet

Suddenly Shaeva, who has been standing to the side, enters the center of the circle and tries to calm Kalika as "Kali". He has been confused by the strange ceremony and does not understand her trance. "Kali" engages him with her fire dance, and they dance an almost violent, passionate, and confrontational dance in which Kali can only be subdued by her active seduction of Shaeva (Shiva). He is aware of this process and never takes his eyes off of her, deflecting her advances with dips, embraces and lifts. It has become a savage tango. The

Pas de Deux is frightening, auspicious, transformational for everyone present, as Kali lifts up Shiva, turns, slides him down onto the floor, steps up on top of his body, and lifts her arms. The music ends. There is silence. The Goddess speaks.[45]

Kali: The King is sacrificed so that winter will end, and the crops will grow.[46] I grant light and liberation to all who can walk through my dark valley. Obey this command. You must follow the Red Angels and be fearless!!!!!

Shiva: Jai Ma!

And Kalika falls out of trance upon Shaeva's words. She is disoriented and falls to the ground. Shaeva embraces her. Kalima comes to her daughter, lifts her, and blows in her ears.

Kalima: Tell me your name.

She responds slowly, knowing the routine.

Kalika: Kalika Kalderone, I'm 23 years old, and you are Kalima my mother, and … *She looks around at all the people watching her — She looks at Shaeva.* And you are my Shiva. *She collapses into her mother's arms.*

Kalima: Take her into the tent please. *Shaeva picks her up and takes her into the tent.* Rama, strike up that Hungarian Pergetes number so we can all dance, OK??

Rama: OK boys lets hit the "Khelimaske Dyila" …….. 5 6 7 8 [47]

People pair off and dance until dawn as the light fades.

Scene V — Refugee Camp — Next Morning — The Red Angels

Scene 5a. Arrival of the Red Angels

The lights come up on the immobile debauch of the previous evening. Everyone is asleep. The only motion is in the smoldering fire where little Misha who is playing with Kali's flower necklace. The camp resembles a cremation ground with all the bodies and trash— It is a refugee camp wasteland. In the background we hear the sound of bombs that segues with the sound of a truck getting closer, coming to a stop, and being turned off. American voices are heard. The Red Angels have arrived, weary from their long voyage.

Nico: I can't believe we're actually here. How old is this truck? Girls wake up!

Carmen: Oh my God, this is like a war zone. I think I'm gonna cry.

Su-Ling: Carmen, control yourself and don't stare.

Sofia: Excuse me sir, we are looking for the Red Cross Tent?

Meanwhile, back at the campfire....

Misha: Mommy wake up, wake up, the RED ANGELS are here . . . .

Yana: Tell Mommy about that later OK honey? Let Mommy sleep.

The American girls drive through the camp, hauling a huge wooden flatbed loaded with baskets of rice, nuts, raisins, coconut, and clay and metal pots. They are wearing red sports sweats and baseball hats. The refugees can't believe what they are seeing.

Tsara: *Seeing Misha she approaches.* Excuse me little girl, do you speak English?

Misha is shy but she is fascinated and nods yes.

Tsara: Can you tell us where the Red Cross Tent is?

Misha: Are you the Red Angels?

Silence— as the seven girls stop in amazement and look at each other.

Misha: We've been waiting for you right here. Kali told us you were coming.

Nico: Yes, we are the red angels, and are we in the twilight zone?

More and more refugees have begun to wake up and notice the group of American girls dressed in red. They eyeball the truck with curiosity and hunger.

Sophia: Good morning, ladies and gentlemen. Yes, we are the Red Angels from San Francisco, California, and we are here to make a Pongala with you.

Silence . . ..

Tsara: Do you all know what a Pongala is?

More silence

Nadia: Maybe we ought to try another approach . . .

Kalima: *Stepping forward.* I am Kalima and I know what Pongala is . . .. and I believe you were sent by Queen Kali— the Black Mother? Could I possibly be right?

The Red Angels smile in disbelief, their eyes popping . . ..

Tsara: How did you know that Kali sent us?

Kalima: Because we spent the whole night calling her, and when she arrived, she told us to look out for the Red Angels. And now you are here to make the Women's Pongala. Thank you, Mother Kali!!!!

Sophia: Kalima, do you know about St. Sarah la Kali in St. Maries de la Mer?

Kalima: We were on our way there when the Serbs caught us. We go every year and meet our entire Kumpania there.

Sophia: We are dancers on our way to dance and document that festival. You must come with us…... somehow.

Kalima: Thank you for bringing the Pongala. Maybe this will give us the strength to make the pilgrimage. Maybe this is Kali's miracle message.

Juliette *to Sophia*: How are we going to feed 3,000 refugees with one cart of food?

Sophia: I don't know. I don't know how any of this happened, but here we are and, and The Goddess wants us to break bread with these hungry people, and that's what we will do. Right Kalima???

Kalima: Of course, in the name of Kali I thank you.

Tsara: Can you help us with the Pongala setup, Kalima?

Kalima: Of course! Let's get to work.

They shake hands. Sophia pulls out her camera to film.

Scene 5b. Pongala Preparation

As they unload the truck......

Kalika: My mother is the Phurai Dai [48] of the Romani Kumpania Kalderone. She knows well the ways of our ancient gypsy ancestors in India. You have surely been sent to us by a Kali miracle.

Nadia: We really want to help you. So, girls, how are we going to choreograph this cooking routine?

Tsara: Kalima and I will demonstrate the Pongala, and then we will distribute the materials to all the women to make their own fires in a huge circle around this spot.

Kalima: First we must draw a huge Kali Yantra with a big fire as the "bindu"[49] in the center.

Shaeva: I will take care of that mother— teach your Pongala to the women.

Kalima gets up on the truck and demonstrates as Tsara assists.

Kalima: Ladies gather round. You will need three rocks or bricks like this, and sufficient firewood for an hour. The recipe calls for 3 cups of rice, 6 cups of water, a pinch of salt, a cup of coconut, one of raisins, and one of nuts. You watch it boil and pray for miracles. If it boils over, your wishes come true. And if Kali wishes, your rice will multiply, and all will be satisfied.

Kalika: Who will draw the Rangolis mama?

Kalima: Shaeva will draw the Kali Yantra, and everybody must draw their own designs around to please the goddess. *They draw designs with drizzled flour on the earth.*

The Red Angels help distribute pots and rice, and a circle of small fireplaces are set up around the larger fire. The Kali Yantra is being drawn by Shaeva on the ground with flour. The young girls bring in another Kumbha (clay pot) full of water. Women search for their 3 rocks, and set up their spots, drawing their designs around the pots (rangolis). The musicians begin to play a haunting ballad. And the bombs continue to drop in the near distance. Everybody interacts with mixed fear and desperation. Su-Ling now holds the camera on Sophia, in reporter mode, with the Pongala activity in the background.

Sophia: Hurry up Su-Ling— I've got to get this!

Su-Ling: I can't tell if there's enough light.

Sophia: There's enough light, trust me— Try to keep me in the corner of a medium two shot with all this in the background, OK? Ready?

Su-Ling: OK— action! Do it!

Sophia: Good morning. This is Sophia Knolls for KSTV in the Cegrane Refugee Camp on the Kosovo-Macedonian border, where hundreds of homeless refugees are arriving every day. Sincere efforts are being made by the Red Cross to make people as comfortable as possible in a next to impossible situation. And despite all of the grief and misery, people are helping each other in ways that will hopefully redeem some of the darkness that has caused this ethnic cleansing. We see Albanians and Macedonians, Catholics and Muslims, Gypsies and Turks, Bosnians and Croatians, wealthy and poor all together— homeless. Today the Red Angels, from San Francisco, California, have momentarily shifted the dark mood on these Macedonian Cremation Grounds. What you see behind me is the cooperative organization of a "Pongala" ceremony - an exclusive female East Indian ritual inherited from Pre-

Aryan tribes of a matrilineal society. It is being revived and practiced in Southern India. But the Roma people, who are also descendants of these ancient people, have carried many of the Hindu customs throughout Europe and particularly throughout this part of Eastern Europe. So, with the assistance of Kalima Kalderone, the "Phurai Dai" of the Romani tribe here, and my assistants the Red Angels, we will attempt to stretch 1000 pots of rice across this sea of hunger tonight at midnight. Our prayer— ladies and gentlemen? To turn around hunger with food— and hate with love. Stay tuned this evening for the ceremony. And remember, most of the world does not enjoy the freedom we have in the USA . . .

Sophia Knolls for KSTV in Skopje, Macedonia . . .

Did you get it Su-Ling?

Su-Ling: I shot some beautiful tape. You want to see it?

Sophia: No, I've got to get to the airport to send this to San Francisco. Start a new tape and keep shooting. I'll be back.

Scene 5c. A Romani "Kris"[50]

Kalima and the Roma men (the musicians) are gathering for a "Kris" (Romani for private meeting). Carmen, overhears the conversation.

Rudra: Kalima, you are the "Phurai Dai", but all this ceremony is making us hungrier. My wife is pregnant, and the festival is 2000 miles away. We have to go Kalima.

Krishna: Yes mother, and I have a plan, and you must ask Mother Kali for support.

Kalima: I will not make any violence Krishna. The Macedonians are trying to help.

Durga: Yes, but we are in cages. This could be endless.

Kalima: OK Krishna, what is your plan?

Krishna: Tonight . . . .. when the fires for the Pongala are lit, we will play the "Gharba" song, and you will dance in the smoke. When the rice is cooked, and the cloud is thick, we must ask Kali to lead us out of this place in a procession West — to France — with whomever wants to come. We will go peacefully as a group. Nobody will harm us if Kali is with us.

Kalima: You are brilliant, and if I hadn't seen you come out of my womb with my own eyes, I would have thought you were born to Kali herself — as was Kalika. Go then and find the best way out. I will pray.

Carmen, who has been collecting firewood, has overheard this conversation, and is overwhelmed with the information.

Scene 5d. Shaeva and Kalika

Shaeva finds Kalika by the creek filling the Kumbha with water.

Shaeva: You can't carry that by yourself, let me help you.

Kalika: I'm not ready to go yet, I have to bathe— come join me.

Shaeva: It's cold here for May.

Kalika: You were pretty hot last night I understand.

Shaeva: Weren't you there?

Kalika: Kali was there.

Shaeva: Where were you?

Kalika: I was in spirit, asleep.

Shaeva: And where are you now?

Kalika: I'm right here, looking at you.

They kiss, and two girls giggle who are nearby.

Kalika: They are laughing at us again.[51]

Shaeva: I don't care what anybody thinks anymore, ever again. I want to go where I want, touch who wants to touch me, pray to whomever I wish, and have real love instead of fear in my life. I'm young and strong, and I want a woman— a beautiful dark woman— who isn't afraid— like you Kalika. I want to be with you.

Kalika: This is not good. Krishna is not happy about last night, when you danced with "Kali". You are a gadjo. It is against the rules.

Shaeva: I had to dance with *you* last night, I was afraid you'd burn yourself in the fire.

Kalika: *suddenly angry* – Shaeva – I had to dance for my people …to bring Kali to my people! *She breaks down.* The Roma people cannot be trapped like this!!! And I know they are planning something tonight.

Shaeva: I promise to protect you, whatever happens. *He embraces her.*

Scene 5e. The Red Angels Huddle

Carmen: Tsara we have to get the girls ready to dance. Where's Sophia?

Tsara: She's gone to the airport to ship the tape.

Carmen: We've got to call her. It's important.

Nico: Yes, call her and tell her to pick up some barbecued chicken, mash potatoes, and good old American corn on the cob— I am starved.

Nadia: Could you also ask her to buy some Tampax?

Nico: Oh no— you know what that means …….. you get it, then I get it, then Carmen….

Tsara: *(interrupting)* Girls, can we get serious here? Now —
The pongala preparations seem to be going OK. Obviously, there isn't enough rice for everybody.

Juliette: Hey…. I believe in miracles . . . maybe it will multiply like with Jesus.

Nico: Oy Juliette, come down to earth.

Carmen: Umm, girls? I've got to get this off my shoulders . . .

Tsara: What is wrong Carmen?

Carmen: I overheard the Roma men talking about busting out of here tonight, when we light the fires. They want to escape right out of here, and onwards to the sea.

Juliette: Wow, I don't know whether to be freaked out or excited!

Su-Ling: That's crazy, how can anybody bust out of here? These people have been walking for days— they are already tired, sick, undernourished, and confused.

Nico: I think it's an inspiration… clearly, there is no future here in a refugee camp.

Carmen: AND the musicians will play the Garba folk dance to signal the exodus.

Tsara: That's the dance we do with the clay pots. You know this could maybe work… a mass movement…. A parade, a pilgrimage…

Tsara urgently dials Sophia on the cell phone.

Nadia: You guys are for real!! Dancing for the revolution, are we?

Sue-Ling: It's a good thing my father can't see me now.

Juliette: My father cannot see me now because he was killed by Rwandan dictators. *Pause and transformation.* We are supposed to be here to bring attention to this cause of ethnic cleansing.

Nico: *Pointing into the sky.* There he is Juliette, looking at you right now, and he's proud.

Tsara: *(on telephone)* Sophia, this is Tsara— Well, there have been some new developments, so you need to get back as soon as possible— Yes, Su-Ling has been shooting tape. Sophia listens. Bring the Garba costumes with you from the airport on your way back. Yes, we're going to dance tonight, in full regalia, to distract the guards along with the pongala, and help these people make an escape pilgrimage out of the camp to work our way to France. Yes, I said escape. *Pause... she hangs up.* She's on her way girls.

Scene 5e. The Company Hunger Hymn to Kali – THE PONGALA

The women have all taken their positions at their fires. The conch is blown, everything is ready. Kalima enters, dressed in ceremonial robes, with lots of jewelry. She is a Priestess and is breathtaking with her full priestess regalia. She bows to the fire and leads everyone in an opening hymn:

Kalima: *(singing/praying)*

"O Mother of the Universe!
  You who provide basic sustenance
  and subtle nourishment for all creatures!

  Please feed us, Holy Mother! *(others join in)*
  Satisfy every level of our hunger!
  I know the mother always feeds her hungry child,
  regardless of their foolishness or carelessness.

  Goddess Kali, grant the child who sings this song
  your supreme blessing of total illumination of the way.
  Today is the most auspicious day!
  Please, Mother, do not delay! *(all)*

  Goddess Tara, my pangs of hunger for reality
  are becoming unbearable.
  Mother! Mother! Mother! *(all)*
  You are the longing and the longed for!
  You cannot refuse your child's earnest prayers."
             Ramprasad [52]

St. Sara la Kali Queen of the Gypsies

Scene 5g. Personal Prayers.

The conch is blown again. The women shrill. and everyone goes into prayer Sophia enters with suitcases. Su-Ling gives her the camera and the Red Angels Disappear inside Kalima's tent to change. Sophia shoots video.

Misha is in the arms of her Grandfather Yoshada. He kneels down to pray.

Yoshada: Allah, please forgive us our sins, and the sins of others. I beg you for my health. Give us our families, our land. Thank you for our daily food and for the blessings that come in every day. Thank you for my beautiful wife and children, and my Misha— the light of our lives.

Misha: And I pray that all the guns of the world would just crumble up and disappear.

Painful silence, as Yoshada carries her away.

Nanda: *(to Yana)* I see your brother has an eye for this gypsy dancer.

Yana: None of us have any privacy whatsoever.

Nanda: I hope he's not making a mistake.

Yana: Mother don't judge Shaeva for this love he has. It's really the only thing to look forward to, no matter where you are— Don't you remember? You were young once. I certainly remember how strong that love can be, and now my true love is gone.

Nanda: Yes, I know my darling. These are terrible times.

Yana: Give Shaeva you're blessing. He is Albanian and she is Roma, but Kalika is like our family. They grew up on our farm Mother.

Nanda: I am only worried about his future. But you are right Yana. We cannot transfer our experience of abuse based on their blood line. We must not let the Serbs stir our anger. Our family has been living there for so long, with our Albanian traditions. This is evil this fighting. This war will never end— over blood and religion. I can't stand it. And the bombing, when will it end? What possible good does it do? *She breaks down in confusion.*

Yana: Mother, this is about family. Kalika is Roma, and we are gypsies like her now. Shaeva feels true love for Kalika, and I am happy for him. We must honor this now. Who knows how long any of us have anyway?

Scene 5h. The Garba dance of The Red Angels (Matrikas)
(Matrikas are a group of Hindu Goddesses who fight demons)

The musicians are tuning and count off the "Garba" which cues a dramatic entrance from the tent of the Red Angels, completely transformed into Tribal Indian Gypsies with their jewelry, regalia, and clay pots on their heads. They circle around ceremoniously, creating a mystical ambiance despite the desperation of the moment. Both the Gypsies and the refugees are initially taken by surprise, until they too become mesmerized. The Roma knows the music, have seen this dance before and join in, circling with the pots on their heads, and making the gestures.

The Albanian women also join in and before long, everybody is smiling.

Scene 5i. Sophia Reports— Take # 1
— INVOCATION to Light the PONGALA FIRES

Krishna sounds off the conch shell again— The drummer plays a drumroll. Kalima says her prayers tossing herbs into the fire. **The pots go on the fires.** *Sophia hands the camera to Shaeva and she begins to speak, dressed in belly dance regalia.*

Sophia: Welcome to the full moon at the Cegrane refugee camp in Macedonia. What you are about to see ladies and gentlemen— is the simultaneous ceremonial lighting of the Pongala fires, intended to illuminate the personal and family karma of every woman who participates. In India, thousands of women celebrate this ritual together. This ancient Indian custom has been brought to all the Kosovo refugees by the Roma gypsies and the Red Angels at this time. It is a symbol of hope for a new future, where the clay pot becomes the tomb and the womb, where there is a blurring of distinctions between the living and the dead. We are about to light the fires with the Maestra of Ceremonies, Kalima Kalderone, a Romani gypsy of distant Hindu descendance, who seems completely familiar with the Pongala, and the ways of the Mother Goddess, Kali. Queen Kali provides the thread in this entire journey as the Red Angels attempt to lead the way out of refugee hell on the pilgrimage to the sacred church of St. Sarah— la Kali, in St. Maries de la Mer, France. Take a look at sacred fire!

Kalima: Come help me, Red Angels. You are now Kali's Matrikas!
Kalima leads the chant; Sophia signals the Red Angels entrance as they snake dance around the fire in full costume and wild rhythm and color.

OM KALI AI NAMAUHE *(3 times)*

GREAT KALIMA

MOTHER MISTRESS OF ENDINGS, SLAYINGS AND RELEASE
GODDESS OF DEATH AND MOTHER OF PEACE
WE CALL YOU BY THE VORTEX
OF DEATH, DYING AND SORROW
SPREADING OUT
WE CALL YOU TO HALT THIS MASS DEATH INFERNO
SAVE OUR PLANET GREAT GODDESS
MOTHER OF BONES AND EARTH
AS DEATH FORMS WITHIN LIFE
AND LIFE WITHIN DEATH

Kalima holds a torch high in her hands and lights the central fire. The Gypsies and Red Angels come to the central fire to light a stick, which they take to their fires. The other refugee women form a circle around this with their pongala fires. And the smoke, incense, music and dancing that ensues create a dreamworld ambiance in which all of the players become entranced. They dance in a circle around their fires letting their hands hover over the heat. They dance with each other. Clearly, all of the women are in blissful trance, including the Red Angels. Shaeva continues to shoot videotape, and is concentrating on Kalika, whose dance has taken on the postures of Goddess Kali once again. He gives the camera back to Sophia, enters the dance floor, and takes Kalika on his shoulders. The pots begin to boil over, and with heavy rags, the women begin to dance with the hot pots on their heads.

Scene 5j. The Escape— Gypsy Queen Parade

An exile parade forms, with refugees like lemmings, being led by Kalika, Shaeva, Kalima, the musicians, and the Red Angels. They begin another song about the Gypsy Queen and the rhythm accelerates.

GYPSY QUEEN

> "Arise Roma, for the moon is shining to see your face,
> And the caravan awaits your call,
> a journey to become a
> Brown Baked Gypsy Queen . . . Fly! . . . .
> Run away into the arms of sunset
> waiting just over the next horizon.
> You bow to the sign of the open road
> and yearn for a thousand miles before the day is done
> the highways call your name
> and the earth sings a song to guide you.
> Be free Gypsy Queen …. March on to Freedom.
> Free your gypsy soul
> Free of the fetter's life imposes
> Free to pursue the secret heart we all keep hidden........
> Run wild through the forests playing with the rain
> Let the drops wash away the stains that tarnish your heart,
> Cleansing the battered side of your soul
> Brown Baked Gypsy Queen
> You have everything you need—You must only look to find it."
> March on to   Freedom....

Scott Applegate[53]

The Red Angels become Kali's "MATRIKAS"[54] and lead the way under the chain link fence, and onto the long and winding road around Kosovo and towards the sea. Sophia continues to shoot video as the entire refugee camp escapes under the fence and down the road singing and dancing.

END ACT I

St. Sara la Kali Queen of the Gypsies

ACT TWO

— THE PILGRIMAGE

Scene I— Minstrels on the Road in a Musical "Dunyavi"[55] Odyssey
Scene 1a. The Parade

Act two begins with a musical ODYSSEY of refugees led by Kali, the Romas, and the Red Angel Matrikas on to Albania, and towards the sea.

The pilgrimage takes the form of a dreamlike parade of wasted minstrels who have come close to death but are in the bliss despite their homelessness. The Red Angel Matrikas and the Gypsies dance together in the fusion of European Europe Folk Dance, Middle Eastern Belly Dance, Tribal American Belly Dance, Flamenco, Kathakali Indian, and Italian Tarantella (dances all derived from India). We hear the audio of a radio broadcast mixed in over the music.

Scene 1b. Gypsy Update— Take # 2

Sophia is in broadcast mode with Su-ling shooting on the side of the stage.

Sophia: An unbelievable exodus of Albanian Muslims and Romani Gypsies has taken place over the past three days from the refugee camp in Cegrane, Macedonia, when they all made a miraculous exit singing and dancing in the decoy smoke of Pongala fires. Macedonian and Albanian citizens are providing support and accepting refugee families along the way. Rumor has it that this is a KLA publicity stunt, but facts closer to the truth suggest the more pacifist tactics of Mahatma Ghandi, as the company is miraculously marathoning its way peacefully to the Mediterranean without obstacles, singing and dancing. The Red Angels are an American group of dancers from California who are accompanying the Romani Refugees to France where Gypsies make their annual pilgrimage, worship, and celebration around their matron saint Sara— la Kali, in Les St. Maries de La Mer. This dramatic statement has sent a wave of sympathy throughout local communities on route, who have accepted pilgrims who are too weak to continue. The music and the dancing have not stopped for three days. And that is just as well because soon they will be boarding a tanker, courtesy of the French government, which will carry 500 Romanis, refugees, and pilgrims to their shrine at the Rhone River, Delta Island of Camargue. This entire event, ladies and gentlemen, has been a remarkable example of unbelievable spiritual strength, tenacity and humanitarian support, exhibited under extremely difficult conditions. Stay tuned for more updates on the Gypsy Pilgrimage to the Cave of Queen Kali— St. Sara— the Black Madonna.

The parade has taken itself up and down the aisles of the theater, with all of its serendipitous minstrel color, giving the stage an opportunity to be changed into the interior of an ancient church, while the curtains are closed. (This is in the event that an indoor theater is used. An amphitheater would clearly be more suitable to a procession.) They arrive at the dock where the boat waits. The procession returns to the stage to climb up the stairs onto "the French Tanker, "La Liberte". They line up in front of the curtain as if they were looking at the shore from on board.

Scene II— The Mediterranean Sea Voyage—
Scene 2a. Quest

Stretched across the edge of the stage, looking out to sea, are the Red Angels, the remains of the Albanian family— Yana, Misha, Shaeva, and Parents; and the Roma family, visibly including Kalima, Kalika, Krishna, Rama, Sita, Ganesha, Hanuman, Druga, Rudra, Bima and Lakshi.

We hear the sounds of ocean waves.

Yoshada: Goodbye sweet Balkans, my only home, valley of bombs and blood, land of constant struggle and burning desire. Goodbye.

Nanda: Oh no— We will be back. We grew too much corn on that land to give it away. My children must be safe, however, and for the moment, we are in exile.

Yoshada: How can I calm my heart when the destination is not our home?

Nadia: You are making a pilgrimage with us to ask for help.

Yoshada: By the time I get there, I'm really going to need it.

Yana: Rest here father, we have a long trip.

Scene 2b. The Legend of St. Maries de la Mer; and St. Sara la Kali

Misha: Where are we going Aunt Kalima?

Kalima: We are going to a very special church called Notre Dame de Les Saintes Maries de la Mer— Our Lady of the Saint Maries of the Sea . . .

Su-ling begins to shoot tape while Sophia gets on her laptop. They are still on the boat.

Misha: And does Kali live there?

Kalima: Queen Kali has a home there, yes.

Misha: I thought she lived in India.

Tsara: Kali was born in India and has always traveled with the gypsies.

Sophia: Tell us more about the festival and how it started Kalima. *She begins to film.*

Kalima: OK, everybody… listen closely, and let me take you back a thousand years, in 42 AD. After the death of Christ, Mary, the mother of Christ, Marie-Salome, and Marie-Jacobe, the mothers of St. James and St. John, with Lazarus and a dark gypsy woman, servant of Mary's named Sara, were forced to flee the Holy Land by boat. After storms and a perilous journey across the Mediterranean Sea, the boat capsized in the ocean, and the young gypsy woman Sara, managed to save the two Maries, Salome and Jacobe, in a small rowboat, landing at what now has become a shrine upon which an ancient church stands.[56] The two Maries have their shrine upstairs in the church, where we will watch them lower their bones and relics in a coffin on May 24th.

Misha: Is this a true story, or pretend?

Kalika: We Romas believe it is true Misha.

Sophia: *Looking at her laptop.* Not to interrupt, but I am quite pleased to inform everyone that in the fifteenth century, King Rene, Count of Provence, intrigued by the still-living legend that two Marys had been buried beneath the church, decided to see for himself it was true. In 1448 he began to excavate.

Kalima: *Picking up the story as they settle into the sea journey.* Before long they uncover two female bodies with their hands crossed over their hearts. All the church officials were summoned, who all proclaimed on December 22, 1448, that the bodies were indeed Mary Jacobe and Mary Salome, the aunts of Jesus Christ. The very next day, the bones were installed in the upper chapel. And ever since then Gypsies come from all over the world on May 24th and 25th to touch the bones and celebrate Kali as the Black Madonna.

Juliette: OK. And what about Sara the servant?

Sophia: Oh, they found her too, and gave her the mysterious, dark, cold, cave like crypt in the basement, since she was a Black Madonna, and obviously could not be mistaken for the Virgin Mary, whom they never found. She is conflated with Sara the servant who saved them.

Nico: I'm confused. Who is Sara and Who is Kali?

Tsara: There are many stories about Sara, as the mother of Abraham, or some slave from Egypt, but I'll tell you the real truth. Sara la Kali is the Black Gypsy Queen from ancient India whose destructive form is Kali and Creative form is the goddess Tara, her sister. "Tsara", is also a Romani word for wagon,[57] and I believe that "Sara la Kali", is a cryptic derivation of "Tara la Kali" combined in all her universal glory, as the Gypsy's Black Hindu Goddess.[58]

Nico: Only you would know Tsara. Cause she is your namesake.

Kalima: I completely agree. The Black Madonna is our Queen Kali, even though they keep her in the church dungeon. They clean her up for the Christians and the Gadjos, but we truly believe she makes miracles. Look where we are now, because of Kali and her Matrikas. It is only right that we make pilgrimage and homage to her and pray for our future. Thank you, Kali Ma!

Scene 2c. Shaeva and Kalika— Part 3

Kalika: Look, Shaeva, up there is the constellation of Virgo, where Kali comes from; and the gypsies say that all the French cathedrals were arranged so as to mirror, on the earth, the design of that constellation so they would always be under her sacred protection.[59]

Shaeva: Do you really believe that Kali lives in all of these places?

Kalika: *Carrying on her romantic drama-* "We Gypsies are the Lords of the Universe, of fields, fruits, crops, forests, mountains, of rivers and springs, of the stars, and all the elements." [60] (Pg 42 Esty) Of course I believe! The Goddess is everywhere, and nature is her manifestation!!

Shaeva: *Joking* - So is this Virgo Queen of Heaven a virgin?

Kalika: Well Kali is a virgin in the sense that no man dominates her.

Shaeva: Oh, I see. Are you a feminist?

Kalika: You are making fun of me. Her virginity is different than the Virgin Mary. "Our mind is different from you gadjos; our understanding makes us older than our years. We sail over strange seas and turn to a pole-star unknown to you;"[61] for it is by natural magic that we live… and these things, a gadjo can't touch!

Shaeva: I just wondered if Kali was a Virgin . . .

Kalika: Well, if you are really asking about me, Shaeva Dunav, the answer is yes, and that's the way it will be until I am married.

Shaeva: So, I understand. I guess we'll just have to perfect what you call our Shiva-Shakti [62] dance. When can we practice that again?

Kalika: Whenever the spirit is moved, I suppose.

Shaeva: And what about your spirit Kalika? What do you want?

Kalika: I don't know how to answer that. My survival with family is all I know. And that I love the warm sunshine, and a good fire on a moonlit night.

Shaeva: I'll keep you warm Kalika.

Kalika: *She looks at his palm and then his eyes.* I know that you are a good man Shaeva. But it will take a lot more than dancing Shiva/Shakti to convince my mother to let me go.

Scene 2d. Kali Revelation

Sophia takes the camera. They are still on the boat".

Kalima: We Roma worships the Christian Virgin the same way that the Hindu's worship Kali. She is our mother goddess. It is in the Hindu and Gypsy tradition to offer blood. But we only do that amongst each other. Just as the Christians drink the blood of Christ, we offer Kali blood.

Su-Ling: You mean real animal sacrifice?

Kalima: Usually we offer the heads of pigeons, although it used to be goats and ox.

Nico: Not only am I seasick, but I think I'll have to make a trip to the powder room if we're going to continue discussing animal sacrifice, OK?

Juliette: Is this why Kali is so frightening, with those teeth, and the bloody tongue, and that meat cleaver that makes you tremble in her shadow?

Tsara: Kali dominates time (Kala). She is the darkness, before time and the formless dark that will come again. After she devours all time and destroys the universe, she then again recreates it for the next cycle.

Nico: Ah yes, Terrible Black Kali, I can see her now with her long red tongue lolling out of her mouth, a necklace of skulls, earrings of children's bodies, a belt of human hands, her four arms wielding weapons, hair flying black, matted and wild, naked and blue in the midst of an ecstatic dance, standing on her lover. Imagine her on Bay Watch.

Kalima: Yes, that is Kali— and the Tantra of Great Liberation can only be achieved by understanding her power as Creator, Protector and Destroyer all in one. The whole Universe springs from her dark womb, also known as the lotus, and the chakra symbol, as well as the sacred mandala, and our symbol for the gypsy wagon wheel.

Kalika: "For us woman is like the earth. The earth is our mother and so is woman. The seed of life comes from the ground."[63]

Carmen: So how does the Yantra fit with the Tantra?

Kalima: The triangle is our symbol for Kali in her three forms of maiden, mother, and crone— like the phases of the moon. The Matriarchal mother, sister, Queen is the "Phurai Dai", the source of all Romany blood. In Tantra we meditate on the Kali Yantra, on the triangles of life. We used to have priests and priestesses of Kali who were trained to perform the Great Tantric Rite, "Maharutti," known in India as "Maithuna," or what you call sex without male orgasm.[64]

Sophia: Now that's interesting, but I don't think I'll be able to broadcast this.

Nadia: Don't interrupt.

Shaeva: Do you know about this Kalika?

Kalika: No, I don't.

Yana: Maybe she's waiting for the right guy.

Kalima: Suitable Gypsy men are taught that occult coition is a means of increasing psychic powers. Love power generated by controlled sex was thought necessary for the training of a sage. My grandmother always said, "If a Roma man really wants to possess the power of love, he should always give more than he takes."[65]

Juliette: I can't believe that actually exists.

Nadia: It definitely wouldn't go over big in corporate America.

Yana: Are you getting that Shaeva?

Shaeva: Yes Mam, what I don't understand, is why your Queen doesn't give you a home.

Kalika: India is our homeland.

Shaeva: Then why don't you live there?

Krishna: Because we live on the road. We are in constant exile, and that is our lot ever since the days of the caste system. There are hundreds of folk tales, legends, and songs about our curse to wander eternally. The Tribal Indians didn't want to fight for the Hindu or the Muslims. They wanted their freedom to make music and be close to the earth, and the road is the only place we find it. We stay as long as we can.

Scene 2e. Freedom Song— the Roma

Krishna strikes a chord on his guitar and continues singing, and accompanying solos to the poetry of Spatzo, an Italian Sinti Gypsy, persecuted during the Holocaust.

Krishna: "We Gypsies have only one religion: freedom. In exchange for this freedom, we renounce riches, power, science, and glory. We live each day as if it were the last.

Rama: *(singing)* When one dies, one loses all. A miserable caravan is just as valuable as a great empire. And we believe that in that moment it is much better to have been a Gypsy than a king.

Sita: *(singing)* We don't think about death. We don't fear it. Our secret is to enjoy every day— the little things that life offers, and that other people don't know how to appreciate.

Kalika: *Singing* A sunny morning— a bath in the spring, the glance of someone who loves you.

Kalima: It is hard to understand these things, I know. One is born a gypsy.

Durga: It pleases us to walk under the stars. They talk to Gypsies.

Kalima: Like how to read the future, and how to make love potions.

Rudra: Most people don't believe in things they can't explain.

Durga: We instead don't try to explain the things we believe in.

Kalima: Ours is a simple, primitive life.

Kalika: It is enough to have the sky as a roof.

Sita: The fire to warm us ……… and our songs when we are sad."
Spatzo (Vittorao Mayer Pasquale)[66]

Krishna strikes a final chord on the guitar.

Scene 2g. Vision of the Black Gypsy, St. Sara

A storm suddenly begins to build. There is thunder, lightning, and the boat begins to rock dramatically. Everyone attempts to hang on to each other as they are whipped across the deck by the wind and the waves. As if these pilgrims haven't been through enough. Sophia decides to seize the moment and gives the camera to Su Ling.

Sophia: *Barely able to hold her balance.* Su Ling, are we rolling?

Sue ling: We are rolling in many ways. Go for it, you crazy witch!

Sophia: *Shouting over the wind and the rain.* This Black Madonna, Sara la Kali IS the Hindu Goddess Kali. "Kali's best-known forms are dark and wild. I think of her as a way that Hinduism has found to affirm and include all that has been rejected. She is a symbol not only of death but of life and victory over death. Fearlessness is the boon she grants. She is the fierce feminine personified, Queen of the Void, vast as space itself."[67]

Sophia continues trying to keep her balance: She will smash your ego to smithereens!!! You don't know she's there until your life is falling apart, being stripped away, and you're trying desperately to hold on, but everything you touch falls away!!!!! And then . . .

Su-Ling: You've run out of tape here Sophia.

There is a sudden flash of light and Carmen points towards the hull of the boat in disbelief.

Carmen: Dios mio, que es eso? Santisima Madre, ayuda mis ojos!

They all look in the direction where Carmen is pointing out to sea.

Juliette: I don't believe my eyes— There's a big black gypsy with a gold cape hauling the tanker!

Tsara: It's her!! It's Saint Sara la Kali— and she is walking on the water, and... *Looking up.*

Kalima: And the storm is dying, and the ocean is calm.

Sophia: Great. We are witnessing a miracle, and I am out of tape.

Nico: *With her sunglasses.* Have all of you completely lost your mind? What are you looking at? I don't see any black gypsy.

Nadia: Get with the program Nico. Take off your sunglasses.

Nico: Oh my God, or Goddess?

The ocean calms down and parts to reveal the port of Camargue. They all start yelling at once.

All: "We love you Kali, Long live St. Sara la Kali, JAI MA!"

The sound switches from storm, to birds, and then to Gothic, French Gregorian chants and they arrive in the upstairs sanctuary of Notre Dame de la Mer, at the Rhine River delta, on the island of Camargue, France.

Scene III-Notre Dame de Les Saintes Maries de la Mer -May 24/99

Scene 3a. The Lowering of the Relics with Father Paz

The Catholic Father Priest *praying*: Bienvenue Madames et Monsieurs. Bienvenue au le plus vieux pelegrinage du France, que nous celebrons chaque annee lorsque 1427.[68] Bienvenue especialment aux toutes les Gitanes: Les Manouches; Les Romas; Les Sintis: et Les Gitanos de España. Sin vous autres, cette fete ne vivirais pas. Merci, et que commence le homage aux Les Saintes Maries de La Mers. (*Welcome to the oldest pilgrimage in France that we celebrate annually since 1427. A special welcome to the Gypsy families, without whom this holiday would not exist. Thank you, and let the festivities begin!*)

Everyone crowds into the chapel craning their necks toward the ceiling as the priest speaks. From an opening in the stone wall high above the altar men begin to lower two coffins.

Priest: These coffins contain the remains of Mary Salome and Mary Jacobe, the aunts of Jesus and Sisters of Mary.

A stillness falls over the crowd. Solemn organ music fills the air as the coffins slowly descend, trailing ropes entwined with garlands of flowers. As it comes within reach, we hear from the crowd.

CROWD: Vivent Les Saintes Maries!!!

GYPSIES: Vive la Sainte Sara-Kali!!!

It becomes a free for all as worshippers extend their thin white candles high in the air to snuff the flame against the bottom of the box for good luck. Parents hold their babies up to touch the box before it hits the ground. The sick and the lame are lifted to touch the box. On a very high altar sit the statues of the two Maries. Even the Albanian families bow to the floor in reverence. Everyone is suddenly lifted by the blessed mythology of the moment as the old Latin Christian hymn comes to a close.

Sophia: *Whispering, as she shoots her camera.* Kalima, where is Saint Sara?

Kalima: Under the church in a cave. We will go there next, but I want to ask the father if we can sleep there.

Nadia: Come on Kalima, let's go together.

Nadia approaches Father Paz with Kalima and her Kumpania.

Nadia: Father, thank you for such a beautiful service. We have just arrived with this Roma Family.

Father: I know Kalima. She never misses the festival.

Kalima: Hello Father Paz … *She hugs him as tears come to her eyes.*

Father Paz: I've been trying to convert Kalima and her family for 20 years, but she is dedicated to her Kali.

Kalima: Will you let us keep the vigil there tonight, Father? Our people from the Balkans have many prayers to make as they too are in exile.

Father Paz: We have been following your cross-continent pilgrimage on the news, and we were honored to have orchestrated the tanker in Corfu, courtesy of our Camargue Mayor, who of course, recognizes the cultural and financial benefits of the Gypsy event. We not only open our hearts to you but offer you food and shelter during these holy days under God's roof. And since you are the Grand "Phurai Dai", I will give you the key for two days.[69]

Kalima: Thank you Father.

Father Paz: I hope to see you in confession tomorrow.

Kalima: Yes Father. Do you remember my daughter Kalika?

Father Paz: Of course, the dancer. *They hug.*

Kalika: Thank you, Father. I want you to meet the Dunav family from Kosovo, who have fled the refugee camps with us because of Serbian Ethnic cleansing. They are Muslim, and there are thousands like them. We want to help them.

Yoshada: Thank you Father for taking us in.

Father: Welcome all of you.........I am sorry for your tragedy, and we open our hearts and arms to you. "The poor are honored, the rejected welcomed, and the unloved comforted."[70] Please be my guest and come downstairs to see Saint Sara, your Queen Kali.

Sophia: Father, can you tell me about Saint Sara?
Sophia walks with Father Paz to the crypt of St. Sara La Kali)

Father: No one knows if she really existed. The evidence has been lost to time, blown out to sea.

Sophia: I am not so sure of that. We saw a black woman in the sea while on the boat. It was not an illusion.

Father: I don't know about that my dear. But we do know that there was worship of Ra, the Egyptian sun god here, and that there is a pre- Christian, Mithraic altar dating back to the fourth century BC that is down in the crypt where sacrifices were made. This has been a pilgrimage site since at least the sixth century BC, and this church was built in the ninth century around the old altar and columns. Women's skulls were found here from the first century, from the Middle East. The advent of the Maries arriving here in a boat in the first century marks the first entrance of Christianity into France. This place is very sacred.[71] And the Gypsies feel the magic, despite all the commercialism. They come here for guidance and the familiar security of their brothers and sisters. And we welcome them.[72]

Sophia: And what about these Middle Eastern women's skulls father?

Father: Some believe that the worship of Sara is an ancient race memory of the gypsies going way back to the worship of a mother cult fertility goddess in India. The procession to the sea, which you will see tomorrow, has the air of an old puja baptism rite. There is a pagan streak in these gypsy people. Some scholars believe they worship the sun and fire, the moon and the stars, and all the other fairy tale spirits that go with that.[73] St Sara's crypt is like an old Indian temple, thousands of miles from a Catholic Church. *A Flamenco wail is heard.*

Sophia: I can't wait to go in and start filming. Thank you, Father Paz, for your warm hospitality.

Father: Bless you sister, for your courage in Kosovo.

Sophia: I only hope that you can continue to help Gypsy refugees, because they have been oppressed by both sides in this war.

Scene IV— The crypt of St. Sara la K ali

Scene 4a. Prayers

We can hear Rudra's accordion crying from the crypt of St. Sara. As the lights come up in her chapel, we can feel the intense heat, the stillness and the presence of serenity.

The shrine of Saintes-Maries-de-la-Mer Saint Sarah, also known as Sara la Kali.

To the right of the altar is St. Sara, a dark-faced, Black Madonna, smiling. She is about five feet tall, slightly elevated on a stand. She is dressed in blue black and has midnight black hair. Many a rosary, jewel, and dress have been offered to her wardrobe. The layers of clothes and numbers of trinkets left by generations of gypsies have transformed the statue into a Romani caricature of themselves. A small carved wooden shrine beside her statue holds small shoes and letters honoring her miracles. There are children's crutches, canes and metal braces laid up against the wall behind her, as testaments to her healing. Krishna goes up to St. Sara with a complete lack of self-

consciousness, and very intimately he parts her elaborate robes and finds a way through her dress to the statue underneath. She is suddenly flesh, the way he touches her, gently caressing her. Then he leans over closer, whispers something private to her, kisses her on the lips, and steps away. It is a breathless moment. The Gypsy guitar music continues.

Krishna: Thank you, Mother Kali, for saving our lives. Help us find our way in this darkness. Thank you for the fire, the moments of illumination, and the promise of liberation. I love you dearly. Please help our family and all the others in exile.

Kalima: Oh, Great Mother; we stand now in your dark womb, the source of the spring of life that flows over the gypsy race from which all my children were born. Grant us a new beginning. We are destitute and at your mercy. It has been your feminine power which has given me the strength to carry on. I give you my heart as always. Jai Ma!

In the stifling, smoky crypt, charged with mystical incense, hot with the wax of white candles, and magical light, Rama picks at his guitar and begins the spontaneous religious drama with an impromptu musical line.

Scene 4b. Offerings of dance
— The Red Angels, Flamenco, Middle Eastern, etc.

Other musicians and dancers join, and Flamenco flavors take over. The fervor rises, roles change; spectators become performers, hands and feet become instruments, and gypsy men and women pour out their hearts to St. Sara-Kali, their Queen. It is an all-night vigil, and we are taken on a magical musical mystery tour through the Middle East, Eastern and Western Europe, and the Mediterranean, with Gypsy dancers of every persuasion. Flamenco, Turkish, Hungarian, Egyptian, Polish, and native Tribal Indian dance is woven into the offerings made to Queen Kali. Even the Red Angels perform their belly dance for the Goddess as offering.

Throughout the evening, Gypsies approach the Goddess and leave offerings (flowers, notes, bottles of wine, jewelry, watches, crosses, etc.), kissing their hands and raising them to her mouth, then kissing their hand again. (Similar to Hindu puja activity around statues of the Gods) Some offer the heads of sacrificed fowls, piled up in front of her altar.[74] The American girls are both thrilled and shocked witnessing this ancient rite.

Su-Ling: This is the part I can't stand.

Kalika explains: You see ....the Goddess must have blood, since it is she who first bestowed the life blood.

Carmen: Like death and rebirth, right?

Kalima: Exactly, and it is by the full moon that a gypsy woman becomes pregnant, to bring life back out of the darkness, for the moon manages the flow of our blood, as does Kali manage our fertility. Before there was electricity all women bled on the full moon.

Sophia: OK I get it .... A dead soul goes back to the moon and the stars to be recycled again someday in a new body, like in the old mystery religions.

Kalima: Very good, Gadjo— you are a brilliant student.

Sophia: Oh, Kalima teach me how to read palms, or tarot cards. I think I'm ready.

Kalima: This is a secret talent you find inside yourself........I cannot teach you this. But I will read your cards, in exchange for your earrings maybe?

Scene 4c. An Unprecedented Proposal of marriage

Holding Kalika's hand, and with his family by his side, Shaeva interrupts Kalima and requests her to approach the altar

Kalika: Mother, Shaeva wants to ask you something.

Shaeva: Kalima, I am a gadjo, but I have known your family since I was a boy. Your husband would sometimes drink wine with my father. Politics drove us apart. Blood and caste separated our hearts. The tragedy of war has by accident caused us to find each other again. And now, under the darkest of circumstances, the bright light around your daughter has caused me to fall in love, and I want to marry her. I have nothing to offer except my heart and my loyalty, as now, none of us has anything but each other. I only ask for your blessing in the eyes of your Madonna, as I seize the moment and proclaim my love for Kalika. Kalima, I am asking you for her hand in marriage.

There is a long silence as Kalima thinks carefully.

Kalima: Mr. And Mrs. Dunav, We both know of the love that can be generated between a young man and a young woman under adverse conditions. We Roma are used to adverse conditions, and this is why we keep our marriages within the "family". Kalika is a Gypsy.

Nanda: Our nuptial rites have many similarities Kalima .... and although we have nothing to offer your bride, we can offer our love and our blessings.

Kalima: Since the Balkan folklore has been so influenced by the Turkish ways, the bride does go to the groom's family with the Roma tradition there. However, I come from the Tribal NW Indian Tradition, in which the man joins the family of the woman, and thereby supports the woman's family. And since my husband is not with us, I would have to ask in his name, that Shaeva join our family. That is, of course, if you can do without him.

Shaeva: They can't do without me because I am the physical strength in my family now and they need me. But my strength is motivated by my love for Kalika, and I want to make a life with her, and to offer her a real home. I know that I must attend to the safety of my family. But I am still certain of my love for Kalika, and I ask you for some blessing.
Kalima: I just don't know about this… breaking tradition.

Kalika: Mother, we were hoping that you would consider this proposal in the presence of Kali and all of our other Kumpania to perform the first half of the ceremony here, so that we are initially bonded by both families.

Kalima: The entire routine? "The weeping of the bride", "the henna ceremony," and "the Dance of the Virgin Tamborine."[75]

Nanda: I think that's an excellent solution, like an engagement.

Kalima: What about the dowry, the display, the eating of the sugar and salt bread, the Ceremony of Honey, the banquet, the Dance of the Bread, the Dance of the Apron, the consummation rites, AND the exhibiting of the stained sheet with the Dance of the Fertilized Tambourine????? What about tradition???? This is my Roma Kalika we are talking about.

Shaeva: At the moment, all I can offer is the virgin tambourine, which I bought new from a Gypsy in front of the church outside. Ultimately, I want only the best for her, and I will respect her virginity until we marry.

Kalima: This is an unusual situation— no dowry. Your father Vishnu is not here.

Kalika: But I am in love Mother, and our love will contribute to the Peace.

Shaeva: And I will be strong for my new combined family.

Kalima: *Kalima takes a very long moment to pray internally staring into the fire.* I must remember that love conquers all…We must not perpetuate separation and racism. Let the ceremony begin ladies. And with this, the Kalderones and the Dunavs will initiate union.

A loud cheer is heard from everybody in the sanctuary.

Scene 4d. Engagement Choreography:
Weeping Bride; Henna Ceremony; Virgin Tambourine

The following is a choreography which includes the three traditions mentioned in the script, abstracted into dance form. The weeping of the bride is a ceremony where the bride sits in the center of the room with the women around her. Kalika wears a purple dress. Kalima begins to play the virgin tambourine (eventually others join her in an elaborate rhythm) while Kalika sobs out loud with her head and face covered by the handkerchief, in the presence of her family who alternately laughs or weeps with her in the language of dance. Kalika, in a state of semi-consciousness, close to a trance from weeping, throws herself in front of the statue of Kali, as the women sing and play the tambourine. The text of the song in Romani is in fact that of a funeral lament. They are losing a daughter. She dances, weeping and sobbing to the beat of the tambourines.

> **They sing:** How good you were, and now you're here no longer
>
> You washed your father's feet, and now you're here no longer
>
> You washed your mother's feet, and now you're here no longer
>
> You prepared good things to eat, and now you're here no longer[76]

The music changes to a slow steady accordion drone.

The grandmother brings in a bowl of henna paste [77] and begins to smear it on Kalika's hands, which are then covered with special mittens. Kalika performs a solo dance while Krishna sings and the musicians play "Oh Young One".[78] She dances ceremoniously in front of St. Sara la Kali, and in front of Shaeva without touching him. She then returns to her family who removes the gloves and assists her to leave the imprint of her hands on a towel, which is given to Shaeva. Her head is covered with a red veil which comes from St. Sara's statue. An apple is sliced and the bride and groom, each eat half.[79] Kalika and Shaeva finally dance without touching (fandango), surrounded by the entire Kumpania. The music winds down as everyone falls asleep, and the young couple continues to dance their slow, dramatic, and passionate fandango.

Scene V— The Procession to the Sea
Scene 5a. Parade of the Three Saints

With the dawn comes the rousing sound of Krishna's long horn, the "zurla," and the gayly costumed dancing girls from Arles, Les Arliesiennes, perform to awaken the crowd. They lead the procession to the sea with a huge cross. The statue of St. Sara la Kali is hoisted onto the men's shoulders, and the procession officially begins when she falls in line behind the other two Maries.

We can hear all the **Gypsies chanting**:

"St. Sara help us Gypsies. Heal us, help us to be better!"

This is a moving scene, because the chanting goes on in French, Spanish, English, Hungarian, Roma, Sinti, Calo, etc. Outfitted in brightly colored shirts and mounted on white Arab horses, local cowboys called "gardiens" lead the way, and the procession dances through town to the sea escorting the black Madonna.

Immersion and Blessings

Upon arrival at the sea, the horses line up in a semi-circle pretending to escort the Three Saints into the sea. The statues are carried out into the water, submerged three times, and then presented to the Archbishop of Aix, who is sitting in a small rowboat a little way offshore. The congregation of Gypsies has reached the climax of their pilgrimage as they all immerse themselves in the water. There is a profound spiritual ambiance on the shoreline.[80] *The Archbishop blesses the sea, but it is the Gypsies who sing hymns untiringly and shout thousands of times "Vive Saint Sara-Kali!" The Gypsies all attempt to touch or kiss her clothing or her face to soak up her magic.*[81]

Gypsies call out from the crowd individually.

Blast the hinderers and slave masters!
Cut ignorance and blindness!
Halt starvation and swarming!
Limit mankind's spreading and destroying!
Enlighten all who are seeking!
Put to flight all who torture and kill!

This dramatic ritual on the beach and in the water is a religious experience for the Roma. They travel far to be emboldened by St. Sara La Kali... to transcend their insecure lives.

Scene 5c. FINALE ** COMPANY CRY TO KALI

From the water we hear everyone chanting

FINALE MANTRA TO KALI—

**GREAT DANCING K ALI, DANCING ONTHE EARTH
KRIM KRIM KRIM
HOLY MOTHER FULL OF STARS COVERING THE EARTH
HUM HUM
LOVING MOTHER SUCKLING THE EARTH
HRIM HRIM
WILD MOTHER LAUGHING, CLEANSING
FREE THE EARTH,
DAKSHINEE KALIKEE!!**

This next part should be sung as raw, Flamenco, Gypsy "cante jondo", which sounds "like gushing blood" (**Garcia Lorca**)[82]

**KALI WE CALL YOU
WE ARE YOUR CHILDREN
TERRIFIED AND LOVING AND HELPLESS
BEFORE YOUR WRATH HOLD US AND PROTECT US
TEACH US AND SHOW US, REVEAL TO US THE
SECRETS THAT LIE IN THE HEART OF YOUR DARKNESS
FROM YOU COME ALL THINGS TO YOU GO ALL THINGS
MOTHER PRIMAL
TIME AND TIDE AND INFINITY
WE FIND YOU HERE— DEEP INSIDE US
GREAT MOTHER GRANT US THE
WISDOM TO BETTER THE EARTH
TO LIMIT THE PLAGUES OF
PEOPLE THAT ARE DEVOURING
THE EARTH TO FIND THE LIMITS**

OF YOUR MERCY AND CULTIVATE
YOUR MAGIC.
WE SEE IN DEATH AND DECAY
THE IMAGE OF THE DOORWAY TO LIFE
AND SO FEAR NOTHING

IN THE WARM PROTECTION OF YOUR LOVING ARMS
YOU CAN STOP THE WAR, QUEEN KALI!!
JAI KALI! JAI KALI! JAI KALI! VICTORY TO HER!

Scene 5d. "I Will Carry You"— The Benediction song to Tara/Kali

As the sun sets, the women surround the Black Madonna singing the final transformation to the TARA side of KALI:

"I Will Carry You" *(Amy Grant)*

CHORUS

> Lay down your burden
> I will carry you,
> I will carry you my child
> I can walk on water and calm the restless sea
> I've done a thousand things you've never done ...
> Now I'm weary watching,
> while you struggle on your own
> If you call my name, I'll come

CHORUS

> I give vision to the blind man,
> I can raise the dead
> I've seen the darker side of hell, and I
> returned I see these sleepless nights
> and I count every tear you cry
> I know ... some lessons hurt to learn ... [83]

CHORUS

Instrumental segue to Gypsy music and dance finale

St. Sara la Kali Queen of the Gypsies
5e. True Gypsy Finale

The Red Angels join the Gypsies with a belly dance ballet, building in repetition. Soon everyone is dancing in concentric circles, merging many dance techniques and cultures.

This finale becomes a wild and joyous company number on the shores of the Mediterranean Sea with a moment of common bondage between people of many colors.

Voiceover: Perhaps we are all Gypsies seeking the solace of a refuge protected by a fierce but holy mother...

THE END

BIBLIOGRAPHY

St. Sara la Kali, Queen of the Gypsies

Barraclough, G., <u>Atlas of World History,</u> Times Books Ltd., London, 1998

Bhardwaj, S., <u>Hindu Places of Plilgrimage in India,</u> U of Cal Press, Berkeley, 1973

Bhavnani, E. <u>The Dance in India,</u> Taraporevala & Sons, Bombay, India 1965

Crooke, W., <u>The Popular Religion and Folklore of Northern India,</u> Liberty Art Press, Pataudi House, Delhi, 1968

Esty, Katharine, <u>The Gypsies, Wanderers in Time,</u> Meredith Press, NY, 1969

Fonseca, Isabel, <u>Bury Me Standing,</u> FirstVintage Departures Edition, Random House, NY 1996

Galland, China, <u>The Bond Between Women,</u> Riverhead Books, Penguin Putnam Inc. NY 1998

Galland, C., <u>Longing For Darkness,</u> Penguin Books, NY, 1991 Harding, Elizabeth U., <u>K ALI, Black Goddess of Dakshineswar,</u>

Samuel Weiser, Maine, 1993

Hixon, Lex, <u>Mother of the Universe, Visions of the Goddess and Tantric Hymns of Enlightenment,</u> Quest Books, England 1994

Jayakar, P., <u>The Earth Mother,</u> Harper and Rowe, San Francisco, 1990

Jenett, Dianne, <u>"Red Rice for Bhagavati",</u> Revision Magazine, Winter 1998, Vol.20

Kinsley, D., <u>Hindu Goddesses,</u> U of Cal Press, Berkelesy, 1988 Kinsley, D., <u>Tantric Visions of the Divine Feminine,</u> U of Cal Press, Berkeley, 1997

Leland, C., <u>The English Gypsies and Their Language,</u> Trubner & Co. London, 1874 and Gale Research Co., Book Tower, Detroit, 1969

McDowell, Bart, <u>GY PSIES, Wanderers of the World,</u> National Geographic Society, 1970

Mookerjee, Ajit, <u>K ali, The Feminine Force,</u> Destiny Books, NY 1988

Slobin, Mark, "Europe/Peasant Music-Cultures of Eastern Europe", Worlds of Music, Schirmer Books, NY, 1992

Thomas, P., Hindu Religion, Customs and Manners, D BTaraporevala Sons & Co., Ltd., Bombay, India

Tomasevic, Nebojsa, Gypsies of theWorld, Jugoslovenska revija, Belgrade, 1988

Tong, Diane, Gypsy Folk Tales, Harcourt Brace, Orlando, Fla, 1989 Walker, B.,The Secrets of the Tarot, Harper Collins, NY, 1984 Walker, B.,The Woman's Encyclopedia of Myths and Secrets, Harpers, SF,1983

ENDNOTES

St. Sara la Kali, Queen of the Gypsies

1 "Fonesca pg. 96-97— "Since their first appearance in the Middle Ages, the Balkan provinces have been a kind of homeland to the Gypsies...With their ability to move between radically segregated classes, between peasant and landowner, and to serve both, they managed to dig out for themselves an economic niche."
(Tinsmiths, coppersmiths, blacksmiths, musicians, entertainers, fortune tellers, horse care and breeding)

2 Tomasevic—Tree Worship amongst the Burbeti, Kalderash, and Kales tribes in India— "Bibijaka", or Black Sara, is honored in March around a fruit tree, most often a pear, which is then named Bibi. The tree is decorated with ribbons and flowers, and offerings are laid on the ground. Candles are lit, prayers are chanted to a divinity who lives in forests and in high mountains, is golden and beautiful, never speaks or eats.

3 The Roma flag uses blue to represent the sky, green for the grass on which they spend most of their lives, and the red wheel for the chakra and the wagon wheel, representing the eternal movement of the Roma from India, to the end of the world. (see image)

4 Harding, pg. 80-The Goddess Kali in her yantra form (mystical diagram), holds life energy in her central point, the "bindu", enclosed by five inverted concentric triangles which represent the fifteen psychophysical states of the senses, the organs, and the breathing points. The circle is the cycle of life and death which we must pierce to achieve "moksa", or liberation. The eight petals stand for the eight elements of Prakriti— earth, air, ether, fire, mind, intellect, and the ego.

5 Fonesca, pg. 100— "Rom" is how the gypsies refer to themselves and literally means man or husband. Rom is used among European Gypsies, "lom" in Armenian Romani; and "ḍom" in Persian and Syrian dialects. Rom, Lom, and Dom all correspond to the sanksrit word domba, and the modern Indian word dom, which means "man of low caste living by singing and music." In

Panjabi, dom means "strolling musician", and the concept exists since the sixth centrury.

6   "Tzigane" is another name for Gypsies (Tsigani, Ziguener, Ciganos, Tigani)

7   Tchalai— Preface to Tzigane Tarot http//www.romani.org/rtchalai.html

8   Slobin, pg. 189 "Ganga" is a village group of singers from Bosnia, Yugoslavia where peasant women sing with great emotional intensity and impact. Also, the "Ganges" river in India is a holy stream and its waters are said to be capable of washing away all sins. Perhaps this linguistic connection could be made because of migrations from India.

9   The Dunav Balkan music group— http://www.classical artists com/dunav-balkan

10 "Kumpania" is Rom for a grouping together of families not necessarily united by kinship, but all belonging to the same group, and the same subgroup, which is all based on tribes leaving India. Beyond the nuclear family there is the extended family or "vista", derived from the word vine, or family tree. The vista represents the fingers of the same hand. Several hands create a Kumpania

11 Poem by Tchalai

12 Tomasevic, pg. 155— "Thousands had moved here from Kosovo, in southern Yugoslavia, which they had left not only because of poverty, but also because of pressure from the local Albanians who wanted an ethnically ""pure" "province."

13 Tomasevic— In the suburb of Belgrade called Karaburna, a huge, unheated, unplumbed, ramshackle Gypsy settlement sprang up after 1980 when the ethnic Albanians drove the Roma out of Kosovo.

14 McDowell, pg 102— "Chingerdyi"— is a Hungarian dance with clapping hadns, smacking of ankles, scuffing shoes on the earth in rhythms. It has an Eastern sound with sliding quarter tones, glissandos, and a kind of bagpipe bottom.

15 Bhavani— "Tandava" is a forceful, more masculine dance from Kathakali technique in which the dancer strikes the earth barefooted in complex and rapid patterns. It is often a dance of anger or aggression. And is also used to speak symbolically.

16 Walker Tarot, pg 17

17 Kathak is the classical dance school of North India.

18 Thomas, pg 116—The "Garba" is a well-known women's dance in India originating in Gujarat. During the nine days of this festival an earthen pot, or "Garbi" with beautifully painted designs, is kept in a place of honor with a wick burning scented oil in it. The girls carry these earthen pots on their heads and go from house to house singing, clapping, and dancing. This is a dance often done during Holi week, and is devotional.

19 Kingsley, (Tantric), pg. 109

20 Fonesca, Pg. 100

21 ibid, pg. 103

22 Thomas, pg. 115— "Dancing from the very early Vedic rituals, was connected with worship in India. In later times dancing before idols formed part of daily worship in all well-known temples. It is in the temple that classical dance of India developed. In the mythology of the Hindus, the celestials have their professional dancing girls (Apsaras) and musicians (Kinnaras and Ghandarvas)."

23 Ibid pg 117— "Although music and dancing are believed to have been originated and patronized by gods themselves, professional musicians and dancers have been held in contempt by the Hindus especially in the Middle Ages. Manu, the law-giver speaks of them as persons not fit to be associated with by decent Aryans. In the mythology of the Hindus the Apsaras and Ghandarvas (celestial dancers and musicians) are depicted as 'impure' inhabiting the mountains and valleys bordering on the celestial regions." This low social status gave rise among the Hindus a stigma attached to minstrels who traveled.

24 The Roma— Origins and Diaspora— http//www.romani.org/toronto/diaspora_rl.html

25 San Francisco Chronical— May 28, 1999

26 Esty, pg. 80

27 The Roma, Origins and Diaspora pg 2

28 28 Jenett, D., pg 37 The "Pongala" is an ancient Indian woman's rice cooking

ceremony, dedicated to Bhadrakali, which has been revived with more and more popularity now in Southern India (Kerala).

29 Bhardwaj pg 2— "The nature of Hindu pilgrimage is capsuled in the Indian expression tirtha-yatra, which literally means "undertaking journey to river fords." Pg 98— "The fourth type of sacred places (for ritual purification) are those that have been sanctified theoretically by the rulers of solar and lunar dynasties. These are the tirthas where the rulers established a temple and duly consecrated it. Etymologically, the expression 'MANUSA TIRTHA' should mean the 'human sacred place'" In France the Gypsies call themselves "MANOUCHE"— which indicates that the tradition of making pilgrimage to St. Maries by Gypsies from India seems obvious.

30 Harding, pg. 2

31 Tomasevic, pg 140— "Skadarlija, the old Bohemian part of Belgrade, is sometimes visited by bear tamers. The Gypsies brought this profession with them from Turkey, and before that, India, where Gypsy bear tamers can still be seen. Ursari, in Romany (bear leaders) occupied almost the lowerst rung of the Gypsy ladder, just above the beggars. On national and religious holidays, they used to tour villages and suburbs performing their tricks." Animal cruelty acts have outlawed this activity in Europe now.

32 McDowell, pg. 110

33 Fortune telling, and particularly the reading of hands has been the skill of Roma women for many years. The reading of palms comes from India where the mudras (hand gestures) are very important in spiritual worship. The adornment of hands with symbolic designs and symbols is done with Henna in India. Vedic texts from India allude to telling a man's fate from the shape, lines and patterns on his hand, taking us back some 3,000 years. This art was probably connected to the Atharved system of determining illness through the examination of the pulse in the hand.

34 Gypsy women have been famous for their herbal remedies for physical and magical effects since their origins in tribal India. As Nature-worshippers, Gypsy women had exceptional mastery over the use of plants, and occult recipes for transformation are passed down in the family.

35 Tomsevic— Balkan gypsies often serve hedgehog and snakes with beer and whiskey.

36 Harding, pg. 125— Most Kali pujas take place on Tuesdays.

37 "Puja" is an elaborate religious ceremony of the Hindu in which they worship a deity with great devotion.

38 Harding, pg. 101

39 ibid, pg. 134

40 ibid, pg. 94

41 Hixon, pg. 127

42 Tomasevic pg 69— "Falling in trance is a holy act signifying that the spirit or deity has enteted into the sorceress and that she alone is able to comjune with him for the good of the whole village." This takes place among the Banjarra tribal Indians in NW India.

43 Bhavani, pg. 202

44 ibid, pg. 203

45 Kingsley, Pg. 119-120

46 Slavonic Web— Balkan Folklore— http://www.slavonic web.org/folklore/dances.htm, pg 3 On Korcula island in Croatia there is a sword dance called the "Kumpanija" which stems from old pagan springtime fertility rites. The traditional Slavic figurees of the kolo or circle symbolize the sun and new life.

   Not only does Shiva dance with Kali to subdue her madness, but also to insure fertility. There is always great dramatic tension in this folk dance.

47 McDowell, pg. 97—The "Khelimaske Dyila" is a romping Hungarian dance number which is mostly sung and accompanied by stamping feet, clicking tongues, the tapping of spoons, and rapping of knuckles on tables.

48 Phurai Dai— Queen/Goddess leader of the caravan.

49 A "bindu" is literally, "particle, dot, spot"; a symbol representing the universe in its unmanifest form, and placed in the center of the Kali Yantra.

50 VURDON, pg. 11— "The kiris (krisnitori) is a true Romani court made up of the elder members of the group, and it meets to resolve problems.

51 Fonesca, pg.24— In Albania there is no intermarriage between Muslims

and Gypsies.

52 Hixon, pg. 32

53 Gypsy Folk Tales, Tong pg 89

54 Kingsley, Tantra— pg. 153—The "Matrikas" were the seven aspects of Kali as fierce female warriors who help Durga. The word also represents the motherly sounds representative of the alphabets in Kali's skull necklace. *I have used the Matrikas as a metaphor to identify the seven American dancers in the Red Angels, because they become Kali's symbolic warriors as catalysts to the St. Marie Pilgrimage.

55 Dunyavi— means world in sanskrit/roma, and has been used to entitle this Act II opening number because it is a medley of Gypsy music and dance forms.

56 Esty, pg. 80-81

57 Tomasevic— Banjarra Indians section

58 Galland, Longing for Darkness, pg. 30

59 Walker, Myths and Secrets pg. 890—Virgo Paritura means "Virgin Giving Birth". It is the name of the constellation where Kali comes from. The Druid Grotto underneath the Chartres Cathedral used to be occupied by the image of a black Goddess giving birth, similar to certain images of Kali. The cathedrals were constructed around the same design as the Virgo constellation. Gypsies therefore connect the stars with their worship of Kali.

60 Esty, pg. 42

61 ibid

62 "Shakti" is divine female energy. Shiva is worshipped in relationship to Kali and Shakti by the sexual practice of Tantra.

63 Walker, Encyclopedia— pg. 360

64 Walker, Tarot pg. 16

65 ibid

66 VURDON, pg 15 http://www.dag.it/franzeze/English.HTM— poetry of Gypsy prisoners

67 Galland, Bonds— pg 109-110

68 McDowell, pg. 45—Translation—Welcome, Ladies and Gentlemen to the oldest pilgrimage in France. Welcome especially to the Gypsies— the
Manouche, the Romas, the Sintis, and the Gitanos of Spain. Without you, this festival would not live. Thank you and let the tribute to the three St. Maries begin.

69 Esty, pg. 84

70 Galland, Longing, pg. 176

71 ibid, pg 177

72 Bhardwaj pg 227 "The deities at the shrines of pilgrimages tend to become highly personalized and are propitiated for specific material gains and for the resolution of anxiety arising out of the problems of everyday life."

73 Esty, pg. 83

74 Walker, Encyclopedia pg 892— "Gypsies celebrate the Feast of the Assumption of the Blessed Virgin by piling up the heads of sacrificed fowls in front of her church, as Kali's votaries in India piled up the heads of sacrificed animals."

75 Nuptial Rites of the Roma— pg. 2— http://137.204.140.151/period MA/index/number2/rom/rom3nup.htm
"The tambourine in the Near and Middle East and in the whole of the Mediteranean is linked to the female gods, to female ecstatic rites, and to sexual inversions practiced in ritual occasions during which men symbolically transform themselves into women by playing the tambourine— whose inner parts, the hollow body and the diaphragm are perceived as representations of respectively, a female belly and hymen."

76 ibid

77 McDowell pg. 130

78 Songs of a Macedonian Gypsy, pg 2— http:tsetse.cs.eartlham.edu/dusko/InfoMak/culture/gypsy.html
"OhYoung One"— Abre Ramche— is a Macedonian Gypsy folk song which says:Young one, my beautiful young one, why do you run away from me? You know that I love you very much. Do not leave me lest my youth withers away. Do not forget our true love. You tell me that I should wait until I am grown, and then we will know happiness. I cannot wait.

79 Walker, Encyclopedia pg 363 -"Eves Apple"
80 Bhardway, pg 149 "The life-giving water, 'amrita', is not merely present in symbolic form. For the pilgrims, a whole cosmic event is being reenacted, one in which they actually feel that they are participating. The myth is reactualized, at the specific time and at the specific place. The pilgrim is bathing in the original "amrita".
81 Esty, pg. 85
82 Angus, Forces for Change, pg 205— Here is Spanish Flamenco Gypsy music with Byzantine liturgical, Arab and Gypsy elements, according to Manuel de Falla. The motifs include defiance, love, loyalty, pride, jealousy, revenge, freedom, persecution, sorrow, and death. The stamping in Flamenco is clearly traced to the "tandava" of India.
83 "I Will Carry You", written and recorded by Amy Grant

Sacred Journey

Cecilia Anne Gruessing, M.A.

Sacred Journey

The Eleusinian Mysteries

A Mystical Musical Drama

Ceil Gruessing, Fall 1999

Sacred Journey

Persephone

Demeter

The Grotto

The Abduction of Persephone

Demeter and Persephone

Cecilia Anne Gruessing, M.A.

INTRODUCTORY NOTES

Ever since I first read the Demeter— Persephone myth from "A Child's Book of Greek Myths" at the age of 12, I have been fascinated by the Eleusinian Mysteries. I have reached out for every book possible on the subject, and then some. At Antioch College, in my early twenties studying dance and theater, I performed the part of Persephone at the "Yellow Spring" in Ohio, rising up out of the rock to bring rebirth, life, music, flowers, and joy to the world. My dear friend, Lisa Vander Sluis was also fascinated by the inside story on the Eleusinian Mysteries, and we would pour over books with raised eyebrows, sharing propositions of the secret mysteries. As a choreographer, I have dreamt about dancing in a ballet that re-enacted the secrets of the unspoken rituals that took place inside the temple initiation ceremonies. At one point I interviewed with a young Greek director in New York who wanted to mount a modern interpretation of the mysteries as musical spectacle and drama. There have been many signs pointing me in the direction of this story.

Six months ago, I left my family and home on the advice of an old friend, Victoria Ransom. She is a psychic channel for a 3000-year-old spirit, Illyania Moirae Effane (which means daughter of the fates, but we call her "Grandmother"). This spirit is also called the Crone of Eleusis, High Priestess and Initiator in the Temple of Mysteries.[1] Grandmother advised me to leave my home life behind and go to San Francisco to get a master's degree— to become diplomaed, and to begin the long transitionary road from show business and teaching to a respectable career in Sacred Dance and Theater and healing. I also was told stories about my time as an Eleusinian priestess in a past life. I am extremely grateful to Victoria and Grandmother for making me aware of that past life connection as an initiate to the mysteries, and to my mission as a priestess and spiritual artist in this life. Part of the process has involved my own healing, as a death and rebirth experience, envelops my entire spirit right now.

Taking the class with Mara Keller (The Eleusinian Mysteries at California Institute of Integral Studies in SF) has been comforting and a confirmation at the end of a long rainbow journey for me. Because of her intelligence, her scholarship, and her nurturing presence as an educator, Mara has opened my eyes to my own personal journey back to the feminine. I am deeply connected to this myth and to this material.

The Demeter and Persephone story is another ancient agricultural myth about death and rebirth and the seasons. Fall comes, the flowers die, and we mourn the loss of beauty and life on the earth until the flowers return in the spring, and once again there is sun. Persephone is a f lower Goddess and daughter to Demeter and Zeus. She is abducted and raped by the underground God of Hades, Pluto. Demeter, her mother, and the Greek Goddess of Agriculture is stricken with grief, unable to function, and wanders the earth in sorrow. Consequently, the earth has no fertility, no plant life.

The Eleusinian mysteries celebrated this myth and its relationship to agriculture and the evolution of the soul. The Greeks celebrated a special initiation twice a year involving the lesser and greater mysteries of Demeter and fertility, which began in 1500BC and lasted for over 1000 years until the advent of Christianity. Nobles and citizens from all over the ancient world passed through these initiations the Eleusinian Mysteries. An important prerequisite for the initiates, or "mystae", was never to have committed murder. The ceremony required fasting, cleansing, sacrifice, worship, and pilgrimage to the city of Eleusis, where they entered an underground temple. Initiates were sworn to secrecy regarding the activity inside the temple. (I often think that the inheritance of this death and rebirth mystery went to the modern-day carnival fun house -a dark and scary journey, ending with sunlight, and a return to reality.)

This piece of work, has been written as a treatment for a musical mythic film, because it is a mystical Mediterranean fairy tale which needs every cinematic trick possible to render the beauty and magic of each location, both real and fictional. Even though the story opens in a grounded European setting with "real people", the fantasy develops with the arrival of the god characters shortly into the third scene. I have taken certain liberties with the original story to maintain a theatrical rhythm.

The musical numbers have not yet been fully explored, as I am seeking a composer that can embrace the music to make this work come alive. Musical mixing of the Greek and American cultures, with contemporary film technology could promote this as a classic movie fairytale.

The mysteries of Eleusis are about descent and the darkness. Something must die off, to become part of the soil and then create a new life. It is the death and rebirth theme of many religious and cultural mysteries, all originating in the importance of the agricultural cycle of fertility. The god and goddess archetypes reveal so much about us, and I am clearly connected to these characters. With open heart, I am grateful and content to have been given the opportunity to create this drama about Demeter and Persephone from material I have been exploring for many lifetimes.

Thank you,
Cecilia Diaz Gruessing,
Fall, 1998 San Francisco

Sacred Journey

CAST OF CHARACTERS

- **Demeter**— blond mother type (30-45), runs a bakery in a coastal Greek town. An active member of the community. Persephone's mother, Demeter represents the Earth Mother, Goddess of agriculture, grain fertility, harvest, Sacred Law and the seasonal cycle of life and death.

- **Persephone**— Demeter's teenage daughter (16), sells flowers in front of her mother's bakery. Loves to dance and run with her friends on the beach. Blond, thin, beautiful, maiden like— Goddess of Spring and Flowers, representing youth, beauty and life. She is the abducted wife of Hades, Winter Queen of the Underworld.

- **Seven Priestess/Girlfriends**— One for each color of the rainbow and Persephone is the red/pink. These are Persephone's 6 friends & Demeter's priestess -singer dancers.

- **Extras**— (about 10)— as bakery customers, gypsies, and Initiates

- **Old Woman /Baubo** — small, but energetic older woman with lots of hutzpah who plays the customer, Maria, in the first scene, as well as Baubo, Demeter's companion, nurse, and comic relief later.

- **Pluto**— King of Hades—A very strong, attractive, dark, well built man (50's), mobster king pin, lives the material life of the flesh. King of the dead and the Underworld, Abducts Persephone

- **Dionysus**— A beautiful young man (early 20's) racy lifestyle, but has a kind heart. Brings Persephone back from the Underworld. God of the grape, wine, fertility, and prophecy, vegetation, pleasure, festivity, madness and wild frenzy.

- **Hecate**— A very witty and expressive older woman (sixties) and Demeter's older sister, who helps her find her lost daughter. Known as a moon goddess of the three paths, Earth, Sea and Sky…She is also the Guardian of the hearth and household, protector of everything newly born, and the goddess of witchcraft.

- **Hierophant**— An older man presiding as High Priest over the mystery ceremonies.

Cecilia Anne Gruessing, M.A.

SCENE BREAKDOWN

1. **OPENING** — Demeter's Bakery..page 276
2. **TO THE SEA** ....page 276
3. **TO THE MEADOW**— Sacred Tree & Sacred Stump....................page 278
4. **ABDUCTION** — RAPE of Persephone ....page 281
5. **THE SACRED WAY TO ELEUSIS**...page 282
6. **DANCE OF THE KERNAS** ....page 283
7. **GYPSY CAMP** ....page 284
8. **THE TEMPLE OF HECATE** ....page 285
9. **HECATE & DIONYSUS** ....page 288
10. **THE PILGRIMAGE PARADE** ....page 290
11. **DANCE AROUND THE WELL** ....page 291
12. **THE DESCENT**..page 292
13. **THE RETURN Ritual and— THE SACRED MARRIAGE** .....page 296
14. **THE REUNION** — Maypole ....page 296

Sacred Journey

Scene 1. OPENING — DEMETER'S BAKERY

We are in a fictitious Greek fishing and agricultural town on the Mediterranean Sea near Athens any time in the late Twentieth century. It is a fall Sunday in September, and harvest time has set in for the farmers. It's business as usual at "Demeter's Bakery" in the marketplace on the waterfront where everybody buys their baked goods and produce. Demeter's daughter, Persephone, sells flowers on the street in front of the bakery. Today is her 16th birthday, and her six girlfriends are gathering to kick off the special traveling party to the beach with their dogs. On the sidewalk, they practice their street dances until Demeter can lock up the bakery and take them to the beach for the last swim in the sea before winter. Her last customer is an old woman (also plays Baubo) who has a special request of Demeter. Members of the community come to her for spiritual guidance because of her name, profession, and faith in her namesake, the great Goddess Demeter.

>**Old Woman—** Dimi can I give you a candle to light for me, to the Holy Mother Demeter, so that my corn will seed well and grow strong in the spring, as well as the baby that grows within my granddaughter? Can you do this Dimi?

>**Demeter—** Right now I will do this for you Maria, because my mother loved you so much, and because you are so beautiful.

Demeter kisses the old woman and invites her to the back room where she lights a new candle on her altar saying a final prayer to the original mother goddess Demeter, before leaving.

Photographs are taken outside the bakery of the friends and relatives there to celebrate Persephone's birthday. They mount their special baskets upon their heads which Demeter has prepared and hike off to the sea with their dogs.

Scene 2. TO THE SEA

Adolescent girls see the water, the open beach, and run like gleefully with their dogs, to the shoreline, screaming, leaping, dancing, and liberating their city souls for the magic of the moment. They drop their baskets, tear off their clothing, and plunge into the ocean, dogs yelping at their heels.[2](originally as pigs / now dogs) Demeter rushes up the rear with the rest of the gear, winded from the chase, and anxious to lifeguard the swimming. What joy to watch them play together like children, bonded by the water, free and uninhibited. They begin to dig in the sand ambitiously, constructing a huge sea castle with moats and bridges, pools and walls, windows and balconies. Demeter feeds them figs, apples, and bread, hand to mouth, bypassing their sandy hands.

As they are engrossed in this earth and water activity, two men conspicuously cross their paths on the shoreline. Demeter knows these men, and nods without offering any opportunity to converse. The younger man, with long curls approaches Demeter.

Dionysus— Mother Demeter, I believe you know me, and I have always loved you and your daughter, and would like to make my peace with you and offer my services to you whenever desired. Allow me to make this gift to your daughter— my sister, on this her 16th birthday to bless you both with love, divine vision, and fertility. *It appears to be a fennel wand,* **called** *a* **Thyrsus,** *carved with inscriptions, wrapped in ivy, and topped with a pinecone, with trinkets dangling.*

Demeter: You share the blood of your father Zeus, but I would hardly call her sister. She comes from a completely different upbringing and philosophy.

Dionysus: She is still my half-sister, and very beautiful -
A goddess of flowers, in every way. Please give this to her.

He gives her this mysterious Thyrsys and disappears. The other man has already passed on. Demeter is disturbed and turns away, to conceal the wand as Persephone returns. .

Persephone: Mother, who were those men, and why have you withdrawn your smile from the joy of these festivities?

Demeter: *(reluctantly explains)* The older gentleman is your father's brother Hank Pluto, who runs an upscale house of ill repute downtown. The younger man is Dionysus, his nephew. I don't know him well, and don't want to know him. Since divorcing your father, I have worked hard to be independent of that family and their machismo thank you very much.

Persephone: OK, momma, but who is Dionysus?

Demeter: He is Zeus's son by his first marriage.

Persephone: So, he is my brother?

Demeter: Half-brother, and that's all he will ever be, understand? Your father's family is very powerful, but I choose not to support the manner in which they achieve their power. And I tell you as sure as my name is Demeter, that his family is connected to underground mysteries which are deep in the shadow world, such as alcohol, drugs, scandal, pornography, and mafia. As long as I am your mother, I will ask you to avoid this world, understood?

Persephone: Yes Mother. Can we go to the meadow now to celebrate?

Demeter: Yes of course, the sun is falling, let's not forget the baskets.

Scene 3. TO THE MEADOW

They dance off to the meadow, where stands a beautiful Sacred old oak tree next to a grotto, which is a favorite spot to rest and contemplate the view and the last of the fall flowers. As soon as they arrive, the girls begin to gather poppies which they weave into garlands, beautiful wreathes and bouquets, incorporating the dried elements of fall vegetation. They set up a harvest altar around the tree trunk and begin a dance around the tree. In Cyprus maidens danced around trees as a ritual of fertility. [3] *Demeter presents a cake to her daughter with candles. They sing and eat. Some of the girls are dancing in the field vaulting bulls by their horns, which is a fertility ritual inherited from Knossos and Crete.* [4].

Persephone's friends propose a game of hide and seek, in which the person who hides must gather as many unusual wildflowers as possible during her search for a hiding place. Persephone goes to hide first. The girls sing with their eyes closed. Persephone runs wildly towards the grotto near the banks of the river which is not far from the oak tree. There by the banks of the river[5] *Cyane, on the path ahead is a huge tree* stump *covered with myrtle*[6]*, with a beautiful yellow flower growing at its root. There is a heavenly sweet fragrance in the air that only an exotic flower such as this could produce. Overcome with its beauty, Persephone stops to pick the flower.*

A voice: I wouldn't pick that flower if I were you.

Persephone: Who are you?

Pluto: I'm Pluto, King of the underworld, and you would be disturbing roots in my territory if you pick that flower. It's a Narcissus.[7]

Persephone: Aren't you, my uncle?

Pluto: I don't believe we've ever met before . . . but I am willing to make you an offer. If you pick that flower, you can come with me.

Persephone: Come where? And why should I?

Pluto: To a magical place where flowers are born, and where women like you take good care of themselves and share their beauty with the world. I'm looking for someone like you to be my wife. You're so beautiful, so innocent, such a bright light in the darkness. Please come with me. I'll take good care of you.

Persephone: Do come and talk to my mother and meet my friends. . . . *(she hears the girls calling her)* They're looking for me. I'm supposed to be hiding.

Pluto: I know where you can hide, Come with me. *(He lifts her, and they disappear into the grotto cave behind the tree stump)*

Persephone resists, screaming, and kicking, as she descends with Pluto down the grotto abyss. Persephone's screams are magnified to a horrific pitch, bringing Demeter and her friends to the grotto and the tree stump. They find Persephone's garlands on the ground nearby as her voice fades.

Demeter: Oh, dear gods, where is my precious daughter? *(clutching her flower crown)* Who has taken her? I feel some great evil has taken place here against my sweet young Persephone whose innocence knows not the voice of danger. Oh, what must I do, my heart is breaking, I can't go on— where is my baby?

She weeps and wails, the girls are in shock, and out of nowhere Dionysus appears.

Dionysus: What horror is taking place here that calls me from my path with such urgency?

Girlfriend: Persephone has disappeared, and we only saw her 5 minutes go.

Demeter: She has not just vanished. I know that someone has taken her by force. I feel it.

She begins to pace madly, speaking hysterically to herself. Dionysus is feeling conflicted as he recalls his Uncle Pluto's attraction to Persephone. He listens to Demeter rant on and on.

Demeter: Some uncouth evil is at work here, and I am helpless. Despite all my divine senses, I cannot detect where my most precious daughter has gone to. I carried her nine months and gave her life sixteen years ago today, and have loved and protected her, since the day her seed sprouted inside me. She is my daughter, and I must find her, or I cannot live.

Dionysus: Try to be logical, let us think clearly.

Demeter: It must be that devil Pluto, or worse Zeus himself playing with the innocence of my precious Persi. Could it be Dionysus? Your uncle?

Dionysus: We parted ways, and I saw nothing. I don't have the power to see into Hades. But since you have kept my thyrsus wand for Persephone, I will take that as a sign that I must help you find her.

Demeter: I must go to my sister Hecate at her temple in Eleusis to ask for help. Only she can see inside the world of the Gods. And who will run the bakery? And what about Persephone's flower cart? What am I to do? And how will I get there?

Dionysus: If the Gods are offering me this opportunity to make things right between us, I must seize this moment now, lest it never appear again. I, Lady Demeter, will escort you to Eleusis, and protect you along the way. We will find your daughter.

Persephone's friends all volunteer to escort Demeter back to her home. as she weeps hysterically.

Scene 4. ABDUCTION— THE RAPE of PERSEPHONE

Perséphone in Hades, the Underground

The sound of Demeter's musical weeping cross fades with the sounds of Persephone's screams for help. She struggles, strapped in a roller coaster car next to Pluto, which is barreling at top speed through a dark tunnel.[8] Nauseous from the frantic velocity, Persephone eventually becomes stunned. Periodically they slow down to pull up to a window looking upon various scenes of femme fatal archetypes dancing like fashion take-offs of the Harpies, Sirens, Gorgons, Furies, Erinyes. The darkness has elements of seductive yet menacing burlesque and sexual displays, which clearly shocks the young Persephone.

Suddenly the car comes to a halt, and a dark chamber is visible with two thrones and a big bed. Pluto escorts her to the throne. He now becomes more powerful in the Underworld of his kingdom territory, and takes on a more magical, beastly character. He puts on tango music and Persephone dances with him reluctantly. She follows Pluto like a shadow, fascinated by his impeccable direction, and becomes more and more mesmerized... until the music climaxes and he forces her onto the bed. She is not ready for this and refuses. He gags her and ties her up.

Music and blood curling screams fill the blackout and Pluto rapes Persephone.[9]

When the lights come back up, Pluto is untying Persephone. She watches him like a tiger. He gives her a red satin robe to wear and tells her to sit upon the throne of the Queen. He offers her drink in a chalice. Persephone is clearly horrified, her innocence defiled yet says nothing - She stares at him in hate and disbelief.

> **Persephone:** Only water please .... *(she pours the chalice contents on the floor)* How can I trust you?
>
> **Pluto:** It is the juice of pomegranate. Drink maiden.
>
> *Again, he offers her the goblet of dark juice* [10]
>
> **Persephone:** I am dying of thirst and pain......... What do you want with me? *She hesitates and then drinks the pomegranate juice.*

Pluto: I want you to be my Queen. I need you desperately here in my kingdom. Lost souls come to us looking for help, and they need a woman's love when they go through this tunnel. They'll pay anything to be treated with love and kindness. I don't know how. I'm burned out, and I need a woman like you to put flowers back into my life as well as my kingdom. I am a wealthy man, and I can take good care of you. Please let me see your body. You have been blessed with blood and are no longer a child.

Persephone: *Bleeding from the loss of her virginity, Persephone is clearly upset.* You are a beast. I long for my mother and my friends, for they are all I know. Your world is dark and cold, and full of secret desire which I don't understand. Please let me go back, I cannot help you.

Pluto: Yes, you can, and you will. Now you are a woman. Congratulations, and I am proud to have been instrumental in that development. Forgive me if you feel violated, but I wanted you very much, and now I need you. Your heart is great like your mother's, and there is no doubt that your love will benefit many more than just myself. Furthermore, you have eaten the sacred pomegranate and must remain here in the underworld for the gestation of several thousand souls who need your immediate attention. I am sorry you don't love me. Perhaps you can learn. Nevertheless, we have work to do— you must dress and come with me.

Persephone: My mother will find me, and I will leave this place!

Scene 5 — The SEARCH FOR PERSEPHONE AND THE SACRED JOURNEY TO ELEUSIS

Lights up and Dionysus leads the way down the barren road with the young girls singing his dirge like song, "Dionysus Dionysus, Lead us to Elysia" and the sound of funeral procession music[11]. A solemn parade of women priestesses carrying their baskets follows, surrounding the blue-hooded Demeter, who walks with heavy heart. She has transformed into an old woman, to disguise her pain.

It is a full moon, and the girls dance wildly, whipping their hair and beating upon their breasts to exorcize the pain of losing Persephone. It is a way to express in ritual form "a majestic and dignified grief".[12]

"The myrtle boughs in the hair and in the hands of the mystai, following 'Dionysus,' along with the mystical torchlight by which the procession reached its destination... was a sight to behold."[13]

The company makes OFFERINGS AT VARIOUS NATURAL ALTARS as mini ritual drama/ ballets. They have clearly been traveling for many hours and have made many offerings to many shrines along the sacred way to Eleusis. They are hungry from fasting, and cold, and rest after an offering to Artemis at the creek.

Demeter addresses Dionysus....

Demeter: Take me to the ocean to camp for the night, so that the sound of the waves drowns out my tears and exhausts me to sleep. I cannot make much more of this journey today.

Dionysus: Follow this way, Mother Demeter and we will be there shortly to make our offerings to the sea and dance in the moonlight with the head torches.[14] (Referred to as Kernas in Euripides Ion)

The girls continue singing as they follow Dionysus down the hill towards the ocean. Baubo takes Demeter's arm.

Scene 6 — DANCE OF THE KERNAS (crowns with candles)

Baubo – Demeter's comic relief

When they arrive at the beach they form a circle, and the music begins. The priestesses prepare the fires in their clay pots/as crowns, which are like small hearths (kernas), mounted on their heads designed to see in the night.

"The night was spent upon the shore during which dances were performed with flaming torches representing Demeter's search for her lost daughter."[15]

Her servant, Baubo, who is a baudy, comic older woman, dances for Demeter to make her smile. She lifts her dress above her head revealing makeup on her naked body which depicts her breasts as eyes, her belly button as a nose, and her vulva as a mouth ... the ultimate belly dance!!

Demeter cannot resist laughter and is inspired to keep on traveling in the light of the full moon.

Demeter: Ah sweet Baubo, how you make me laugh. I feel hope again.

Baubo: Never forget my lady, that comedy has its roots in tragedy, and somehow it helps us cope. You must have faith. Breathe for me, laugh Mother Demi . . .

Demeter: The ocean, this ritual, and your love have renewed my damaged soul, and I am inspired and determined to press on to the home of my sister, Hecate, in the hills of Eleusis, where she has been known to do prophecy in her temple cave. She will surely know what has become of my Persephone. We are not far, and there will be warmth and nourishment at the home of my sister. The moon is full, and we are fired up and ready to go.

They move on once again with a slow march and processional music.

Despite their exhaustion, the company continues, until the point of weariness, when they hear the sound of gypsy music in the near distance. They see fire and decide to approach.

Dionysus: Look beyond this river. There is a gypsy camp with fire and food. Perhaps we could rest there and proceed in the morning.

Demeter: Of course, my dear Dionysus. The girls are tired and so am I.

Baubo: I think you may like this place Madame.

Scene 7. THE GYPSY CAMP

The music cross fades again into the fiery and passionate sound of fiddles, guitars, clarinets, accordions and drums thrown together gypsy style by a night camp of traveling gypsies. Their fire is roaring, and their dancers are hot. The priestesses are hypnotized immediately, and want to join in. Dionysus begins to drink, sing, and dance and the circle really comes to life, as he turns into the original gypsy brujo. They are offered food and drink at the gathering. Demeter speaks to Dionysus.

Demeter: I will go up to speak to my sister Hecate in the hills. You can see the fire in her temple from here. If all of you do not arrive before I sleep, I will come to find you, so please stay together.

Dionysus: Take my wand with you as you climb. I will make sure that they arrive there safely tonight.

Demeter: Thank you, Dionysus, ...They are my only family now.

The girls take off their cloaks and join the gypsy festivities with joy and curiosity. The band strikes up another song, and the 6 corn princesses (Persephone's girlfriends) do a moon dance of fertility with Greek belly dancing qualities.[16]

Scene 8. THE TEMPLE OF HECATE

Outside the cave entrance, Demeter calls out to her sister.

Demeter: Hecate!! Are you there, dear sister, please be here now. I have traveled long and weary to find you and need your words of wisdom at this tragic fork in my road.

Hecate: Here I am sister. Welcome to my cave. I do believe this is the first time that your feet cross my door. What can I do for you . . . you seem distraught.

Demeter: I have lost my daughter Persephone, and I hear her cries in the night, calling out to me, and I cannot find her. Hecate, I am sick with pain. I have been walking for days, searching everywhere, calling her, making prayers and offerings, but there is no sign of her life. What can it be Hecate? What secret is there that I should know now about my precious daughter. You would know. I must know she is alive. For if she lives, I will then know how to find her.

Hecate: *She walks to her altar, lights a candle, and bows her head... turning...*Very well my sister, I will give you the truth, as long as you do not blame me for the delivery of bad news.

Sacred Journey

Demeter: If you know that she is alive, I will be eternally grateful.

Hecate: Yes Demeter...she lives. It is Pluto who has seized Persephone, by the order of your ex-husband Zeus. And Zeus has given her to Pluto as his wife. They have made some kind of deal.

Demeter can barely contain her rage. Hecate tries to subdue her.

Demeter: What?!! That monster, that python, The King of hell! Wretched animal... How could he do this? Where is there any respect anywhere for children with these macho gods! I will twist his head off. Where is he?

She pauses.... And Hades....... is the only region into which I cannot descend!

Hecate: Demeter, look at it this way. Pluto is not such a bad husband.

Demeter: He's her uncle, old enough to be her father, and with a reputation that I find lacking in honor.

Hecate: He is Zeus's brother and very rich, and Persephone will be Queen of Hades.

Demeter: She is your 16-year-old niece. Please Hecate, have mercy!!!!

Hecate: It's not that bad down there. After all, it is better to be a queen in the underworld, than a slave around the gods.

Demeter: "My immortal, beautiful daughter, dragged down among the dead! The pure Virgin deflowered in the arms of the insatiable Pluton! Her memories of Heaven effaced in those star-like eyes, those eyes of hers which would close under my kisses and reopen to reflect the whole firmament! Parted forever from my daughter! Infinite grief and bottomless horror! What are the miseries of men beside ours. We do not forget. They die, but we are immortal! The grief of a god shakes the Universe. Our capacity to suffer is eternal like our capacity for joy. To put an end to our grief, a world would have to crumble and another to be born out of its wreck!"[17]

Hecate: Weep no more sister. I will help you. The people are starving without your bread. You must get back to work. There are others with daughters too, that are starving because of your grief, which is destroying the land.

Demeter: I cannot think of that now……Will you please help me retrieve my daughter from the underworld?

Hecate: You know Zeus will be furious, if we don't discuss this with him.

Demeter: Do not do this to me Hecate. You know he is brutal and will demand sex for favors to undo his own crimes. He should never have let this happen, and I can no longer spend time or energy reprimanding an abuser. So, with the mercy of the goddess, please tell me how to go down to this place called Hades.

Hecate: Very well. You must rest tonight. I will gather your priestesses here in my temple where they will be safe to sleep. Tomorrow I will talk to Dionysus about guiding you to the gates of the underworld.

Demeter: Very well, I am ready. The sooner the better. He is probably raping her as we speak, miserable bastard!!!

Hecate: But Demeter, I regret to inform you, that you cannot go with them below the surface, or you will not return to see your daughter in this same life. You do not realize the power your alter ego has as a reincarnated Goddess of life. The fields of wheat are dying, and something must be done. Your bakery is closed – people must eat Demeter!!! — Have mercy!!!

Demeter: I cannot work, my heart and soul are frozen.

Hecate: We must send the young Dionysus, whom I will imbibe with the strength to withstand the darkness of Hades and will be regenerated with the strength and vision to guide your priestesses through the initiations of descent, which is like a ritual death and rebirth. Surely you are not strong enough now to survive these trials— trust me in this advice. He will return your precious daughter.

Demeter: Dear Hecate, I thank you for this news of Persephone's life. I have come to you for help, and finally you offer me some chance to see my daughter alive again. Talk to Zeus immediately. Please have mercy on my sweet Persephone. I beg you,

Hecate: My dear sister, I will take care of this. I leave you to sleep, as I gather your girls, and instruct Dionysus for the journey to the well at the cave entrance in Eleusis.

Demeter: Thank you for using your powers dear Sister. Please tell me when the girls are here under this roof as I will not sleep before I know they are safe. When Persephone and I are reunited again I will be able to return to the bakery. Thank you for your help.

Hecate agrees and leaves. Demeter lights a candle, and then sings and dances a lament.

SONG/DANCE— Demeter's solo lament. (*Theme song potential*)

Scene 9. HECATE EMPLOYS DIONYSUS AS GUIDE AND SEEKER

Top of the morning, Dionysus has been called to Hecate's chamber where she is offering him a task.

Hecate: Dionysus, God of the Vine, walker of the underworld, I ask you to continue your service with my sister Demeter. Her grief is affecting our people now, and no other but yourself is suited for the gravity of this mission I am about to present to you. Because of her sadness, she does not realize her power over the earth. The fields are barren, the bakeries closed!!

Dionysus: It is Demeter who makes the wheat, the corn and the flowers grow. She is the mother goddess. I am honored to protect her, for I am not afraid of the darkness, and her lost daughter is my cousin whom I have never known.

Hecate: I have made a special potion for your vision and your strength to ensure your success on this journey. Are you willing to make the descent into the underworld to find and return Persephone, who has been unfairly abducted by Pluto and crowned his Queen?

Dionysus: Yes, I can do this. I am living proof of the seed that is mashed under the fruit of a grape and then tossed into the soil where I can pass many cold days . . . until one day when the warmth of the sun brings joy into my heart, and once again I grow into a new vine, with new leaves, and luscious black grapes. Demeter must be able to see her daughter again, and by the laws of nature and the gods, I will demand her resurrection as the Goddess of Flowers, and she will reappear before the first robin's song to spring.

Hecate: Then it is settled – Drink this potion as I recite this sacred blessing. "With the omnipotence of the Mother Goddess and her most powerful ambrosia, we activate the magnetism of this infusion for the guidance, vision and power of Dionysus."

Dionysus swallows the sacred potion and kneels in front of Hecate's altar and becomes entranced as Hecate lays out his directions.

Hecate: Tomorrow at dawn you will take Demeter and her priestesses to the well down the hill next to the temple which King Keleos[18] has begun to construct in her honor. You will descend to Hades in Eleusis at the Sacred Well,[19] and participate in the mysteries. Then you will ascend with Persephone and her nymph/priestesses at the grotto by the fig tree stump[20] where she originally descended with Pluto. This path must be retraced to honor Persephone's return. Do you hear me Dionysus?

Dionysus: Yes, every word. Continue.

Hecate: Demeter will not descend, but she will meet you and Persephone at the grotto. However, Persephone will only have 6 months of freedom under the sun, and then she must return to the underworld in the fall.

Dionysus: But why must the young Persephone return again to the world of King Hades? Demeter will not like this.

Hecate: This you already know as God of the vine because of your own parallel death and rebirth issues with nature and the underworld. This is the mystery that you will remember upon seeking Persephone. Do not ask any more questions. Be fearless and go. I will protect you by the power of the moon and this potion. Take my torch. Sleep well my son. *She blows out the candle.*

Scene 10. THE PILGRIMAGE TO ELEUSIS

It is morning in the temple of Hecate, and the brigade is ready to travel — Demeter, Dionysus, the priestesses and Baubo. Baubo is helping Demeter dress. Hecate introduces everybody.

Hecate— I leave you in the hands of the young, immortal God, Dionysus, gypsy brujo, divine dancer, and deity of nature and wine. He knows the underworld well and fears it not and will take the priestesses to the entrance near the well. You will enter and leave with him. After the initiation mystery you will emerge into the Elysian fields on the Mediterranean, where Persephone originally descended at the grotto by the tree stump. There she will be reunited with her mother once again should our plan succeed. I have prepared some of the initiate's Kykeon[21] for you and the princess initiates to take before you descend. Madame Baubo[22] will accompany Demeter as her nurse and companion on this journey.

The company drinks the kykeon (A ceremonial drink made of fermented barley, water and mint), and then begins the ceremonial pilgrimage to the sacred well. This becomes a strange, mystical, crusade, juxtaposed by Baubo and her clownlike antics to amuse Demeter[23]. The company of priestesses proceeds in the stately and solemn demeanor climbing the hill to the gates of Eleusis. Baubo's dance ties in with the "Kordax", a type of dance in Greek Drama. It was a dance of comedy and has been described as obscene and ignoble; it involved suggestive rotations of the body, kicking one's buttocks, slapping the chest and thighs.[24] In the case of Baubo, she would lift her skirt to reveal a face painted on her torso with her breasts as eyes and her vulva as a mouth. This continues to make Demeter laugh and distract her from her misery.

Scene 11. DANCE AT THE WELL

The Kallichoron or "Well of Beautiful Dances", "The Virgins Well"[25], or "The Fountain of Maidenhood"[26]

Upon arriving at the well, we see that there is a new temple which has been built in honor of Demeter.

Dionysus: Lady Demeter, behold this temple which has been constructed in your name to honor your sorrow, and respect your powers as an Earth Goddess. We must dance here around the well to generate energy for the descent.

A circular choreography very much like the "Emmelia" begins, as a sacred ritual preparing the initiates to descend. The Emmelia was a grave, serious type of dance typically used for tragic themes; it embodied a code of symbolic gestures through which the dancer could tell the entire story of a dramatic work without speaking.[27]

Demeter: Dear Dionysus. I thank you for your bravery and kindness. Only the success of your journey will heal my broken heart. I am a mother, and my sadness seems so infinite. Such joy will be mine when I see my dear Persephone again. Thank you for saving my child.

Dionysus: I do this for you and the needs of my people. The bakery needs you, and the gods need you to bring happiness and sustenance to the world again. The girls will become initiates of the Eleusinian mysteries, and I will come back with your daughter.

They embrace, and Demeter stays with Baubo as she says goodbye to Dionysus and the girls. They silently stand side by side watching the dancers, as they all one by one follow Dionysus down the stairs of the well.

Sacred Journey

Scene 12— THE DESCENT

The music changes to one of wind, echo, drum and bell. The initiates, called the "mystae", are blind-folded with veils, falling through space, tumbling amongst one another, screaming and losing all control. They go through a dark labyrinth that is lined with frightening characters.

The following three exquisite quotes are taken from Edouard Schure—
" The Great Initiate". And read as a voiceover of the **Hierophant.**

"The Mystae personally went through the terrors of hell, or rather the trials of purgatory, according to Christian terminology. Dense night enveloped them. Hands laid hold upon them and dragged them away in the darkness. Then, like blinding flashes of lightning, sinister visions pierced the blackness. Some caught glimpses of Sisyphus crushed beneath a rock; others of Ixion broken beneath his wheel. Men were seen hurled to the ground by monstrous serpents which encircled their bodies. And hideous larvae appeared and disappeared, barring the way. Were they going forward or backward? No one knew. Around the groping and distracted Mystae, the unbroken hissing of the wind mingled with plaintive cries."[28]

Voice OF PLUTO: "Here the passions you have created are living entities. The beast which you have fostered chooses you for its prey. You who are ambitious, cruel, lewd, wicked and hypocritical, defend yourselves against your own offspring!" [29]

They are suddenly brought together by centrifugal force and unveiled to watch a series of slides depicting the slaughter of humanity, animals, nature, and mother earth committed by man in his disrespect for life on the planet— They are then forced to look at the suffering, pollution, torture, war, and disease created by this irreverence for life. It is one big nightmare, bad movie, nobody wants to watch. "Ancient esoterism believed in the existence of elemental spirits without an individualized soul and without reason. Half conscious, they fill the earthly atmosphere and are in some way the souls of the elements. Magic, which will put into action in the manipulation of secret powers, makes these beings visible at times."[30] *Heraclitus said, "Nature* in all places is full of daemons." Plato calls them daemons of the elements. Paracelsus says that elementals attracted by the magnetic atmosphere of man, are electrified and given over to his passions the more he becomes their prey without being aware of it.[31]

ECSTATIC DANCE— *The initiates robes are filthy from the journey. They become frenzied with a shifting soundtrack of drums, causing them to dance frenetically, ecstatically, until they wind up exhausted on the floor in the temple. King Hades (Pluto) struts around laughing, and then exits. All falls silent. The Hierophant enters.*

Hierophant: Those of you still breathing will please rise and bow. You have traversed the trials of the court of King Hades, God of the Underworld, where you have arrived as a result of death. *(He claps twice)* Rise I say!! Rise and be present!! You must shed your tattered rags of journey and put on new white garments.[32] *Manly Hall*

The initiates all change into white robes as the Hierophant continues:

You are on the threshold of Demeter, and you will be permitted to see the mother goddess in all her glory in sun filled fields of flowers and grain. To have survived these ordeals, I commend you and give you the opportunity at rebirth. Behold the great mother!

He gestures to an opening in the earth above.

A vision then appears of the colossal statue of Demeter in gold and ivory, standing in all her majesty and leaning upon a scepter. Her presence is overwhelmingly peaceful. Then "condensed astral Light becomes manifest to the initiates, revealing to them in flashes, through clouds of incense, its inhabitants: archetypes and souls" [33]

Dionysus and the Initiates stand slowly rubbing their eyes, trembling, whimpering, frightened, and vulnerable. Pluto gestures upward, music begins, and a solid light appears at the top of a long stairway. There in the distance stands a radiant image lit with pink and gold of a goddess. The same Demeter, (in her archetypal form) dressed **in white** *as a Goddess, descends the staircase to the sound of flutes and lyres.*

(This is a different form of the baker Demeter... played by the same woman... but more elaborately dressed and presented as a dignified golden Goddess.)

Demeter: In all my mother power and glory, I salute you brave initiates for walking through the storm with courage, facing your demons, destroying your dark sides, and cleansing your souls. You have made it to my garden where you will be reborn into the warm sunlight of Earth.

The sound of a silvery French horn interrupts, then . . ..

Flowers fall from the heavens, and we watch the grand entrance of Persephone in full regalia as Queen of the Underworld. There is no smile on her face, but a mysterious grace and wisdom that rivets the hearts of all who behold her steady gaze.

Mother and daughter are reunited, meeting on the staircase. There is a moment of sheer happiness and ecstasy between mother and daughter. This is a miracle moment. They can now bless the initiates.

The baskets are brought before Demeter, and they ceremoniously reveal their contents.

"The gold objects contained in the basket were the pinecone (symbol of fertility and generation), the spiral serpent (universal evolution of the soul falling into matter and redeemed by the spirit), and the egg (recalling the sphere of divine perfection, the goal of man.)"[34] There is also an ear of corn which is ceremoniously revealed.

Persephone: "Death is only a passage to another life, and as I rise again every spring, so might you too pass on to your next blooming, with my sacred promise of protection. May all your desires be fulfilled. Return to the universal Soul!"[35]

After this comes the sacrament. Each initiate partakes of the corn cake and drinks from the Kykeon bowl, the special mixture of barley water mixed with mint. They are then crowned with myrtle and dismissed with the words.

Demeter: "Go in peace and be pure from evil"[36]

Pluto: *Enters and approaches Persephone to kiss her, but Persephone backs off.* My queen, what is it?

Persephone: I must go. It is already April, Pluto .... Spring can wait no more.

Pluto: No. I forbid this.

Dionysus: *(Stepping in)* — It is true my Lord, Persephone's Earth mother, Demeter, has waited, after leaving the earth barren for six months, grieving the loss of her daughter. Zeus has sent me with her dearest friends to arbitrate this negotiation in the name of all living things on the earth. Her grieving has upset the balance of nature.

Pluto: She is my wife. She must remain here. We need Persephone here to transform the souls. Her place is with me in Hades.

Dionysus: I'm sorry, Pluto. Zeus is your older brother. He has spoken, and his word is the way. She will return in October. Step aside. Her mother is waiting and so is spring

Pluto: I will have words with Zeus about this. *Long pause as he circles Persephone.* Very well then, my queen Persephone. I will see you when the days are short, and the nights are long… without fail.

Persephone runs to Dionysus and then embraces her friends with happiness. She has returned to her former adolescence.

Persephone: Dionysus, I don't know how to thank you . . . Where is my mother?

Dionysus: She is waiting for you princess, and I will bring you together.

The following scene, which ends the play, is enacted as a full-on Ballet, to resolve the story in which Persephone and Dionysus perform a consensual Sacred Marriage, and then Demeter is reunited with her daughter.

Pluto steps aside. Persephone led by Dionysus and followed by the six priestesses; all repeat a portion of the labyrinthic Emmeleia dance that brought them down the well stairs originally. Then, as the initiates ascend towards the light, Persephone and Dionysus linger behind.[37]

Sacred Journey

Scene 13. THE SACRED MARRIAGE & THE RETURN DUET—

Persephone: My dear Dionysus, thank you for this rescue. I want us to perform the sacred marriage dance before seeing my mother again. I believe that your love is pure, and I only hope that you still find me beautiful.

Dionysus: I have watched you grow for years from a distance, and my heart wants to right all that has gone wrong. May the gods come through us and bless the land with your mother's fertility. Dance with me Persephone. Your beauty and the flowers of your soul are irresistible. And I have fallen in love with you.

Persephone and Dionysus begin to dance a romantic pas de deux which takes them to the grotto at the tree stump[38] where she had originally descended in the field of flowers. It begins to rain, symbolizing earth fertility called by the Sacred Marriage [39]. There is a sibling quality to this love tribute which transcends their gender at times in the choreography. Yet their attraction is passionate and sincere.

This is a serious modern ballet duet.

Scene 14. THE REUNION

The priestesses arrive ahead of the travelling company in the Elysian Fields to the grotto in the meadow where they had originally celebrated Persephone's birthday. They leap and dance for joy in anticipation of reuniting their dear friend Persephone with Demeter again.

Persephone hears her mother calling from above and calls out. Demeter runs towards the grotto and the voice of her daughter. Baubo (now the older woman from the bakery) and the other girls wait in joyous anticipation. A huge altar of flowers has been built at the grotto to greet Persephone.

Persephone suddenly appears in the sunlight and embraces her mother. It is a joyous moment. When Persephone and Demeter have sufficiently reunited a MAYPOLE is brought in and everybody prepares to dance. Dionysus accompanies her. Persephone becomes the May Queen representing the resurrection from death, bringing life, color, and merriment back to the earth. In this dance the ribbons are interwoven, to represent the colorful foliage of the bare tree with bright colored leaves, flowers and fruits, all gifts of the goddess of fertility in spring.[40]

EVERYBODY DANCES THE MAYPOLE DANCE— decorated in flowers and overflowing with life. The ceremony finishes when Dionysus brings in two immense jars of wine, which are flung down upon the roots of the sacred tree and broken.

"And the wine flowed out into the Earth as a last libation of praise to the goddess of the mysteries of life and death as the maidens danced around the sacred tree into the sunset and the waning moon."[41]

All who witness the great tragedy and joy of Demeter and Persephone, and the Eleusinian Mysteries will never forget the great lesson of the blessing of life. We must live and love to the fullest.

THE END

BIBLIOGRAPHY

Sacred Journey, The Eleusinian Mysteries

Dover, Sir Kenneth, Trans., Aristophanes— THE FROGS, Clarendon Press, Oxford, 1997

Foley, Helene, Editor, The Homeric Hymn To Demeter, Princeton U Press, 1994

Frazer, Sir James George, The Golden Bough, MacMillan Pub, NY, 1922

Ginner, Ruby— Gateway To The Dance, Newman Neame Ltd., London, 1960

Grove, Mrs. Lilly, DANCING, Singing Tree Press, Detroit, 1969

Hall, Manly P., The Adepts; Part One— The Initiates of Greece & Rome, The Philosophical Research Society, Inc., LA, Ca., 1981

Harding, M. Esther, Women's Mysteries, Harper and Row, NY, 1971

James, E O, The Cult of The Mother Goddess, Fred A. Praeger, Pub., NY 1959

Keller, Mara Lynn, The Greater Mysteries of Demeter and Persephone, 1998

Kerenyi, Karl, Eleusis, Archetypal Images of Mother and Daughter, Princeton U Press, Princeton, NJ, 1967

Kraus, Richard, The History of The Dance in Art and Education, Prentice Hall, Inc. Englewood Cliffs, NJ, 1969

Lawler, Lillian, The Dance in Ancient Greece, Wesleyan U Press, Middleton, Conn. 1964

Lawler, Lillian, The Dance of the Ancient Greek Theater, U of Iowa Press, Iowa City, 1964

Lubell, WM, The Metamorphosis of Baubo, Vanderbilt U Press, Nashville, Tenn., 1994

Meyer, Marvin W., Editor, The Ancient Mysteries, Harper and Row, NY 1987

Ransom, Victoria, The Crone Oracles, Samuel Weiser, Inc. York Beach, Maine 1994

Sachs, Curt, World History of the Dance, The Norton Company, NY 1937

Schure, Edouard, The Genesis of Tragedy and The Sacred Drama of Eleusis,

Rudolph Steiner Pub, London, 1936

Schure, Edouard, <u>The Great Initiates</u>, Harper and Row, NY, 1961

Taylor, Thomas, <u>The Eleusinian and Bacchic Mysteries— A Dissertation,</u> JW Bouton, NY 1875

ENDNOTES

Sacred Journey, The Eleusinian Mysteries

1. Ransom, prologue
2. Ginner, pg. 126—"On the second day of the initiation they went in procession to the sea, each driving a young pig which was to be bathed in the water in preparation for the sacrifice on the following day. The Mystae (initiates) also bathed themselves in the sea as an act of purification."
3. Grove, pg. 36
4. James, pg 246
5. Hall, pg. 19
6. Kerenyi, pg. 64
7. Meyer, pg. 21
8. When I was a teenager, I remember a re-occurring dream I would have about a secret trap door at the roots of any apple tree outside my bedroom window. This Tree bordered a dark forest where I used to play. At night, I would sneak out into the yard and open the door and climb into a cable car which would take me down into the earth stopping at secret rooms along the way, where people would meet and dance.
9. Ibid Pg. 107-8
10. Foley, Pg. 56-57
11. Aristophanes, Frogs, pg. 31
12. Ginner pg. 52-53
13. Kerenyi pg.63
14. Ibid, pg. 184-86
15. Ginner, pg. 126
16. Kerenyi, pg. 9
17. Ibid
18. Foley, pg. 142

19 Kerenyi, pg. 39
20 Ginner, pg. 57. "Dionysus was summoned to return through the trees. A mask was nailed to a tree stump; draperies were hung beneath it, a table of offerings placed before it and round this rude image of the god they danced in order that their dancing might raise him to life again."
21 Kerenyi, pg. 40
22 Lubell, pg. 14
23 Ibid, pg. 16
24 Kraus, pg. 39
25 Kerenyi, pg. 36
26 James, pg. 155
27 Kraus, pg. 39
28 Schure, pg. 254
29 Ibid
30 Schure, The Great Initiate pg. 520 #66
31 Ibid
32 Hall pg. 27
33 Schure Sacred Drama pg. 257
34 Schure, Great Initiates, pg. 521 #68
35 Ibid pg. 521 #69
36 Ginner, pg. 127
37 Schure, Sacred Drama, pg. 298
38 Ginner Pg. 57
39 Meyer, Pg. 19
40 Harding, pg. 45
41 Ginner, pg. 128
42 Schure Sacred Drama pg. 257
43 Schure, Great Initiates, pg. 521 #68
44 Ibid pg. 521 #69

45 Ginner, pg. 127
46 Schure, Sacred Drama, pg. 298
47 Ginner Pg. 57
48 Meyer, Pg. 19
49 Harding, pg. 45
50 Ginner, pg. 128

Cecilia Anne Gruessing, M.A.

St. Cecilia's Circle of Lost Souls

A Musical Mystery Play in One Act
Ceil Gruessing   August 25, 1998

From CLOWNS OF THE HOPI

"In a single performance, the sacred clown can serve many purposes. Their play can offer a psychotherapeutic release for the audience through amusement. At the same time, they may intensify a ritual in progress by contrasting the sublime and the ridiculous. They can also control non-conformist behavior in either groups or individuals through comic object lessons, as well as avert evil or the actions of witches. These outrageous actions— performing what is essentially a dangerous departure from acceptable behavior— must be sanctioned in some fashion by the group. In consequence, it is usually believed that they are representatives of SOME POWERFUL PRIMORDIAL BEING WITH WHOM THEY INTERACT."

Barton Wright

Cecilia Anne Gruessing, M.A.

INTRODUCTORY NOTES

This one act musical, mystery play, "St. Cecilia's Circle of Lost Souls", has been written upon inspiration from Chris Bache and his book, "Dark Night, Early Dawn— Steps to a Deep Ecology of Mind", The dark dramatic action of the play reflects much of the material in his book. It is like film noir.

The work is somewhat in progress in that all the details for production are not specifically outlined (musical arrangements, lyrics, and choreography) However, the one act contains all the elements of a story about a group of people who are working off intense karma in their poverty and stress-related lives.

St. Cecilia is the namesake of the main character, who was not only the patron saint of music, but she was also a martyr for her undying devotion to Christ. In this case, Ceci Ningun is dysfunctional in her devotion to the performing arts (at the expense of marriage), as well as her unrealistic dedication to improving the lives of her resident "artists".

I found myself addressing autobiographical issues about "hell" and personal failure that have become obvious to me after this had been written. I want to suggest that my character, Ceci Ningun, finds herself struggling with the death of her ego as she sees her confused humanitarian ambitions avalanche into a landslide of poverty, unrealistic dreams, misfortune, debauch, and group despair. Each of the characters under her wing is living with their own individual karma, self-sabotage, and personal "hells". Because of their karmic "family" connections to each other, they are swept into an altered group state when participating in Ceci's ritual dance during a Day of the Dead celebration.

Tamara, a pregnant prostitute in denial, becomes the catalyst for a dark miscarriage group experience, when she dies in childbirth. Her baby then will become Ceci's daughter. Each of the other "resident artists" represents failure and hope run amuck, despite their interesting characters and desperate attempts at salvation.

The comic, grotesque buffoonery that opens the show with its cartoon, carnaval flavor, finds it's resolution in darkness and the tragedy of death and homelessness, despite all of their futile attempts at improving their lives. The only lesson one can take away from this situation, is to avoid falling into this abyss, or to accept one's fate and live with it. In drama, we call this tragedy. I have used character models from the sacred clowns of the Hopi Indians to introduce the "morality play" ambiance.

It has been an interesting opportunity to write this play, as it is something I would not normally have created within the perimeters of my previous work. These people are victims of a society that does not include them. This concerns me artistically and politically as a child of the sixties. My greatest fear was always to become a bag lady.

Although I have had the fortune to see much of my work produced on stage and film, I believe that my written work has some form of life through my interest in the "Goddess" and the inspiration she has given me. Each of these characters have interesting potential roles for male and female actors. I hope you enjoy the work, as comedy finds its roots in tragedy.

Thank you.

Ceil Gruessing August 1998

CHARACTERS

- **CECI NINGUN**— is the eccentric proprietress of the defunct dancing school housed in a run-down church. She is a cross-cultural American artist diva who still holds free rent and dance classes for her company members. Ceci lives in her self-constructed, underground fantasy world that maintains the regular "Sunday Mass Journey Service", which draws misfits from all over the city. She feels no pain and generates the comic side show wherever she goes in the name of peace and love. She has no children and has never been married.
- **ST. JOSEPH**— is the guardian angel of St. Cecilia's. He was Ceci's father in his last incarnation. He appears in the form of a street sweeper, with all the wise character of an elder. Although invisible, he is always vigilant on stage…and never speaks.
- **MARIA DE LA ROSA**—is a middle-aged neighborhood social worker She is a previous dance student of Ceci's, who visits the congregation faithfully every Sunday to bring food and supplies, and to attend the Ballet-Mass. She is a frustrated socialist.

St. Cecilia's Circle of Lost Souls

CIRCLE OF ROGUES

- **TAMARA ESPERANZA**— An attractive, Latina, early 30's. She is romantic, naïve, and makes her money as a prostitute. She is in full pregnancy and is in denial about the father and the future of her child.

- **LAKEESHA**— A beautiful, young black girl, around 23, who is butch, bitter, and hooked on drugs. She works the street with Tamara, and knows her temper is bad. She was an abused child, dislikes men, and dreams of cash.

- **MAI LYNN**—A middle aged Native American Medicine woman, 35, who is a mystical healer, and a true gypsy friend of Ceci's from many years. She has the gift of second sight, and helps Ceci, but has no blood family in the city.

- **SHAMAT**— African American Reggae Veteran. He is a pimp, 45, talker, scam artist by trade who plays congas and likes to dance. He has good intentions despite his occasional nonviolent crimes. He wants to retire in Jamaica with all his children and wives.

- **JASON**— A young white, suburban teenager, 18, who has run away from home. He had bad grades, bad attitude, but great moves on the basketball court and on the dance floor. He is surging with energy, emotions, and appetites. He is looking for contact.

- **MAURICE**— Queen like homosexual, entrepreneur, tango teacher, continental gigolo, pseudo-elegant, alcoholic, who occasionally cross-dresses after sufficient vodka. He has the background of a European whose addiction has taken him to the poorhouse which he denies. while dabbling in illusions of grandeur and class. He loves to eat and drink and dress up.

SCENES AND MUSICAL NUMBERS

SCENE 1— OVERTURE .... **page 311**
    Musical Entrance of the Circle of Rogues .... page 311
    Song "Carnaval Finale" .... page 313
    Trio of Dialogues (Maurice & MaeLynn),
        (Jason &Lakeesha), (Tamara & Shamat) .... page 315
    Street sweeper & Song/Hymn .... page 320

SCENE 11— The Show Must Go On .... **page 321**
    Wake-up monologue .... page 321
    Day of the Dead Song .... page 321
    The Call, The Complaints .... page 323
    The Cards— (MaeLynn & Tamara) .... page 325

SCENE 111— SISTER ROSA .... **page 326**
    The Confrontation— (Ceci & Rosa) .... page 326

SCENE 1V— REHEARSAL .... **page 328**
    Greetings .... page 328
    Charge of the Goddess .... page 329
    Initiation Rehearsal Warm-Up .... page 330

SCENE V— THE SHADOW .... **page 330**

SCENE VI— CECI'S LAMENT .... **page 332**

    Ceci's Soliloquy Crash (St. Joseph & Ceci)..page 332
    Ceci asks for redemption ....page 333

SCENE VII— THE INVOCATION.. **page 334**

    Entrance— Offerings— Four Directions ....page 334
    Musical Prayers— Embrace the Change, The Upanishads......................page 335

SCENE VIII— SHOWTIME HELL .... **page 336**

    The Spiral Journey— Song— "Into the Labyrinth"...............................page 336
    Tango de L'amour et Le Mort— Jason & Lakeesha ....page 337

    I Love To Be Fat— Maurice & backups ....page 338
    Mai Lynn's Prayer..page 339
    The Cartoon Wedding Day—Tamara & Shamat ....page 339

SCENE IX— THE DELIVERY .... **page 340**

    The Birth..page 340
    The Death— Slow Dance and "Goddess of Death,
        God of Grain"..page 341

SCENE X— THE BENEDICTION .... **page 342**

    Funeral Dirge and Baptism..page 342
    Prayer to Wakan Tanka ....page 342
    Christian Hymn...page 342
    Reprise: Carnival Finale Parade Exit ....page 343

SETTING—The year is 2012 in the bowels of an American Industrial city.

Setting— A painted scrim depicts the EXTERIOR of the ruins of a church, St. Cecilia's, flanked by a bar, a car-repair garage, and a rundown apartment building. The image clearly depicts the international, crowded ghetto with all its incantations of "hell". The arena supports the ambiance of Dionysian festivals with the Bacchic rites and orgiastic dancing taking place in the midst of moral and physical decay. The style of the entire production is dark, comic, and grotesque, portraying clownish aggressors and victims with a resemblance to Hopi Kachina Dolls. Plants are blue, smog in the sky, declining architecture, and the smell of death and burning wood permeates everything. A corner shows us some young children playing amidst the ruins, still innocent to the debauch around them.

The INTERIOR stage reveals a church, semi-remodeled to accommodate a dance studio/ temple. There are cracked mirrors, with ballet bars. A large tree creates a center altar point in the dance floor. It holds candles, plastic flowers, and a variety of saints, gods, and goddesses from around the world. The choir pit houses the pews for the actors to rest, as well as a baby grand piano which holds a mattress and serves as a "throne" for Ceci. There is a large, open, central area for performing, around which the audience could be seated. This area feels like a graveyard yet is dressed as a campground for the various members of the church company.

SCENE 1— OVERTURE

1A— Musical Entrance of the CIRCLE OF ROGUES

Sirens, traffic, monster trucks, electronic and industrial noise and mechanical rhythm underscore the scrim's image of inner-city madness on a Saturday night in November 2012. It is a city reflecting blue collar, factory land, USA— just before dawn with all of the disenfranchised elements in the fringe of this dilapidated street scene.

St. Cecilia's Church exterior, sits in the center of the block, tumbling like an anachronism amidst the industrial squalor and crime of an old city neighborhood.

The street fills with the cast exhibiting, through song, dance and character, their "Pulp Fiction" criminal, yet clownish behavior. A live drumbeat accompanies their Carnaval parade at night, colored by bizarre, comedia del arte costumes, and a completely abandoned state of mind.

Shamat enters drumming in his blue zoot suit as the leader. Tamara, pregnant, in a sexy green dress, and Lakeesha in disco orange, follow like show girls in step. Mai Lynn as the Mystic Indian Queen in dark violet, follows. She is partnered by Colonel Maurice Mustard, in yellow, who holds his well combed head high (like Liberace) with fabulous pomposity. Jason, like a clown, jogs around in a red workout suit, carrying the paper mache image of a larger-than-life sized woman's naked torso painted like a face with a veil over it. This originates in the Greek Tale of Baubo, about a woman who amuses the public by revealing a painted face on her naked belly. This uninhibited expression resembles many ancient, archetypal myths about celebration of the dark side (the Maenads, the Bachic Rites). There is a certain madness to this "eat, drink, and be merry, for tomorrow we die" parade of rogues and misfits. The comedy of their clown-like innocence is equaled only by the darkness of their creepy buffoonery.

Ms. Cecilia makes her entrance carrying groceries and is anxious to get going on the festivities of the day. She unlocks the church door, and everybody enters.

Director's note:

The instrumental introduction will be constructed in WORKSHOP manner from improvised rehearsals in which good choreography and dialogue is kept and scripted. Once characters are defined, there are several locations in the script which should be developed in this improvisational method, for both dialogue and choreography. This work requires a scribe and choreographer, who will unconditionally devote organizational, secretarial, and creative attention towards a finalized script, with a director who will make artistic choices. These scripts are born from the interpretations of the actors who play the parts, along with their interactive dynamics, whose variations on the theme will always be welcome. All performers must sing and dance and act extraordinarily.

1B. Song "CARNAVAL FINALE"

The following lyrics have opening number musical pizazz, with an instrumental beginning, and comic dance breaks. Macabre as the tone is, the clown like qualities will carry the mood. This song takes them from an instrumental intro on the street, all the way into the church.

**Jump strut you clowns, and
catch the train
Grab a seat, get a drink and join the game
Be ready to dance with crazy and strange
It's the Carnaval Finale,
returning once again**

**Join the King and the Queen,
the Herald, the Jester,
and the Hopi clowns who dance,
come escape your mind,
Leave the past behind and
Give your libido a chance.**

**The King is like a wizard
The Queen looks like a
whore
The psychic has an uncommon frown
and the Bride and the Groom are at war**

**It's the Carnaval Finale
Hurry up & catch the train
You think you know the step,
then it changes once again**

**We dance all night, in a show without end
Looking for a place to let our hearts mend
The road is twisted, debts must be paid,
We are livin in a traffic jam day after day.**

**Seems like Karma's recreation,
just to put me through this test
How long will I be floating,
just give me time to rest!**

I rack my brain and body,
every day to find a bed,
If only I could get a break,
before I wind up dead

Jump strut lost souls, grab a seat, join the game
It's the Carnaval Finale & it's never the same
Miss a little step? Forget your regrets
It's the Carnaval Finale
Remember why you came

Jump strut lost souls,
grab a seat, join the game
Catch that last train to hell
cause it's leaving in the rain

Can you keep the beat?
Can you stand the heat?
Can you live without security?
Sooner or later, you pay the fee,
Cause unfortunately, life ain't free

Give up the glory, forget the shame,
And get a front seat at the Carnaval games
It's the Carnival Finale, returning once again
It's the Carnival Finale - Remember why you came!
Ceil Gruessing

This "Party's Over" ambiance eventually unwinds into dialogue revealing the manic and mysterious moods, misdemeanors and misadventures, of a desperate 21st century band of survivors. They are all stretched to their capacity with exhaustion, inebriation and delusional laughter. The beat subsides and they paid off. Ceci emerges from this commedia del arte throng, and introduces herself as the MC. Upon her entrance they all freeze. She speaks to the audience.

Ceci: Good evening, ladies and gentlemen. Welcome to St. Cecilia's performing arts center of worship and our current celebration of the Dia de los Muertos. I am Cecilia Ningun and I am the director of this esteemed institution of high art. St. Cecilia is my namesake, as she was the patron saint of celestial music. She is one of God's holy helpers and hopefully joins us tonight in spirit for our Day of the Dead Celebration.

This evening, we are very proud to bring you some of the work we have been preparing for this 2013 Day of the Dead Mass. Once again it is fall, the leaves are turning colors, the air is colder, and we snuggle up, and think about endings and new beginnings. And what better opportunity to talk about death and rebirth than November first, when the veil is the thinnest between the worlds? This is when souls come back to share their mysteries with us.

You could say that there is great potential for comedy within the sad stories of my congregation. The greatest dramatists of all time manipulated and exaggerated tragedy to evoke laughter from the audience during extreme moments of darkness to make it palatable. And so, it is with heavy joy and pain that I present a contemporary fairy tale of the musical trials and tribulations of St. Cecilia's Circle of Lost Souls. Laugh or cry, you will perhaps understand their stories. On with the show.

1C, Trio of Dialogues

The company comes out of the freeze and begins to move around and talk to each other. Maurice and Mai Lynn take center stage. These dialogues take place in various corners of the church.

1C a. MAURICE and MAILYNN

Maurice: I can assure you Mai Lynn that you have been the most exotic dance partner of my evening.

Mai Lynn: Merci Msr. Mustard, et vous aussi, Comme estce que je peux vous dire, que des toutes mes clientes ce soir, vous avez le masquerade plus grands y plus beaux.

Maurice: *(not understanding any of it)*— Vous etes tres belle ma petite fille.

Mai Lynn: Now Maurice we both know that I am not a petit fille.

Maurice: Ah madame, if you only knew how much....*Switching gears* ....Mai Lynn, can I make a proposition to you?

Mai Lynn: What kind of proposition?

Maurice: A business proposition.

Mai Lynn: What kind of business?

Maurice: Well, there is a little building for rent on Easter Street where I thought I might start a ballroom dancing school on the ground floor, and I thought that perhaps you might like to use the upstairs absolutely decorated to your specifications, for your "Psychic Salon".

Mai Lynn: Maurice, that's really very thoughtful of you, and I am truly touched . . ., but you are a hopeless, alcoholic Romeo and I am an international Native American gypsy. Granted we are BOTH hung up in lost arts, but you have no money, and I don't even have a social security number. And furthermore, what kind of clientele do you suppose we would draw from Easter Street? Certainly not your upper-class buddies.

Maurice: Mai Lynn, just listen to me. I know I've got a winner idea here. We draw from the lonely-hearts club of America, which forms at least 50% of the adult population. I can see it — "DANCING LESSONS and PSYCHIC READINGS"

Mai Lynn: Sounds like an Escort service for the truly desperate!

Maurice: Mai Lynn, try to think like an entrepreneur . . . we could have great success, and be eating at L'etoiles.

Mai Lynn: You know Maurice, I don't care where I eat, as long as I eat.

Maurice: We could also have a beauty salon and a tearoom.

Maurice cozies up to her to dance. She acquiesces and they dance.

Mai Lynn: Now Maurice let's not get carried away, remember, I'm married.

Maurice: Oh yes, Rudolph, and how is the dear boy.

Mai Lynn: I'm not sure where he is.......

They continue dancing and Ceci enters applauding, once again as MC.

Ceci: Thank you, Mai Lynn and Maurice, for your breathtaking choreography and poetry of hope. As artists, we all know that our faith comes from the spirit that carries us through any work we create. This need for creative people to express themselves is as strong as the aggressive, male energy drive to play football. And then sometimes romance comes along the way to inspire and depress us all of us...to juggle our hearts and give our souls wings. Some are blessed and live out their lives in partnership. Some people learn to live without it, for fear of losing their identity and their humble security. Those who find love, graduate to the home and family-making stages of life, with all the tests and rewards of that so called stability. I, Cecilia, director of the Lost Souls Academy, confess that I have learned to live without romantic love. You may wonder how I maintain my personal sanity....(not that I recommend it as a viable career). So, I merely escape into mother love, through theater and making dances for people to inspire their lonely spirits. It's not the best of jobs, but somebody has to do it. Hence, we move on to the complicated, hormonal collision of Jason and Lakeesha, in which they both express their respective love deficiencies. It is difficult to imagine this type of dysfunctional magnetism, but it exists and clearly demonstrates the extreme longing of lost souls.

1C b. JASON & LAKEESHA

The company of actors unfreeze for a moment. Jason has been bouncing his basketball around, and then turns to talk to Lakeesha who has been dancing with Tamara. Everybody else refreezes.

Jason: So how you doin Lakeesha?

Lakeesha: So, what you want boy? You got your nose wide open, been checkin me out all night long with those white boy worried looks. How the fuck do you think I'm doin after 3 tricks with 3 fat fucked up pigs?

Jason: Hey, sorry I asked. But if it helps any you don't really remind me of Goldilocks. That was the Three Pigs right?

Lakeesha: It was the Three Bears you fool!! *She laughs and slams him.* .... And this is not no fairy tale........ What you got Jason? Anything for me baby? I got to get high ..... I hate my life. Will you get me high? Come on Jason, I ain't goin nowhere.

Jason: I know how you feel *(rolling some kind of cigarette).* I especially know about loneliness.

Lakeesha: You do not know how I feel because you are white, and you got a family SOMEWHERE, I'm sure.

Jason: Yea I got family— but they're far away — and I'd kind of like to spend some time with you.

Lakeesha: You gotta have money to "spend" time with me white boy.

Jason: You don't even know who I am, or where I come from. Maybe I just want to talk.

Lakeesha: Talk? *She laughs.* I don't need a private dick to know that you are a class A runaway, and runaway boys are always horny.

Jason: I don't think you are capable of a normal conversation.

Lakeesha: OK, OK, I'm sorry. Gotta admit I'm jaded from the jump start because my Dad was a mother-fucker so I hate men, and I got a shitty job workin the street. SO . . . .. that's where I'm from . . .. How about yourself, Jason?

Jason: *He sits next to her, now encouraged.* You ever heard of Richmond, Virginia? Birthplace of the nation, crossroad of the races, and capitol of the Confederacy?

Lakeesha: Oh, Backbone of the South, I'm sure you can always go home to your basketball, key lime pie, and white suburbia.

Jason: Well, I won't be going home for a while. I just don't fit there.

Lakeesha: Also, one of the original depots of the Slaves. I'll bet you've already had some of that forbidden black slave ambrosia. Did you pay for it, or did you get it free? . . .

Now he's mad, and sexually frustrated.

Jason: OK so what's the deal with that big brick on your shoulder? I don't care what color you are. You want me to be your slave? OK - What do you want? I'll do anything for you. Just ask. Your wish is my command. I just want to see you smile for God's sake!

Lakeesha: You know, I really wish I could believe that.

She kisses him and walks away.

Ceci enters as MC again:

Ceci: And so, we keep trying to find the right fit. Nothing is ever perfect enough. We keep looking. Getting on trains and buses and planes, getting educated, getting high, changing jobs . . . spinning the bottle where it - stops nobody knows . . . . . Falling in and out of love. And then one day . . . you get pregnant and your whole world shifts gears.

1C c. TAMARA & SHAMAT

Tamara is in a bed constructed with fruit crates, covered in red velvet pillows. Shamat wants to join her.

Tamara: No Shamat, I am not sleeping with you tonight, and this is not your baby, so get these ideas out of your head. La fiesta nuestra esta terminada y yo tengo sueno.

Shamat: *Pulling out his black book.* Why do you want to confuse the situation? According to my calendar, it was you and me, on Valentines Day, last February, at the river; we were not working, and Frankie wasn't even on the books at that point.

Tamara: *Ignoring Shamat* I just know this is Frankie's baby. He wants it, he promised me a house, a crib, a bassinet, and a lock on the door. He loves me.

Shamat: May I remind you, who has been taking care of you for the last 2 years . . . Huh, Tamara? Escuchame! Frankie shows up once a week on leave from his wife and kids, and you're in love.

What makes him any different than the other Johns? You need to wake up and smell the coffee — This is my baby, and we are going to have it together.

Tamara: Ok big Hombre, my handsome king pimp! Where we going to put this baby? He needs a chance, better than you and me. And I want a respectable job. My puta days are over— this is worse than hell. Working all night …with a baby on the way. I've got to be crazy. Where's Frankie?

Shamat: Look honey, I told you that as soon as the drumming gig came through, we would stop the trick business, and I would take you back to Jamaica with me…. to my mom's.

Tamara: Yes Shamat, I've got the picture, me in the stable alongside the other three wives, washing clothes in the river. No thank you. And forget the drumming. Better you go back to the extortion jobs. At least we ate well and could afford a doctor then.

Shamat: I don't care what you say. Nobody can love you the way I do, and only the spirit knows the truth, so I'll leave you on that note. Pleasant dreams Juliet.

Tamara: Oh Romeo, Romeo where the hell are you??

Shamat curls up in a corner. He is joined by a sleepy circle of rogues as they settle into their "improvised beds" around the church yard.; The scrim drops for bedtime.

1D. SOLO DANCE — Streetsweeper, St. Joseph

A lonely old STREETSWEEPER pushes his rolling garbage pail across the street

*and begins to clean as he carefully surveys the neighborhood. Before taking his broom, he kneels in front of the Church, says a prayer, and makes the sign of the cross. He is St. Joseph (a Guardian Angel with wings) disguised as an invisible street cleaner, who takes special interest in the well-being of the congregation of the church. He talks to himself, but **nobody sees or hears him**. He has a matter of fact, Mr. Fix-it, Grandfather persona. (He represents the author's father, Joseph.)*

SONG— a typical Catholic, "watchoverya", Saint like hymn, to which St. Joseph, the angel dances solo. He floats in the Bardo space, sweeping the street and praying for victims and sinners. His dance/prayer has a religious church organ quality that juxtaposes the destructive cold sounds of the night. Those sounds segue with the city awakening with sounds of traffic and a garbage truck. Jose Angel remains on stage.

SCENE II— The Show Must Go On – Next day

IIA. Wake up Monologue— Ceci

CECI NINGUN is waking up in her condemned church studio to the sound of a garbage truck. The scrim lifts again to reveal Ceci's bedroom. Ceci is wearing a ragged diaphanous nightgown in her grand piano bed. Above her bed is a huge ticking clock. She has been flung out of her grand piano bed by the sound of the garbage truck, and the collapse of a piano leg. Sliding onto the floor, she tears off her pearly white eye mask, pulls out her ear plugs, and struggles with her unwinding hair rollers. It is not her day. She screams.

Ceci: Oh my God, what time is it? *Looking up.* Why has the clock stopped? What's going on here? *She stands up.* Am I still asleep? No. Thank God, that was a real nightmare. I dreamt I was crushed by a garbage truck and then rose up to heaven right out of my body like a balloon. I have to write this down. But why has the clock stopped? What's today? Oh, I forgot, it's today. That's right it's the Day of the Dead! Ceci wake up!

IIB— Day of the Dead Song

This flips her switch, and the music begins. She sings. It is the DAY OF THE DEAD/HALLOWEEN/ and THANKSGIVING, and she goes into a mad dance of chores and mental memos to prepare for the day's festivities. She lights the candles on her altar, talks to the spirits and the Mother Goddess, brushes her teeth, gets dressed and dances around.

Ceci *sings:*

DAY OF THE DEAD SONG

Hang out the banner, bring out the flowers,
light the candles and sing.
Take out the trash,
drum up the cash
tell everyone what to bring . . . .

Find a photo of Dad, Abuelo and Buddha,
Jesus and Lady Di
We'll be meeting them at the threshold with joy,
there ain't no time to cry.

Chorus

It's the Day of the Dead, and we celebrate
the time when the veil is so thin
between the worlds of life and death,
Let the spirit dance begin.

Candles, cake, tobacco and incense,
and yellow flowers are like signs
My Dad he likes his bourbon,
and My Abuelo, his red wine.

We're inviting all hungry souls,
though our table is humble and modest,
We will dance with all the ancestors,
and the magic of the Goddess.

Chorus

So dress the altar,
Say your prayers, light the holy fire.
We pray for universal love,
there is no higher desire

All souls will graduate tonight

from the fear of crossing the river
Sink or swim, Embrace the dark,
your souls will be delivered.

Chorus   *Ceil Gruessing*

Ceci then RINGS the church bell. Over the loudspeaker she blasts a brassy wake-up call that can be heard through brick walls.

IIC. SUNDAY ANNOUNCEMENT- WAKE UP CALL

Ceci: *Over a bad PA system* — Calling all sleepy rogues, thieves, con-artists, sinners, and whores. Trick or Treat is over and— This is a wake-up call for all you dancing fools on the Day of the Dead— Yes...Party of the year — But may I remind you that this will be a work day for all of us at St. Cecilia's, since it will also serve as our Halloween slash Thanksgiving, with many hungry neighbors, children, and friends to feed. So, wake up, adjust your medications, hangover pills, whatever, ...and throwback the coffee.... because full cast, obligatory mass and warm up starts in 15 minutes.... with NO EXCEPTIONS! May I remind you that I hope you find your accommodations at St. Cecilia's adequate and comfortable. Coffee will be served immediately in the graveyard .... yes Maurice?

They all begin to move in their improvised beds, not responding positively to this audio intrusion of their dream states. Especially since they have only recently hit their junkyard pillows. Ceci can't hear the general hungover aggravation and irreverent replies to her army like wake-up call. DIALOGUE ensues as they get ready for rehearsal, knowing that their beds are available only if they work for the church.

Maurice: Oui, oui, madame! Je viens! Oh, the sweet sound of management. It can never be escaped. *He is having problems disassembling his tent.*

Jason: I'd be happy to help you out Maurice.

Maurice: I hate the sound of an anxious woman in the morning.

Jason: I take it you've been married before.

Maurice: Yes, three times, and they were all marvelous women.

Shamat: You definitely don't have to be married to recognize the sound of the female alarm clock.

Lakeesha: Bitch, bitch, bitch. Listen to the poor little boys, they don't want to go to school. I don't see you with no J O Bs, to justify these complaints. Now it's time for all of us to get up and work.

Shamat: Who asked you anyway woman? The only work you know, is putting on your lipstick and layin on your back.

Lakeesha: Now you know darn well Mr. Pimp Shamat that you put clothes on your back, by layin me on my back. Peace and Love.

Mai Lynn: Come on guys, Halloween and Harvest is the biggest third world holiday celebrated all over the world. An international extravaganza of spirits will be out tonight. We must be ready.

Tamara: Me? I am wiped out . . . I don't know if I can do this dance thing, look at me, I'm about to explode! Where is Frankie?

Mai Lynn: Tamara, how many months are you?

Tamara: Nueve y pico *Crying* Donde esta Frankie?

Shamat: Forget that guy, will ya? Mai Lynn… How much for you to tell me who is the father of that baby inside her. *Long silence.*

Mai Lynn: Leave us alone and run along to rehearsal. Tell Miss Ceci we are coming soon. We will settle this confusion once and for all.

Shamat: Good, it's about time.

Tamara: Why do you want to get inside of this Miss Mae Lynn? This ain't your business.

Mai Lynn*: Feeling the baby.* Tamara, you are very close to delivery, and the moment you get your first contraction, you must go to the hospital. And . . .You need to come clean with this and stop deceiving everybody. Unburden yourself, or you will be hurting many people with this mystery. Who is the father, Tamara?

Tamara: Mai, I don't know. I'm not sure. I mean with a job like this, it could be anybody's!!!

Mai Lynn: OK, OK, so we'll ask spirit to help us.

II D. Reading the TAROT CARDS for Tamara

Mai Lynn lights the candle and shuffles her cards, says her prayer. The others are stretching on the dance floor) Background music begins. Mai Lynn spreads the cards and reads discreetly.

Mai Lynn: *Covered by— 9 of pentacles reversed – a cloud of Bad faith... Possible loss of a valued friendship, threat to your safety.

*Crossed by the Knight of Swords. The man around you is brave and chivalrous... a good heart... he is heroic and shrewd... It is Shamat.

*Crowned by the 10 of cups – Your ideal situation would be the happiness of family life in a home... honor, esteem, reputation, etc.

*Basis of the situation— 8 of swords - Crisis, calamity, conflict, turmoil, bad news, sickness... not good Tamara.

* Behind you— 6 of pentacles - Just recently you have been made a generous offer of true kindness. Don't overlook us, Tamara.

*Before you— 3 of cups - Represents the sisters in your midst who will help resolve the problem.

*Client's position in the Situation – You are in for a major Transformation, Tamara to let go of the past. (*It is the Death card*)

*Mai Lynn conceals her dismay to this card as it is fore shadows Tamara's fate. She is unable to name or discuss **the Death card and** moves on.*

*People around you— The Sun, reversed – loneliness, broken engagement, cancelled plans, a cloudy future."

*Hopes/Fears - The Tower - This is the house falling.. Total loss

*Outcome—The Judgment - This reading clearly indicates you must find a home for this child --that your health is not good. I am sorry for this news. But Tamara, Shamat is the father. Be realistic!

Tamara: Dios Mio! It all sucks Mai Lynn. Why do you do this to me? You think I don't know how fucked up my life is? I am knocked up and *nobody* knows who the dad is!!!

Mai Lynn: Pobrecita! You are not seeing straight chica! Now your job is to bring life to this baby. It is a precious little girl who will always love you. And the baby's father is Shamat - with his angry sword? *She points to the card.* And he does not know how to show you the love you think you want. The spirit of the angels is with you, to guide you on your journey this day. You are surrounded by loved ones. *She takes Tamaras hand —* We all love you Tamara, and we will be strong for you and help you when you need us. Now we must get ready for the show. You will take it easy, and we go to the hospital on the first contraction. *Tamara is stunned. Shamat steps up.*

Shamat: Told you I was the father... I just knew it baby.

Tamara: You mean, Frankie is not comin? *Still in denial.*

Lakeesha: Come on Tamara, I'll help you get dressed.

Everybody is ready in their rehearsal clothes. They are unaware that they are imitating comic, clownlike, ballet takeoffs of Hopi Clown spirits, with mix matched colors and irreverent accessories.

SCENE III— Sister Rosa
The Confrontation

Ceci is checking costumes when Maria de La Rosa enters in her Sunday social worker suit, carrying a huge suitcase of clothing, blankets, and boxes of food. They speak in Spanish.

Rosa: Señora Cecilia, Feliz Dia de la Gracia (Happy Thanksgiving), and whatever else you are doing tonight. Como estas?

Ceci: Ah me siento divina, Tosa. Besos, Feliz Dia de los Muertos tambien. (Happy Day of the Dead as well) *They hug and laugh. Rosa hands her mail* What is this? Another Pay or Quit bill from the power company? Ay, carumba, no wonder the clock doesn't work. No importa, so we'll get more batteries and candles.

Rosa: I brought lots of food, clothing and blankets, and some baby clothes for Tamara.

Ceci: Oh, thank you Rosa. Me alegre que tu estas aqui temprano para ayudar me con la comida. Por favor, Rosa, te pido, haga me el gran favor de dirigir toda la cocina. *(Relieved that Rosa has come early to help with the food, and would she please take responsibility in the kitchen.)*

Rosa: Claro que si! Soy una mesera para la mesa de la vida. No se preocupe. La Madre, Maria de la Rosa ha llegado. (Of course. I am just a waitress at the table of life. Don't worry. The mother, Maria del la Rosa has arrived.) *She lights a candle by the Virgin Mary & begins to organize food.*

Ceci: Mils Gracias hermana.

Rosa: So, tell me how is your health, Ceci? Are you still taking your medicine?

Ceci: Better than ever, but I hate those pills. They make me sleepy.

Rosa: And did you remember to deposit that cash I gave you into your savings account?

Ceci: I still have the cash around here somewhere. I know I do.

Rosa: What?...... Ceci, I'm not going to give you cash if you can't be responsible for it. Now where is it? You are losing your mind Ceci, No te lo veas?

Ceci: You know what I see? I have a Mass to put on and lots of hungry people to feed, and I don't need this right now. What's gotten into you Rosa?

Rosa: Ceci........Hello? This is reality check time. Your days as the Ballet Mistress at St. Cecilia's are almost over. Ceci... Listen to me. Even I am too old to dance with you.

Ceci: Oh, come on, we're never too OLD to dance. *Packing up.*

Rosa: Ceci, I am your friend, and I love your Sunday Ballet-Masses, but the time has come for you to seriously consider committing yourself to Santa Teresa's Retirement Home. You cannot continue like this.

Ceci: Over my dead body chica. No, me molesta con estas cosas ahora. Mi gente tiene hambre, Rosa, por favor. (Don't bother me with these things now. My people are hungry. Please Rosa.)

Rosa: And what about the tardy back property taxes— The city is within one month of bringing a bulldozer to the property, Me oyes, Señora?

Ceci: Rosa, Yo entiendo todas estas problemas, y mas que tu no puedes imaginar. Pero.... The show must go on, and tonight, we will perform. *Ceci gets dressed for rehearsal.*

Rosa: And what about Tamara? She's due any minute. Where is she going to have the baby?

Ceci: Rosa, I have an angel who will be here today to fix everything, and I must get ready for dress rehearsal. *She heads for the chapel.*

SCENE IV— Rehearsal

The company Circle of Rogues enter, dressed comically in their ballet warm up clothes, all faded colors. Yawning, half asleep, angry, and hungover, they join Ceci for the warm-up ceremonial song and dance. Ceci begins...

IV A. Greetings

Ceci: Good morning, ladies and gentlemen. Thank you for your punctuality and enthusiastic vibrations this morning. *They are tired and hung over, despite their overdone attention to dance attire.* May I remind you that today we are celebrating The Day of the Dead, Thanksgiving, and Halloween all at once. In so doing we give thanks to our ancestors, to our Mother Earth, and to the collective Higher Power that steers all of us on our lifeboats. In this case St. Cecilia's will be sailing in the evening mass to the other side, to embrace big transformations, to dance with our ancestors, and to experience the universal heartbeat. In this morning's mass we will prepare ourselves mentally, physically, and spiritually for this evening's event. Let us begin.

IV B. Charge of the Goddess

Mai Lynn sings the traditional **Charge of the Star Goddess**

By Doreen Valiente and adapted by Starhawk

This is to be recited by the congregation, as a dance prayer that accompanies the mantra that Mai Lynn sings. It is a well-known invocation in Women's communities. .

"I who am the beauty of the green earth, and the white moon among the stars and the mysteries of the waters,
I call upon your soul to arise and come unto me.
For I am the soul of nature that gives life to the universe.
From me all things proceed and unto Me they must return.
Let My worship be in the heart that rejoices,
for behold— all acts of love and pleasure are my rituals.

Let there be beauty and strength, power and compassion,
honor and humility, mirth and reverence within you.
And you who seek to know Me,
know that your seeking and yearning will avail you not,
unless you know the Mystery:

For if that which you seek, you find not within yourself,
you will never find it without.
For behold, I have been with you from the beginning,
and I am that which is attained at the end of desire."

IV C. Initiation and Four Directions

SONG & DANCE MASS— (a sound collage of music)

The following action is like a circular dance class with an altar in the middle. There is a 7 circuit Hopi labyrinth drawn on the stage, which is always there. The mass continues with a ritual that acknowledges the four directions. The Labyrinth is incorporated into this design as an initiation path to the ceremony... opening the circle...

There are definite parts to the mass, which can be staged by the choreographer.

1. **Charge of the Goddess**
2. **Mark the 4 Directions**
3. **Prepare and honor central altar (Tree) sing**
4. **Circle Song /Dance to Invoke Spirit**
5. **Sermoness (Ceci) with Prayers and Offerings**
6. **Group Labyrinth Dance— sing**
7. **Benediction— song /dance**

- *Designs in the choreography are subject to the creative style of the director and choreographer. The entire ceremony is not necessary. It is a basic Sunday mass at this church.... with the extra flair of holiday celebration in a radical style.*

- *A preamble to the later evening Event/Performance.*

SCENE V. THE SHADOW - *Ceci gives notes:*

Ceci: OK guys, that wasn't bad. I know that you are truly ALL very talented, and I thank you for your dedication. However, I do know that some of you are hung over. Can you please hold off all booz and drugs until after this evening's holiday mass at 7pm tonight? Yes? When the veil between the worlds is the thinnest?? Remember...All the spirits will be here!

They grunt and improvise discontent about inconvenient abstention. She takes hands.

Ceci: OK, costumes at 6:30 pm and everybody knows their job—
Let the preparation of food, music, and decorations begin! And to the mighty Goddess, we thank you for your bounty and blessings, and to the Great Father Sky we open up our mortal gates tonight to mingle with our ancestors, and great spirits of the worlds. Bless us with white light and love.!! *She exits to the privacy of her altar.*

And the scene sets up for a banquet, with autumn colors and much movement. Costumes change, food arrives, flowers, decorations, altar offerings, candles glow everywhere, the music changes to an earthy dance rhythm. In a corner Tamara Esperanza is noticeably very uncomfortable with her pregnancy. Rosa comes to her aid......

Rosa: I insist that we go to the hospital. This is so dangerous Tamara.

Tamara: *In her stupor denial.* I want to rest and wait for Frankie. He is supposed to come to the Mass. I promised him that I would wait.

Rosa: *At first speechless . . .* Needless to say I am frustrated to see right before my very eyes another Latina woman who allows men to interfere with mother nature.

Shamat: I can't take much more of this either.

Lakeesha: Maybe she's in love big boy.

Rosa: She thinks she's in love. Hey, I'm ready to sign all of you up for the nut house with Ceci first on the list.

Mai Lynn enters from offstage with flowers and listens.

Shamat: Hey now, Miss Ceci has done right by us.

Jason: Yea, I'd be on the street if she didn't take me in.

Ceci enters quietly and overhears from a corner of the studio.

Maurice: She is our hostess and our patroness.

Rosa: What do you plan to do when your bedrolls are taken away as landfill, and the tree is gone, and the altar, and all the fiesta. *She is clearly upset.* Tamara is about to break water in this underworld temple of madness. You've all got to get out of here.

Lakeesha: I'm not going anywhere unless Ceci leaves.

Mai Lynn: I can assure you Rosa that the only way to remove Ceci from St. Cecilia's would be to carry her out. And since the property is legally in her name, we are her guests until she has made the decision to leave.

Rosa: *Firmly...* Perhaps Señora Ceci is not equipped to make the decision, and they may shortly be made for her. Maybe her 1960s delusions about being an artist are beginning to crumble...and you guys wanna go along with it? I am sorry guys... I love Ceci, but, but... well... I want you to remember tonight, because it may be the last and final show for St. Cecilia's church.

Tamara: *Standing up, changing the subject —* I am hungry and ready to help you with the food Rosa. Vamos a la cocina

Mai Lynn: Tamara, you must go to the hospital now

Tamara: No, no.... Que sigue la fiesta!! *She walks with pregnant difficulty to the kitchen.* Ouch!! *Tamara winces... still standing.*

Rosa: That's a contraction Tamara.... I'm going to call an ambulance now. Somebody has to take responsibility here.

Tamara: I will do the show in Ceci's wheelchair and go after dinner OK? Tamara grabs a chicken leg and blows Rosa off waving her other hand. The group disperses to prepare, and Ceci enters, stunned, from what she has overheard.

SCENE VI— Ceci's Lament
VI A.— Ceci's soliloquy crash

Ceci goes to her altar and breaks down. She prays.

Ceci: Oh, dear God, Oh Mother Mary, Mom, Dad ... Where are you? Where are you? I am calling all of you now!!! What have I done here? I need help. This is all my fault - I have brought all these crazy people together with no foundation for a future; The Queen is pregnant ... the tower is falling; my dancers will be homeless and hungry ... What have I done?

St. Joseph enters and listens silently absorbing her dilemma. Ceci continues

Ceci: How have I sunken to this level of survival . . . the absolute bottom . . . a barely criminal world of day-by-day existence . . . with this ridiculous faith in song and dance. Are we all nuts? No... it's just me... This is 2013 . . . only kids sing and dance! Adults are working, paying rent and mortgages, going to Hawaii, buying health insurance. I can't remember the last time I was in a restaurant. Starving Artist is clearly NO LONGER A CAREER, and it is definitely NOT A JOB And I have dragged all these lost souls with me ...... She falls to the floor. St. Joseph comes to her side. And most of all ...... the Queen is Pregnant. right now,.....so I must pray for Tamara and this child.

St. Joseph helps her stand up. This confuses Ceci, as she cannot see him, but feels him. His presence gives her a sense of revelation.

VI B. Ceci asks for Redemption

Ceci fumbles around for a moment to shift gears ... She has composed herself and faces the audience with her wish to redeem herself.

Ceci speaks I know that these are very inconvenient circumstances for a mass or a celebration or even a performance. I know that you have all put your faith in me for hopeful success as artists. I can no longer promise you that dream. I can only give you my spiritual faith in spirt and music and dance and the natural forces of the universe... intangible as they are... I know that we have shared precious moments together despite our desperation in these crazy times of living in the fringe. But I love you all and embrace your hopes and dreams.

So, we will proceed with the last supper...and then our final mass. But first I will pray for all of us. Join me one more time.

Dear Creators, . . .

Father Sky and Mother Earth . . . and the great power of God that injects the spirit into our lives.. Please shine the light on this newborn baby soul that Tamara and Shamat are bringing into this world.

Show this soul a path to safety and sanity…… that she may grow in clean, fertile soil, and become the flower that God intended. I ask for the ability to heal with my hands, that we may all have some joy on this earth in this so fragile of times. Let us cherish what nature offers us, let us cherish what love the universe cares to bestow upon us, and most of all let us cherish the bliss that comes from the understanding that we are all are so very precious, and TRYING AS HARD AS WE CAN to coexist.

And that if our turn has come, that we walk graciously away, strong and proudly towards the light. Oh, Great Spirit, I ask for your presence and guidance on this holy night. And protect our Tamara and her child at this crucial hour.

SCENE VII— THE INVOCATION

A— Entrance – Food Offerings— Four Directions

A fan fare is heard, and one by one 9 priests and priestesses enter in their different colors of the rainbow, each carrying food in baskets upon their heads. Around each of their waists is a 12-foot length of knotted rope in their respective colors.

Red— Jason -
Orange - Lakeesha
Yellow— Maurice
Green— Tamara
Blue— Shamat
Purple— Mai Lynn
White— Ceci
Pink— Rosa
Gold— Jose Angel

They each enter in file, bowing to the four directions, and then making their Thanksgiving food offerings to the altar buffet table, bowing, and proceeding to their positions at the long dinner table facing the audience... They proceed to eat ceremoniously... each reciting their dramatic prose. There is theatrical irony in this scene where they are eating as they are honoring life and death.

VII B Prayers: Embrace the Change; and Upanishads Excerpt

All verse should be put to music to be sung

EMBRACE THE CHANGE   by Starhawk

Ceci recites:

> "All that ever was exists in
> the living body of the being
> we call the universe, Goddess.
> She breathes in— we are born
> She breathes out— we die"

Maurice— " But birth and death are on the same wheel, which is always turning, like the tide, or the changes of the moon"

Shamat— "We become ancestors, the unborn, newborn, the guardians of those to come, Cherish the turning, the letting go and the bringing forth, decay and growth, life and death,"

Tamara— " All points on the wheel are sacred Embrace the change."

*The Pagan Book of Living and Dying Starhawk

They continue prayer with excerpt ideas from the UPANISHADS

Lakeesha: We pray to Mother Earth, Father Sky from whence all living things derive their nourishment,

Jason: And forever we give thanks to the Divine Power that created us and gave us our connection to all living things on earth and in spirit.

Mai Lynn: We ask for deliverance from unkind and unsacred acts towards others and believe that true love of humanity and the planet is love for oneself and the circle of life.

Now that I see in the Mind (Mai-Lynn)
I see myself to be the All (Jason)
I am in beasts and plants (Tamara)
I am a babe in the woods (Lakeesha)
and one who is not yet conceived (Shamat)
And one that has been born (Maurice)
I am present everywhere. (Ceci)

                              Ideas from The Upanishads

Everybody then makes holes in the earth and buries an offering . . .. Jewelry, photos, old cell phones, trinkets, money   Music Begins

SCENE VIII - SHOW TIME IN HELL!!

VIII A— Spiral Journey song, Into the Labyrinth—

Instrumental musical intro

The men and women form two lines opposite each other to dance. There is much coming together and going apart, pairing off, circling, forming snake lines that interweave, returning to gender groups, and then separation.... the music changes with a haunting melody.

*A circle is formed, (Ariadnes Thread) in which all the ropes are tied together except the tails. A labyrinthic chain is created which opens up a spiraling descent into the darkness of the underworld. The music intensifies with melancholy rhythm, expressing the following: They sing:

Into the Labyrinth   C. Gruessing

Into the Labyrinth, To the Tunnel I plunge,
Falling, Spinning, Lost as I lunge
At the mercy of wind so dark and so cold
My turn to dance, This is the Threshold.

Stand up - Fear not your future
Cause this is just a test
Cry not, oh no, my children
Face the music, be your best.

**The party's just beginning,
no time for trips and tears
Get up, work on your chakras
and reconcile your fears.**

CHORUS – **Into the Labyrinth**

**Stand strong and learn the lessons,
how they burn and how they sting,
I'm sorry it ain't over
till the fat lady sings.**

**Sticks and stones can break my bones
Names can't really hurt me,
ashes to ashes, dust to dust,
my soul has kundalini!**

CHORUS (Repeat into the Labyrinth)

VIII B Tango de L'amour el Le Mort— Jason & Lakeesha

The music then turns to a Bloodthirsty Bolero as Red, Jason, and Orange, Lakeesha, tango to Love and Death. (Tango de l'amour et le mort from the French Rock Opera STARMANIA, Lyrics by Luc Plamendon, Music, Michel Berger.) The seduction is intense as Jason, the WARRIOR challenges Lakeesha, the KALI, seductress, destroyer. They dance, scream and yell at each other with all the passion, jealousy, anger, and hatred of two black cats, until they symbolically destroy each other.

<u>Tango De L'amour Et De La Mort</u> – Luc Plamendon - STARMANIA

**Le monde est une femme
Dont on voit la photo
Un jour sur les journaux
Mais quand elle vous poursuit
Au détour de la nuit
Elle passe incognito
Vous, ne soyez pas surpris
Qu'elle vous tire dans le dos
Dans le dos
L'amour est une femme
Qui tue celui qu'elle aime
Avec la même main
Qui caresse si bien
Avec le même bras**

Qui vous serrait si fort
Avec le même bras
Qui vous disait
Je t'adore
Je t'adore
La mort est une femme
Qui danse avec l'amour
Cet éternel tango
Où chacun tour à tour
Rend dingue son partenaire
Cet éternel tango
Qui vous envoie en l'air

Ou bien 6 pieds sous terre
Viens danser viens mort

Ce tango au sang chaud
Est-ce l'amour ou la mort
Qui sera le macho

VIII C — I LOVE TO BE FAT - Maurice

Next, we pass The Royal Fat King (Maurice) admiring his jewels, eating and drinking, and expanding, and burping, and grunting, until he makes himself sick. He sings— **I LOVE TO BE FAT   C. Gruessing**

Feeling sublime, consuming champagne and fine
wine.... Indulgence is my middle name,
I'm fat and I'm proud.

What's the difference if I'm having affairs,
Oh Yes, with chocolate eclairs,
Last night I had coquille St. Jacques with bagels and lox
and cream cheese . . .

I love to be fat, I love to be fat, I love to be fat . . .
Oh yea, Oh yea . . .

Cut the Scarsdale girls and let yourself go
Who would care if you kicked sweet and low?
Just follow your desires . . .
Have fun be OBESE!

**And when everybody sees that you've
grown, in especially erogenous zones...
then they'll know there's more to touch, to rub, to
squeeze, to love.... Mais Oui !!!**

VIII D— Mai Lynn— Native American prayer

D. Mai Lynn sits on her stool with her rattle, feather, sage and regalia, smudging and dancing around a globe of earth surrounded by candles, praying fervently — She is anguished and recites: (from The Sacred Pipe— Black Elk)

Mai Lynn: "And now, sending a voice directly to Wakan-Tanka, we cry: Grandfather, Wakan-Tanka, with the help of all things and all beings we are about to send our voice to you. Be merciful to us! Help us! I place myself upon this sacred path and send my voice to you through the four Powers, which we know are but one Power. Help me in all this! O my grandfather, be merciful to us and our land! Help my people and all things to live in a sacred manner pleasing to You. Help us O Wakan-Tanka to live again!!"

VIII E. The Cartoon Wedding Day— Tamara and Shamat –

"Someday My Prince Will Come"

Next, we see a cartoon scene with a pregnant princess (Tamara) alone in the garden. She is about to pick a rose from the lonely rose tree. In all her splendor and fertility, she is so melancholy and sad to behold. She sings of this missing part of her heart. ("Someday My Prince Will Come"- Walt Disney— Snow White & The Seven Dwarfs). When out of nowhere, the cool blue suited joker (Shamat) arrives with blue plastic violets singing in scat. She is awakened with joy, and listens to his smooth blue lines, falling and weeping into his arms with clown like ecstatic bliss. He whips out a ring, a veil and a top hat, and takes her arm. Suddenly she has a labor pain, and harsh dialogue ensues. Tamara is clearly losing her mind on stage.

Tamara: Oh my God, everybody is here. They have all come back for my wedding. *Looking at her belly.* Frankie, how are we going to get married in front of my mother and father like this?

Shamat: Tamara . . . This is Shamat, the real father, remember? Now you said you wanted me to marry you, and we're getting married!! What is the problem now?

Tamara: Because my father is not going to be able to look you in the eye, after you did this to me. That's what's the problem. *She cries out, holding her belly.*

Shamat*: To the sky.* Oh my God, if you are out there, help me now—

Tamara: Frankie, this just isn't the way I thought my wedding day would be, and I'm depressed— and you, you could care less . . . what is this, your third marriage? I just don't trust you Frankie— I mean, I don't even know how I got pregnant, and I don't know how I got here— somebody handed me a veil, somebody said "marry me", and I said "Yes". *She becomes hysterical.*

Shamat: Baby, it's me Shamat, remember? I love you . . . I am here for you. *Trying to revive her.* Please stop, honey, the wedding march has begun!! *(music)*

Tamara: *She cries out in labor pain holding he belly* My water broke!!!!!

Shamat: Oh my God, not now, please not now, just give us one more day .. Oh no!!

SCENE IX— The Delivery IX A— The Birth

There is a sudden flurry of movement — darkness hits the stage - A wedding march takes on distorted, macabre tones as a symbolic *groaning, painful, and tormented birth labor takes place on stage in abstract, grotesque form. All the dancing lunatics rise to their most exaggerated, monstrous selves, forming a birth tube, moving viciously, screaming, forcing themselves upon one another, until the emotion intensifies to such a climax, that a highly amplified baby's cry pierces the madness, creating a sharp silence and piercing light.*

Ceci presents a baby girl in the white light. Mai Lynn and Rosa have been helping

Ceci with the delivery. They are covered in blood. Shamat rushes to Tamara's side and calls out her name hysterically. But she doesn't answer.

Shamat: Tamara, baby wake up! I am here… I promise to take care of you…

Mai Lynn: She can't answer, her heart has stopped. She has passed on.

IX B — THE BIRTH/DEATH
— Slow Dance & Goddess of Death and Grain

There is a long silence with slow motion movement. Ceci gives the baby to Shamat. She recites the following passage under a white spotlight for Tamara's soul.

GODDESS OF DEATH, GOD OF GRAIN - Starhawk

Ceci:

**"Goddess of death,
you who are the end inherent in the beginning,
scythe to the ripe grain, the fall of berries,
and the coming of night
You are called the Implacable
One, but we know you
as the most gracious Goddess,
Healer, end of sorrow, relief of pain,
Receive our sister, Tamara
May she become a star in your night sky
cauldron and be brewed back to life.
(Lakeesha** *takes over the blessing*)
**God of Grain, God of seed,
You who every year's end are cut down and buried,
you who know the dark places underground,
the way down and way up, the fall and the rising,
Guide our sister Tamara
Show her the long road through the maze
to the place of rebirth
to the place of return."**

Meanwhile St. Joseph, the guardian angel, has lifted the body of Tamara and takes her to the tree altar to pray over her.

Mai Lynn— She's crossed over, the angels have taken her. We must close the circle now.

Shamat has broken down weeping and gives Mai Lynn the baby girl as the sound of ambulance sirens begin. St. Joseph and Ceci carry Tamara to a waiting ambulance whose siren overlaps the scene.

SCENE X— THE BENEDICTION

X. A The Funeral Dirge/ Baptism

A New Orleans type funeral dirge melody begins.
Ceci and Mai Lynn, covered in blood, are baptizing the baby, and the chorus is singing to ritual movement around her. The baby is passed around and returns to Shamat. The cup of wine is passed, and they all hold hands around the tree. In the distance we hear the ever-increasing sound of bulldozers.

XB — Prayer to Wakan Tanka – Sun Dance – Black Elk

Mai Lynn: "Oh Grandfather, Wakan-Tanka, maker of all that is, who always has been, behold us! And you, Grandmother and Mother Earth, you are Wakan and have holy ears; hear me. We have come from You, we are part of you, and we know that our bodies will return to You at the time when our spirits travel upon the great path. By fixing this center in the earth, I remember you, to whom my body will return, but above all I think of Wakan Tanka, with whom our spirits become as one. By purifying ourselves in this way, we wish to make ourselves worthy of You, O wakan-Tanka, that our people may live!!!!!"

XC — Christian Benediction

The music segues into a Christian Hymn and Ceci takes the baby and ties her around her body in a long white sheet. They all sing:

**Glory Be to the father,
And to the Son
And to the Holy Ghost.
As it was in the beginning,
is now and ever shall be,
World without end, Amen, Amen ...**

The sound of the bulldozers increases, as we hear the reprise refrains of the Carnaval Parade song

XD – REPRISE OF CARNAVAL PARADE - FINALE

*St. Joseph and Tamara (dressed in the pale blue/grey) **dance around the graveyard tree in spirit and then lead the group off dancing on the Carnaval Parade that started the show, as the overture melody increases mixed with dirge music and the overlapping sound of a bulldozer.***

Ceci is the last to leave still holding the baby, watching her world collapse. St. Joseph, the angel, accompanies Ceci and the child. She rocks the baby in her arms. St. Joseph puts his arm around her, and she reluctantly leaves the church, walking down the street, while the bulldozer rolls over her piano bed.

LIGHTS FADE—THE END

The Muses and The Maenads

"GRACE AND FURY"

A Grecian-American Musical Mystery Play

Ceil Gruessing   November 1998,
San Francisco, Ca

Apollo and the Nine Muses

Dionysus and the Maenads

The Muses and The Maenads

INTRODUCTORY NOTES

The following One Act Play, THE MUSES AND THE MAENADS, was written to fulfill a written discourse for a class called The History of Western Thought at California Institute of Integral Studies. As my focus and concentration in Philosophy and Religion deals with Sacred dance and theater, I have chosen the medium of a modern, one act, musical play to synthesize and deliver the information I have been exploring about Greek mythology of the Classical age. From earliest times the Greek legends and their literature abounded in references to dancing and dancers in the schools, at the athletic competitions, at the festivals, and as an act of worship. Dance was a language of prayer, praise, and dedication, a means of attaining union with the divinities.

The dichotomy between Apollonian and Dionysian principles, as the combined chemistry for dramatic tragedy, has always fascinated me. Friedrich Nietzsche defined it for me in The Birth of Tragedy . . . that when these two polarities confront each other in life, or on stage, where neither is right nor wrong, it is the recipe for tragedy. And in ancient theater the only way to resolve it was for the chorus to cry out in song. My travels through theater and life have constantly revealed the challenge of this struggle as the impetus for an artist's creativity.

These two brothers, bound by blood, are dedicated to the expression of their completely different souls. Apollo represents precision, lyrical harmony, propriety, tradition, and respect, calling for the light, the establishment and the pursuit of individuation and the heavenly dream. The inspirational Muses are his entourage. The nine muses originate in Greek Myths as deities who gave philosophers, artists and scientists the inspiration to create. Hesiod called them "Moises". In Greek "mosis" means wish or desire.

His brother Dionysus, God of the grape vine and nature, represents the green man, symbolizing death and rebirth, sacrifice, transformation, debauch and madness. He takes us underground with his Maenads to a dark creative world where the spirit merges with the divine. I believe that all human beings reflect and balance these opposite qualities within themselves, in one form or another.

Cecilia Anne Gruessing, M.A.

In my story, Apollo (Paul) is the director of a private high-class school of the arts and sciences where sophisticated girls can become modern day Muses. It is the year 2000. Our story opens at THE MUSES SCHOOL OF ARTS AND SCIENCES in the hills of San Francisco. Under the direction of Paulo Goodman, and his sister Artemisia, the school has pursued the ideals of their late mother, Olympia Mnemosyne, who originally built THE TEMPLE OF DELPHI and founded the school for young women to be highly educated under the disciplinary concepts of the great God Apollo. They are being groomed to compete intellectually and academically with the enlightened power circles of the world in the new millennium. The curriculum is focused on high level math, science, history, philosophy and literature, as well as the classical arts of music, poetry, dance and theater. The nine positions in the company are only open to talented students who fit the characteristics of the nine classical Muses.

Paulo is in conflict with his brother Dion Goodman, who sings in a successful punk rock band, with his female musicians and singer/dancers, the "Maenads". In Greek Mythology, the Maenads were wild "roving women" who followed Dionysus with savage ceremonial rites in nature.

The school is holding a fundraiser in which they invite wealthy intellectuals who represent famous Greek philosophers. Dion shows up at the fundraising performance with his Maenads to set the stage for tragedy as all hell breaks loose. The contrast between the two groups of strikingly different women provides ample possibilities for song, dance, and drama in musical theater format.

The musical numbers are not developed in this work and would be strategically instrumental in developing further expression of the characters and story. Lyrics must eventually be reworked to accommodate original music, and choreography, although classical poetry is used here from public domain sources.

Each dance also enters a mystical realm with homage to antiquity, ritual, and ceremony, providing a philosophical journey for the reader. I have mostly tried to elaborate upon the conceptual dichotomy between Apollo and Dionysus. This mythical dialectic is intended to illustrate the parallel conflicts between Apollonian and Dionysian principles within our own present-day psyches, our relationships, families, and cultures. This is very evident by the contrasts in dress and performance styles of the Muses and the Maenads, as they reflect the philosophical differences.

STYLE AND SET

STYLE— The school area represents a time warp. Visually, the decor demonstrates a synthesis of the old Greek Hellenic era of classical decor mixed with the comforts of 21st century life. As pedestrians, the characters are contemporary, but inside the school, in order to maintain the intellectual Greek spirit, all students, teachers, and guests are asked to dress in the period costume of the day (togas) in this academic/temple setting.

SET— The stage is divided into 4 areas. SR (Stage Right) houses a classroom area surrounded by Grecian columns interspersed with marble statues of the 9 Muses. A large white conference table occupies the triangular, raised area with several Grecian benches and stools. USC (Up Stage Center) sits the hearth and the altar with a huge statue of Apollo central, flanked by the goddess Artemis and Mnemosyne (Goddess of Memory and mother of the Muses) on either side. SL (Stage left) supports another triangular raised platform portraying a Library with bookshelves, TV, computer, and area to sit, study, practice and discuss forum style. The Central stage area is open and reserved for choreography and large group scenes. The pit can be used for "off stage activity" and as an audience.

SCENE BREAKDOWN

1. **Hestia Lights the Fire**..page *352*
2. **Entrance of Artemis** (Misha).................................page 352
3. **Rehearsal** — The Muses ....page 353
4. **Entrance of Apollo** (Paul)—The Announcement.....................page 354
5. **Sibling Rivalry**— Apollo and Dionysus ....page 356
6. **Party Preparation** ....page 358
7. **Arrival of the Guests** —The Greeting Dance...........................page 358
8. **Formal Introductions**..page 358
9. **Hesiod** — The Invocation of the Muses......................page 361
10. **Pythagoras**.. **page** 365
11. **Interlude** — Siblings ....page 367
12. **Plato** .... **page** 368
13. **Euripides** .... **page** 370
14. **Dion Donates** — Paul Acts Out................................page 372
15. **Romantic Duets**...page 376
16. **Ceci Returns**...page 380
17. **Dion and the Maenads** — "The Bacchae"..............page 382
18. **The Pythia Speaks**..page 387
19. **Resurrection and Convocation of
    The Double God by the Triple Goddess** ....page 390

The Muses and The Maenads

CAST OF CHARACTERS

- **Hestia**— The Aunt (sister to Zeus) to Apollo, Artemis, and Dionysus— Grandmother of the school— Crone mother to the Muses, protectress of vestal virgins, guardian of the hearth, cook, house manager— dedicated, humble, gentle, reserved (60 to 70 years old).

- **Apollo**— God of Healing, music, prophecy, the sun. — Son of Zeus, older brother of Artemis. Played by Paul Goodman, Director of The Muse School— ambitious, educated, well-groomed, physically fit, perfectionist, demanding, homosexual, establishment oriented, but artistically driven (mid 40's)

- **Artemis**— Goddess of the Hunt— Apollo's younger sister, MISHA, co-director of school, "older sister" to the Muses, boyish, athletic, nature oriented, choreographer, protective, but formal and distant. (30's)

- **Calliope**— Leader of Muses, her specialty is epic and heroic poetry, holds a writing tablet and stylus, and has a beautiful voice. She is interested in politics, strong, intelligent, basic, no frills.

- **Clio**— Muse of history, holds a roll of parchment. She is academic and the proclaimer, wears glasses, very responsible, knows her facts, and likes to gossip.

- **Euterpe**— Muse of music— she plays flute, sings, and dances well. She is slender and quiet, and extremely lyrical and feminine, hardworking, and attentive.

- **Thalia**— Muse of Comic and Idyllic poetry— holds a comic mask and carries a shepherd's crook. She is a bit overweight, laughs a lot, loves children, flowers, and food.

- **Melpomene**— Muse of tragic poetry— holds a tragic mask— She is dark, beautiful, and dramatic— a woman of few words, she writes, is romantic, heavy, with a strong operatic voice.

- **Polyhymnia**— Muse of Sacred Poetry and Hymns— one finger raised to her lips. Plays the piano, very spiritual, very priestess-like, takes care of the altar.

- **Urania**— Muse of Astronomy and Science— Holds a globe/stethoscope. The astrologer, the science wiz, interested in everybody, healer mentality.
- **Erato**— Muse of lyric and erotic poetry— the beautiful, manicured blond singer dancer who plays guitar and is simply enchanting; always sweet, accommodating, and attractive.
- **Terpsichore**— (Theoclea)— Muse of dance and choral poetry— an adolescent girl who really studied with Pythagoras, who was a dancer and became a pythoness at the Oracle at Delphi. Well-trained dancer/performer
- **Ceci**— The former Terpsichore; a great dancer, who has dropped out of the Muses school to switch over to Dion's rock n roll lifestyle.
- **Plato,** Robert— Philosopher, speaks over exquisitely, a bit snobby, friend of Apollo (40-50)
- **Pythagoras,** Tony — Attractive, spiritual, scientific, open minded, romantic genius (40-50)
- **Hesiod,** Frank— Overweight, conservative, jolly, bald, romantic, friendly poet (50-60)
- **Euripides,** Bill—Young, dark, fashionable, tragic, sarcastic, hip, on the edge writer (30-40)
- **Dionysus/Dion**— God of Wine, Creativity— as DION, younger brother of Apollo, rock singer, dresses wild, long hair, somewhat feminine, outspoken, drinks, excessive, great wit, speaks his mind despite disapproval, loves women, loves himself, knows darkness (20's)
- **Nine Maenads**— originally the wild followers of Dionysus. Here they are the female musicians, singers, and dancers in Dion's band. They are tatooed, pierced, and savage.
- **Three male satyrs**

The Muses and The Maenads

Scene 1— Hestia lights the fire— Dawn Friday 9/27/2000

A solitary torch illuminates an altar USC. As dawn breaks to the sound of stringed instruments, an older woman holding a candle enters the stage dressed as a priestess and begins to activate the altar. She is Hestia[1]. The music progresses and eight young women approach from the back of the theater in contemporary street clothes. In the orchestra pit, they change into their muse tunics and dance regalia which are in lockers. We hear mystical "Madrugada music" in the background as they organize their books, instruments, and Muse props, lyres, flutes, etc. They approach each of their individual Muse statues where they light a candle and then sing their prayers in unison as a chorus.

SONG about inspiration

The dance muse, Terpsichore is missing, and Hestia sees this. She rings the altar bell to cue the introduction of a ritual warm up that connects *them to each other and the altar. The music has a liturgical quality and gradually swells as they begin their stretching choreography.*

Scene 2— Artemis (Misha) Goodman

Misha (Artemis) enters with Theoclea near the end of the warm-up, both dressed in tunic like dance work out clothing.[2] (FN, Ginner, pg 154)

Misha: Good morning, ladies, and thank you for agreeing to this extra early rehearsal hour. As you know, we may have lost our Terpsichore, Ceci, who I understand may drop out to work with our brother Dion (Dionysus). However, I am sure she is nothing more than a glorified groupie in Dion's show, better known on the street as the "Mad Maenads". We are hoping she comes to her senses within the next hour, otherwise…... I must fill the role of Terpsichore immediately.

Theoclea: *With great ambition…* I want you to know Miss Misha that I would do anything in my power to step into this role at any time. This would be a dream for me.

The girls react to this shocking information because Ceci was an important part of the company. They know that there is conflict between the brothers, and they gossip about it.

Misha: We must discuss this with Paulo first, and I thank you for your cooperation. *She turns to the group.* May I remind you girls that the school frowns upon this form of expression for young ladies and we hope that cultural exposure to rock bands such as ***Cybelle and The Korybants, Orpheus and The White Dice, and The Bacchus Babes*** doesn't distract you from your studies and your dedicated worship of Apollonian principles. Nevertheless, we do wish Ceci well one way or the other.

She continues.

Now girls, I would like to introduce you to Theoclea who works with the Nymphs in the Junior class, and she has been chosen to understudy Terpsichore because of her outstanding skills as a dancer and of course her excellent academic work. *Theoclea smiles and stands up tall.* We must recreate the choreography for Theoclea as soon as possible because I suspect that Paul has plans to debut the ballet sooner than we think.

May I have a short meeting with Theoclea, Melpomene, and Thalia to discuss reworking several of the parts she must learn this afternoon after the run-through.

Misha, Theoclea, Melpomene and Thalia go to work introducing Theoclea to Terpsichore's choreography. The other Muses take this break and continue to gossip about Ceci's shift to the Maenads. They agree that she was unhappy and needed more freedom, and that despite all her discipline, she was a dancing fool, drank wine, and was always crazy about Dion.

Misha: *(returning to the group)*— I suggest running through without Terpsichore the first time to estimate the damage and the repair. Are we ready girls? Places please.

Scene 3 — Rehearsal— Invocation of the Muses

REHEARSAL CHOREGRAPHY— The Muse Ballet Rehearsal

Narrated voiceover:

"Born from the skirts of Mnemosyne", the 9 muses emerge to sing, dance, and glorify memory in three movements: Past— Coming out of the mist; Present— reflecting the fleeting moment; Future— Divining our desires and capturing inspiration."

All this is done to a shortened version of **"Invocation to the Muses" by Hesiod** *(in full version in Scene 9), which is recited, sung, danced, acted out and staged with mystical formality.*

Musical Rehearsal Review of the Muse Ballet

The music begins. The girls dance their parts. Artemis takes notes, Theoclea watches nervously dancing behind the choreography. Stopping 2 or 3 times, Artemis tries to explain the entrances and exits to Theoclea as the new Terpsichore. There is tension in the group.

Scene 4— Apollo (Paul) Goodman— The announcement

Paul (Apollo) enters in the final movement of the ballet and is moved, watching his choreography as if it were his own child, falling, flying, hitting the mark, dissolving, struggling for perfection, order and reason. At the end he applauds.

Paul: It is your mission ladies, to inspire the hearts and minds of men to the higher insights of life and love. This evening the perfect opportunity has presented itself with a fundraising dinner we are throwing for four potential patrons who are visiting and would like to see some of our work. *The girls take excited deep breaths and Theoclea panics.* The transits are perfect with the full moon rising at 8pm. Misha, this is indeed a marvelous work in progress to exhibit. Can it be ready at 8pm along with the preparations for the house and dinner?

Misha: I don't know Paul . . . we don't know about Ceci, who really knows the part. She is not here, and this is will not be a quick fix.

Paul: Now Ceci never misses school. She will be here soon.... And fortunately, I see we have an excellent understudy with great technique.

Hestia: Paul darling, what would you like to serve for dinner and for how many?

Apollo: Something delightful and vegetarian Mother Hestia, and of course the girls will help you. Won't we ladies?

*The Muses chatter nervously, delighted with the excitement of a party and a performance. They reassure Theoclea about the choreography and build her up. They talk about missing Ceci. Others talk about the **Dion and the Maenads** concert last night where all the women went crazy.*

Paul: *(louder)* Won't we help Mother Hestia to put the temple together for our grand FESTIVAL OF THE MUSES on this mysterious Fall Friday, Full moon night? Yes Ladies? (*The girls quickly reply positively.*) I have been remiss about committing to a date for our annual fundraiser, and now some famous writers are in town to visit the school. Hence ladies… the Muse ballet opens tonight!!

The girls can't believe they will actually perform tonight. They chatter about that.

Misha: I think they want to know who's coming to the dinner.

The phone rings. She answers it. Paul answers the question.

Paul: It is a surprise for the moment ladies, because you would surely die of nervousness if I told you. Just be on your best behavior, as our future depends on it.

The girls beg him to give them a clue, but he teases them and promises them it will be a night to remember with a full moon and excellent financial transits. He takes the phone.

Misha: Paul, it's Dion, and he wants to come to the party tonight before he goes on tour tomorrow.

Paul rolls his eyes, trying not to lose his train of thought. He covers the phone……

Paul: OK I'm excusing all the Muses from academic study today to concentrate on this very important ballet debut, OK? Does everyone know what to do Misha?

Misha: Yes Paul. Say hello to Theoclea the new girl from the San Francisco Ballet. I have arranged for her to cover for Ceci as Terpsichore, because because . . .. I don't know how to tell you this Paul .

Paul: Straight out with any bad news, OK?

Misha: *She races with the words.* Because we think that Ceci might be dropping out after dancing with Dion's Maenads last night at the rock concert downtown.

Long pause, as Paul digests this.

Paul: Give me the phone. *He shakes Theoclea's hand with misgiving as he takes the phone.* Yes, it's very nice to meet you, welcome to the Muses.

Theoclea: *(nervously)* Of course I am honored Mr. Goodman. Thank you very much. I just hope I can learn all the choreography in a few hours.

Paul: My dear Theo . . . A good muse always rises to the occasion.

He takes the phone aside and shifts character drastically into sibling rivalry with his brother Dion. The Muses continue rehearsing in the background. Misha focuses on Theoclea.

Scene 5 — Sibling Rivalry

Dion appears on the cell phone stuffed into a limousine with his band of exotic Maenad women.

Paul: All right Dion Goodman, this is it— now you are abducting my students?

Dion: Paulo, what are you talking about?

Paul: Ceci Diaz, my Terpsichore and top ballerina, who has been here for three years, went to your concert last night, and in a sudden burst of adolescent passion has switched camps to the world of debauchery and rock and roll. What will I tell her parents? She did not show up today!!! And we have to perform this evening.

Dion: I have no idea who she is Paulo. I sang for thousands of screaming females last night and partied with the Maenads after that. I did not abduct a muse.

Paul: Tell me Dion, what exactly is it that you do on stage? Is it legal? Whatever it is, I know Mom would disapprove. Are you going to your AA Meetings?

Dion: Are you taking your Rogaine? How about that Viagra? I'm sure you've tried that.

Paul: Don't change the subject. I'm missing a Muse Dion.

Dion: Look Paul, I refuse to feel guilty about your missing Muse, which I had no conscious part of— and what's more I'm calling you now, only as your flesh and blood brother. Can you forget all the disapproval for five bloody minutes? I'm doing pretty good now, I've got money, and a following. I want to pay back the money I owe you. Can I come over tonight?

At the sound of money, Paul relinquishes his aggression and opens up.

Paul: Uh huh . . . OK, I just need to calm down. *He breathes.* First of all, I am very happy that you are finally making money. That's good news. So, let's make a deal. I will graciously extend an invitation to you for our fundraising gala that we are throwing this evening, on the condition that you do not try to attract and convert any of the remaining Muses who will be dancing tonight. We will be performing for their parents and some very important celebrity guests.

Dion: A deal is a deal . . . Thank you, big brother, I'm truly honored. And so, what do you suggest I tell my Maenads? Are they invited?

Paul: I'm sorry Dion, that's as far as I can take the spontaneous factor tonight, with you alone. And please wear something civilized … OK?

Dion: Fine, Paul, I'll leave the babes in the bar, and their furs in the car. See you later.

Scene 6 — Party preparations

The Muses are preparing for the event. There is background music with a small orchestra. The pit can be used for this on/off stage activity. Melpomene, Thalia, and the new Terpsichore work on the fractured ballet. Elaborate fruit and flower displays are arranged and hung. Wreathes and garlands are placed on the statues. Hestia puts the girls to work on food and Misha attempts to fit costumes for the evening performance. There is an air of excitement as the festivity fills the temple with aromas, sounds, energy, and inspired creativity.

Scene 7— Arrival of Guests— Greeting Pyrrhic Dance

The music and the lights change as the parents and guests arrive. The Muses take their position next to their statues, and angelic music fills the air, as four very scholarly male guests in togas enter the room. Apollo greets each one and introduces them to the Muses: Frank Hesiod, Tony Pythagoras, Bill Euripides, and Robert Plato. Each guest is greeted by two Muses and escorted to the dance floor. Calliope dances with Apollo, and Artemis leads the group in a Sacred Greeting Dance which first honors the altar with bows and song. Next, the nine Muses circle and honor each other, then proceed in a dance exhibition of strength and dexterity locking, leaning, and lifting each other in civilized yet, martial style. Each guest is invited to interact individually with each Muse in some metaphoric form of combat or dance confrontation known as the **Pyrrhic dance.**[3] *(Lawler pg. 108) The dance becomes fiery and rhythmic, exciting and dangerous, to a climax which has honored the Gods, and broken the ice and a sweat for everybody. Hestia serves water from the sacred spring, famed by the Muses for inspiration.*[4] *(Encyclopedias of Religion & Ethics: Muses pg.4)*

And suddenly Dion appears at the door in full rock regalia.

Scene 8 — Formal Introductions— Artemis and Apollo

There is a hush, until Misha goes to her brother, Dion and greets him. The Muses seat the guests of honor and begin to serve dinner. They are clearly distracted by the appearance of Dion. Some of the Muses form a small orchestra and play softly. Paulo leaves to compose himself off stage and Misha takes her place on stage to speak.

Artemis: Ladies and Gentlemen, Welcome to Delphi, San Francisco, The Muses School of Arts and Sciences, and our annual Festival of the Muses. History has taught us that the Festival of the Muses promoted all the musical and poetic talent of later Greece. The study of the Muses shows us more and more that the origins of our philosophy, art, science, and religion came from the Hellenic period in the Helikon of Ancient Greece. As a school for women in the 21st century we feel an obligation to offer gifted young ladies the best educational opportunity possible to prepare them to lead the work forces of society in the future— To be priestesses, poets, and orators, as they inspire men, women, and children in the form of Deans, CEOs, doctors, lawyers, artists and leaders in the twenty first century.

They are gaining knowledge in math and science, and quantum physics, philosophy, language, history, and the fine, literary, and performing arts with professors who are the most learned educators in these fields. A muse must become suspended between reality and unreality, between history and fantasy, claiming the merits of both. We are free to say whatever we like as Muses, without losing our dedication to myth making. In a sense we are inventing the world we describe.[5] (Redfield, pg. 39) As well-educated women, with the gifts of mother nature, this is our license, and we are proud. This evening, we are especially honored to present the talent and intelligence of our "Nine Elected Muses" with their fine work in the arts. Our performing arts company, "Mousike", which is Greek for early dance, poetry, and singing… will show some of our work this evening. I am very proud to have directed and choreographed this work with my brother, our Director, Paulo Goodman who will now introduce our Muses. *Applause*

Paulo: My most gracious welcome to everyone here. It is sheer synchronicity on this star kissed night of the full moon to commune with some great minds who have been invited to share some of their brilliant knowledge with us. They have also come to witness our work in the art of mousike,[6] which is very much "the art of the Muses". Allow me to introduce our esteemed guests:

These special guests each stand and bow, consecutively.

1. **Frank Hesiod**— Music producer
2. **Tony Pythagoras**— Cosmic Scientist
3. **Robert Plato**— President of Yale
4. **Bill Euripides**— Director of Lincoln Center for the Performing Arts

   Paulo: *continues* Furthermore, The Muses School is rapidly growing. We are proud to educate and refine some of society's most intelligent and gifted young women and dedicate our mission to honoring the grace of our founder, the late Mrs. Olympia Mnemosyne.[7] (Farnell, pg. 437) As you know we are always looking for encouragement from today's philosophers and welcome all blessings in the name of the Gods. At this time, I would like my older sister Hestia to share a sentiment regarding the Muses from Homer and the Iliad—

   Hestia proudly takes her place on stage.

   Hestia: "With Apollo, the Muses choose and inspire those they wish. They are lyre players and singers, orators, dancers, and writers....and are able to make sorrow and grief disappear from mortal hearts with the songs they sing. Thus, when poets sing to Apollo and the Muses at the beginning of their songs, they put themselves under divine protection and inspiration. Invoking the Muse is the price the poet pays in order for his song to be truthful, and in order that he may be blessed with the imperishable memory and knowledge that the Muses alone bestow."[8] *(Encyclopedia of Religion (Muses)*

   Applause

   Paulo: Thank you, Hestia. We hope to train our women to make those contributions to society's poets, scientists, scholars, and statesmen. At this time, I will introduce the great writer Hesiod who has come with his "Invocation of the Muses" from his work, THEOGONY, to immortalize this wonderful ballet with our Muses. This is a great surprise for the girls, as they have been working with his poetic tributes for years, not knowing the man behind the voice. Ladies and Gentlemen, I give you ....Mr. Frank Hesiod and The Invocation of The Muses from Theogony—

Scene 9 — Hesiod, and The Invocation of the Muses Performance

Hesiod rises clutching his cane, and bows to the applause. He gallantly speaks as he struts around Apollo (Paul) who holds his lyre.

Hesiod: "In the midst of the dancers Apollo takes the lyre, beautiful and tall as he strides amongst us, alight with radiance. Brightly shine his feet and his raiment. Thus, he appears as Musagets, - "leader of the muses" and "singer to the lyre". For our ancient storytellers and poets, it is as if the sunlight has been turned into music."[9] (Kerenyi, Gods of the Greeks 149).

Hesiod turns to the audience. I am honored to be here this evening to delight in this divine collaboration with the powers of nine goddesses who have been the source of my inspiration since I have learned to be their servant. They help people forget their troubles and their suffering. Born of Memory also known as Mnemosyne, and Zeus, they graciously establish a moral and political order in the Universe which allows the poet, the politician, the teacher, the artist, or the scientist to draw upon instant knowledge and declare truth as in preaching an oracle. Let us "forget evils and cease all anxieties"[10](Athenian Myths and Inst.) and call upon them now to open this Festival of the Muses, with my very own Muse inspired "Invocation of the Muses."

INVOCATION OF THE MUSES Ballet

The following sequence is the choreographed poetry of Hesiod in the role of a shepherd, as the Muses dance and sing his poem. Apollo continues to play the lyre.

Hesiod: "The muses begin their choral dance on Helikon's summit
Ascend, veiled and misted in palpable air
Treading the night, and in a voice beyond beauty they summon the gods

Then they gave me a staff,
He trades his cane for a shepherd's staff which Thalia gives him.
A branch of good sappy laurel, and they breathed into me a

voice divine, so I might celebrate past and future.
And they told me to celebrate the generation of the eternal gods,
but always to sing of themselves, the Muses, first and last.
They thrill the great mind deep in Olympus,
telling what is, what will be, and what has been,
blending their voices, and weariless the sound
flows sweet from their lips and spreads like lilies,
and all is in bloom as they move in the dance,
intoning the careful ways of the Gods,
celebrating the customs of all the Immortals
in voices enchanting and sweet.
Then they proceed to Olympus,
in a glory of pure Sound and Dance,
and the black earth shrieks with delight as they sing,
and the drum of their footfalls rises like love"

Hesiod's Invocation to the Muses – from Theogeny

Artemis: These are the nine Muses born of Zeus and Mnemosyne:

*Here each girl takes a short **dancing** bow as Artemis presents them individually*

- **Thalia is our cheerful and joyous muse inspiring comedy and poetry.** *She carries a shepherd's staff and a comic mask.*
- **Urania is called "the heavenly one" as the muse of astronomy and is able to read the stars.** *She wears a cloak made of stars and carries a globe.*
- **Melpomene is the Muse of Tragedy and will inspire you to sing your sorrows with lyrical phrases.**
  She carries a tragic mask and a sword.
- **Polyhymnia represents the muse of sacred poetry, divine hymns and spiritual eloquence.** *She is very serious and holds a lyre.*
- **Erato inspires us with lyrical love and erotic poetry and cultivates beauty.** *She holds a golden arrow.*

- **Clio is the Celebrator and the Proclaimer as the muse of history and great deeds.** *She holds a scroll.*
- **Euterpe is our expert in musical instruments and is considered "She Who Pleases" and inspires composers.** *She carries a flute.*
- **Terpsichore makes us dance to express the joyful emotions in our souls.**
- **Calliope as the Muse of Epic Poetry with a beautiful voice, is the leader of the group because she imposes justice.** *She carries a writing tablet.*

Artemis continues:

Artemis: And now I present these lovely ladies in The Muse Ballet, after which we will ask our esteemed guests to speak of their dedication to the arts and sciences.

The music begins and the nine girls recite and dance individually *and choreography takes place behind them.*

From "Theogony" – by Hesiod

Clio: "We keep the company of reverent kings.
as the daughters of great Zeus will honor a lord
Whose lineage is divine, and look upon his birth,
distilling a sweet dew upon his tongue.

Euterpe: And from his mouth words flow like honey.
The people all look to him as he arbitrates settlements
with judgments straight. He speaks out in sure tones
and soon puts an end even to bitter disputes.

Thalia: A sound-minded ruler, when someone is wronged,
Sets things right in the public assembly,
Conciliating both sides with ease.

Melpomene: He comes to the meeting place propitiated as a God,
Treated with respect, preeminent in the crowd,
Knowing that he has been divinely inspired
And wants only to create a safe vessel for his people.

Terpsichore: Such is the Muses sacred gift to men
For though it is singers and lyre players,
that come from the Muses and far-shooting Apollo
Even kings are sent by Zeus, ...

Erato: Happy is any man whom the Muses love.
Sweet flows the voice from his mouth.
For if anyone is grieving, if his heart is sore,
they inspire joy if he is troubled,

Polyhymnia: If he is a singer who serves the Muses
chanting the deeds of past men
Or the blessed gods who have their homes on Olympus,
He soon forgets his heartache, and all his cares.
He remembers none: the goddesses gifts turn them aside.

Urania: We were born of Earth and starry Sky,
And of dusky Night, and of the salty Sea.
We tell how first the gods and earth came into being
and the rivers and the sea, endless and surging,
and the stars shining and the wide sky above.

Calliope: We know how to divide wealth and allot honors
We first possessed the deep-ridged Olympus,
Captivating the mind and soul of all who made the call . . ..
Statesmen, poets, leaders, priests, artists, athletes.
All have come forward, begging for our knowledge
And inspiration . . ..

Hesiod: Sing out these things, Olympian Muses"[11]
Culture bows to your brilliant talents.

(FN Theogony, Hesiod)
The ballet has ended, there is applause, and they all take bows.
Artemis guides Theoclea to the podium giving her notes to make an introduction

Scene 10 — Pythagoras

Theoclea: Good evening, I have been given the high honor this evening as the newest member of the Muses, Terpsichore, to introduce Mr. Anthony Pythagoras. *She tosses her notes and speaks from the heart.* This living genius is not only a brilliant mathematician, scientist, and philosopher, but he also has contributed so much to the validity of the metaphysical arts, which are very close to my heart. I want to thank the gods for bringing me to the doorstep of this wonderful role, as the Muse of the Dance, and now for bringing me to the feet of this great scholar, a man I've wanted to meet all my life *(she bows)* I give you Anthony Pythagoras.

Pythagoras: Thank you, my child. You are too generous. May I be worthy of your beautiful presentation and praise.
(He turns to the audience) "These Muses are only the earthly images of the divine powers whose immaterial and sublime beauty you will contemplate each one in yourself. Just as they have their eyes fixed upon the fire of Hestia, from which they spring, and which gives them movement, rhythm, and melody, so you must plunge into the central fire of the universe into the divine spirit, to mingle with this spirit in its visible manifestations."[12] Yes ladies, thank you for bringing us beauty, truth, and inspiration.

(Pythagoras & The Delphic Mysteries pg 88)

Pythagoras *continues:*

It would be an honor for me to remain here and share my knowledge with you as I am very interested in the Oracle at Delphi and the phenomenon of the Pythia.[13] (Schure, Great Initiates pg 294)

Your natural artistic powers provide me with a doctrine in which the harmony of the celestial spheres leads music toward astronomy and mathematics. Your beautiful song and dance provide the joy in life for our poets and politicians. I also believe that woman represents Nature. And the perfect image of God is not human loneliness. Here we are fascinated by the attraction and intoxication of Love, in which the dream of infinite desires and creations is played out. "Honor be to Woman, on earth as in heaven. She enables us to understand that mighty woman, Mother Nature."[14] *(Pythagoras and Delph Mysteries pg 92)*

*Applause ... **Pythagoras** continues:*

I also would like to pursue with the Muses, a work called the MAGNA GRAECIA, which is a recollection of lifetimes, in which the soul retraces the complete cycle of its former lives and manages to escape the wheel of rebirth. Ultimately one graduates to attain the existence of the Gods.[15] (Greek and Egyptian Myth pg 192)

*Everybody ooohs and aaahs. **Pythagoras** continues*

I am working on theories of prophecy and divination now after much traveling, and I hope to find here amongst you, women who are interested in becoming Pythoness priestess. Is there anyone who would like to pursue this training?

All the girls are thrilled at this sudden opportunity, but Theoclea responds instantly.

Theoclea *(raises her hand)*: Yes Pythagoras, I believe I have the gift for this work and would like nothing more than to serve the Gods in this capacity under your guidance.

Pythagoras: Clearly, I see the violet light around your countenance and would gladly give you every opportunity to serve your countrymen, your school, and your Gods in this divine practice. We will talk more later.

Scene 11— Interlude— siblings

Despite the profound impact of Pythagoras's words, there is a certain discomfort that Paul expresses over the obvious romantic attraction between Pythagoras and Theoclea/Terpsichore.

This is an aside conversation as everyone talks amongst themselves.

Paul *(to Misha)*: I hope we don't lose her next. What is it with these dancers? They are insatiable . . . . They follow anybody . . .

Misha: You've trained them to obey. What do you expect from ballerinas? I say they need to perform more, stop dancing for the mirror, get some real public attention, develop some self-esteem.

Paul: OK..OK..Misha, But right now I'm just worried about their hormones. *He addresses Dion who is sitting next to him.* Do me a favor Dion and make an extra effort to stay away from my girls tonight.

Dion: Hey bro, I don't solicit, beckon, or call anybody, they just arrive at my feet. I don't need girls. I have girls— maids, mothers, and crones, wherever I turn. So, you can be sure that I am not interested in any of your little virgins.

Misha: *(to Dion)* Don't push him, he's very nervous.

Dion: Nervous? He's neurotic. What are you guys doing here? Trying to raise money or jack up the egos of these sheltered teenagers? I don't see anybody writing checks. You want money, let's talk money.

Misha: *(Whispering again to Dion)* We will discuss donations later, OK?

Scene 12— Plato

Calliope has taken the podium.

Calliope: I have been asked to introduce another one of the most famous men in the whole world, the King of Thinking, The Father of Philosophy, and the Prince of Justice. His words are the lyrics to my songs, the wisdom in my heart, and the wings for my melodies. His work has been the epiphany of our culture, chiseling magnificent language from marble into sculpted thought. We are truly blessed to be in his perfect presence. Ladies and Gentlemen, I give you Robert Plato.

With the applause Plato takes the floor ceremoniously before speaking.

Plato: Thank you for inviting me. This is a truly exquisite forum we are so fortunate to attend this evening in the lap of luxury. I am touched by the talent of these young ladies. "Beauty of style and harmony and grace and good rhythm depend upon simplicity. I mean the true simplicity of a rightly and nobly ordered mind and character. If our youth are to do their work in life, must they not make these graces and harmonies their perpetual aim? Let our artists be those who are gifted to discern the true nature of the beautiful and graceful, then will our youth dwell in a land of health amid fair sights and sounds and receive the good in everything."[16] *(Ginner, pg 6)*   *Applause*

As you know, "I have given great attention to the importance of dance in education in my treatise on THE LAWS. That the dance as a whole including song is identical with education as a whole. That the uneducated man is "achoreutos, 'danceless' and that the educated man is one suitably 'endowed with the dance' "kechoreukos". (Plato's discourse on <u>The Laws</u>)

Applause - **Plato** *continues*

Plato: "It is the natural instinct of all creatures to move and especially to move with certain rules of periodicity; for the principle exists within us in the beating of our arteries, and around us in the flight of birds, the canter of horses, the ebb and flow of the sea."[17] *(Grove, pg 36)* However, there are two kinds of dance and music, the noble, what is fine and honorable, and the ignoble, what is mean and ugly.

Dion *(to Paulo)*: OK here we go on the Saint brigade!!

Plato *continues:* "I would have all children, boys and girls alike, instructed from an early age in noble music and dancing, and would spur them on with contests. I would give to official's absolute power to exclude from the schools and from public performances, all unworthy rhythms and harmonies, steps and gestures. Music and dancing should be consecrated to the gods . . . in as much as the gods themselves dance and create dance. Noble dances should confer on the student not only health and agility and beauty of the body, but also goodness of the soul and a well-balanced mind . . ."[18] *(Kraus pg 37)*

Plato throws a special condescending look to Dion.

Dion: Why do I feel I'm about to get roasted?

Plato *continues*: "Dancing serves to moderate four dangerous passions . . . . fear, melancholy, anger, and joy; fear and melancholy are relieved by rendering the body active, supple, light and tractable, while the frenzy of the two other passions is calmed by regular movements. Ideally, dance should be a joy, and a gentle, agreeable agitation caused by the effusion of the spirits which, rising in the heart, spread themselves abundantly through the whole body."[19] *(Vuillier pg. 48)*

As for violent, animal like movement and behavior, attached to orgiastic rituals, I would impose heavy penalties upon these practices and put them to an immediate stop.

Dion: I beg your pardon your eminence. I hope you are not referring to my work sir.

Paul: Dion please!!!

Plato goes on and Paul is very uncomfortable with Misha telling him to relax. Misha pulls Dion away from the festivities.

Plato: "These wild, savage and uncivilized outbursts, however, seem to satisfy an emotional need in these rituals with their violent bodily movements to really free troubled persons from their inner conflicts and frenzy and restore peace to their souls."20 *(Lawler, pg 96)* Crazy madness I call it.

Dion: *shouting from aside—* You know Mr. Plato; you are truly brilliant. Are you having an affair with my brother? He's a perfectionist too you know. I believe you both would get on fabulously.

Plato pretends not to hear, and Paul is about to explode.

Plato: With respect to the work my dear friend, Paul Goodman is doing here, I would like to make a modest donation of $50,000 to The School of the Muses.

Paul has been struggling with Dion's retorts, and finally rises to embrace Plato with deep emotion and honor amidst great applause.

Paul: We are all truly honored by your words, as they have inspired me, they will continue to inspire future generations. I thank you from my heart for your gift. *He bows to Plato.*

Scene 13 — Euripides

Dion: Thank you, professor. May I speak?

Paul: The honorable Mr. Euripides was on the agenda next, I believe.

Misha rises to introduce Euripides, but Dion has taken the stage.

Dion: And with your permission, I would be honored to introduce him. *Dion gestures towards Bill Euripides who stands and bows.*
I wish to honor a great scholar and playwright, now the President of Yale University, and also the author of THE BACCHAE, and many other famous Greek tragedies and comedies. I give the floor to Euripides, nonother than my ally and the chief promotor of 'My Wine Women and Song Retreat', previously known as the Dionysian Mysteries. Mr. Euripides is also the lyricist of our hit songs "Rhapsody Rock" and "The Grapes of Nirvana." Ladies and gentlemen, Give it up for Bill Euripides!!

Euripides: I gladly share this moment with you Dion, as so much of what I have to say about these lovely young ladies relates to the current conflict among young people in society today, especially with regards to your cult.
But first, I must commend the hard work and energy devoted to this glorious Festival with the most exquisite of presentations and libations. I am honored to be here and must certainly write of the blessings of the Muses, for you are truly magical, idyllic, inspirational and seductive for all dreamers. I am a writer. As I invoke the Muses to raise me into truthful light, using my knowledge and wisdom to create some meaning of the human condition, I am also fascinated by the tragedy of life (Oh, yes… the dark side) And I see the function of this polarity provided for natural balance by your God of the Grape and Song, Dionysus.

However, I feel that the Temple of Delphi, is not honestly being represented by these two famous brothers who depict these polarities. I know and respect Apollo well, his devotion to tradition and harmony, strength and reason. But I also know Dionysus, as he was the star of my most famous work, "The Bacchae", which Dion has transformed into a musical hit, now airing on MTV. But, for all you perfectionists out there, you must see the act before you judge it; for the summoning of nature, vegetation, fertility and creativity takes you where you need to go to regulate your dark side.

Euripides *continues:*

How do I know this? Because I have teenage daughters, and I was a teenager once. The Maenads[21] give women a chance to unfold what has been gestating within them: joyous, dark, innocent and savage. In "The Bacchae", Pentheus is drawn to spy on the maenads, frenzied female worship of Dionysus whom Pentheus' mother and aunts have joined, ultimately summoning his own tragic death. Murdered by his mother, Agave, torture of tortures, we see these dark themes living in a brutal tragedy, created by maligned aspirations long fermenting within. These feelings are released by the wine and the dancing and must be absorbed by the universe despite their poisonous exhaust.

What I see is suppression run amuck. Darkness, that is the creative, natural moonlight of mother earth, needs that underground fertility to unfold the root of her seed and nurture the embryo so that it may safely rest and grow in the darkness. I say Paul, we must not exclude that which provides conflicting and polarizing perspectives. We must seek balance.

Dion, how is it, that your Maenads did not accompany you this evening to contribute to this delightful entertainment? I would be so honored to share the success of your musical hit with the ladies who have helped sell it. I would also like to understand how in three short weeks, as the lyricist of a number one hit song, I have made more money than in 2000 years of forty-five published and performed plays!! It may only be rock and roll, but I like it.

And I too would like to contribute $50,000 to the Academy, vis a vis the royalties I have made with Dion Goodman. Ladies and Gentlemen, with great "enthusiasmos" I bring back the man who introduced me to rock n roll an internationally growing musical star, Dion Goodman!!

Scene 14 — Dion Donates— Paul Acts Out

Dion: Thank you, Euripides for your perspective and your support. However, I believe that this evening's function was that of a fundraiser, and not a talent show. Yet I'm actually quite honored to see the work of my brother and sister and know that we all share a common love for music, poetry and the dance. And for that reason, with my own recent success as an entertainer I would like to give $90,000 to the school to continue its fine work with women and the arts.

He gives the check to Hestia.

**The Muses react with big wows, the scholars applaud, Misha and Hestia hug Dion, and Paul is dumbfounded and humbled as he takes the check from Hestia.*

Misha: In the name of the Gods and the School of the Muses we thank you, Plato, Pythagoras, Hesiod, Euripides, and Dion, for your support and divine presence this evening, because your blessings and teachings are what validate our work as the sculptors of tomorrow's female leaders.

There is applause, out of which Paul loses control and explodes.

Paul: It's the madness I can't stand Dion!!! Those women parading around pounding their chests and tearing their hair out— the wild shrieks, and the incessant drumming— the erotic insanity—
Misha tries to restrain him in this public demonstration of emotional insanity, but Paul continues......
the men turn into the animals, the women transform into prostitutes then flip suddenly into freakish demons tearing deer, goats, and live bulls apart with their teeth, and washing it all down with
the juice of nature's grapes, until the blood and the wine mix and embrace everyone in exhausted sleep. This is madness I care not to touch dear brother, not for my family, my students, or my countrymen.

Dion: And what do you call your mighty Oracle with the Pythia sessions which only your chosen priests can witness? I'm told that these poor women sit there on the tripod over the fissure in the rock until any random entity would enter their tired, unprotected vessels, and the priests then read their mumbo jumbo however they jolly well please.

Paul: This work is oracular truth from the Gods. How dare you? And my Muses would never go stark raving mad, attacking anything in their path like savage animals pretending to embody the gods.

Dion growls at him.

Dion: Anybody and anything can enter and dominate a weak spirit.

Pythagoras: Perhaps when there are voices from the other side, they are not always the voices of the Gods, and it is not madness at all, but the voices of disincarnate humans claiming the character of Apollo—as riveting as the Maenad's are when they are possessed by the very spirits of hungry animals.

Paul: No, my brother is just plain crazy that's all. He can't feel anything unless it is loud, chaotic, bestial, and black.

Dion: Take that back or I'll sig my girls on you.

Dion and Paul continue a private argument during Plato's following monologue.

Plato: Since we are discussing this madness, which seems to be a mysterious human characteristic, I have some studies to share with you. I believe that there are four distinctive states of mind at work when the creative forces of the human mind become sensitive to the messages from the spirit world. I would like to offer some clarity to the situation perhaps. *(Dodds pg. 64)*

We have first Prophetic expression from the patron God Apollo;
Telestic or ritual expression from Dionysus.
Poetic expression coming from the Muses.
And erotic expression with Aphrodite and Eros[22] *(pg. 69 Dodds)*

Plato *continues:*

I propose that Apollonian mediumship is the rare gift of chosen individuals. The Dionysiac experience is essentially congregational and is so far from being a rare gift that it is highly infectious. The use of wine and religious dance has no part whatever in the induction of Apollonian ecstasy.

Dion: And now ladies and gentlemen, we blame the grape. What happened to intellectual discourse and the passion of dichotomy?

Hesiod steps in to intervene.

Hesiod: Dionysus offers all of us catharsis— one can be cleansed of those infectious irrational impulses which, when dammed up, have given rise, as they have done in outbreaks of dancing mania and collective hysteria. This trance relieves them by providing them with a ritual outlet. Both Dionysus and Apollo are social necessities ministering in their own ways to the anxiety's characteristic of a privileged culture. Apollo promises security: "Know thyself, Nothing in Excess; Understand your station as man; do as the father tells you, and you will be safe tomorrow." Dionysus offers us freedom. Forget the difference, and you will find the identity, join the parade and be happy today"[23]. *(Dodd pg 76)*

They both have taught us the true meaning of "enthusiasmos"— to be filled with the spirit of the Gods.[24] *(Lawler, Ancient Greeks pg. 76)*

Dion: Thank you, dear Hesiod, for your words of clarity. *Dion fills his Glass.* Would anyone like more wine?

Pythagoras: Fill my glass and let me speak. "In Orphic thought, Dionysus and Apollo were two different revelations of the same divinity. Dionysus represented esoteric truth, the foundation and interior of things open to initiates alone. He held the mysteries of life, past and future existences, the relations between soul and body, heaven and earth. Apollo personified the same truth applied to life on earth and social order. The inspirer of poetry, medicine, and laws, he was science by divination, beauty by art, peace among nations by justice, and harmony between soul and body by purification. Dionysus means nothing less than the evolving divine spirit in the universe, and Apollo his manifestation to earthly man.[25] *(Pythagoras, Delphic Mysteries pg. 34)*

Euripides: I propose that you, Dionysus, round up your famous revel-rousing Maenads and Bacchantes, and invite them - as we speak, to come partake of our festivities and perform their talents in our presence for us to witness this magic. That is of course, Paulo, if you have no objections.

Paul: *With sarcasm...* I must apologize, as I am clearly in my brother's grace, *(handing him the cell phone).* Therefore, I open these temple doors to the music and art of my brother Dion on one strict and formal condition. A promise that no blood will be shed on these floors now or ever.

Dion: And I accept this invitation, if of course your precious Muses will grant the stage to my wild Maenads and the bloodless reenactment of the Dionysian Rites with the festival of Thiasos.[26] (Ginner pg. 57)

Muses: *They squeal out loud uncontrollably, looking for Paul's approval.*

Paul: Agreed *(he sighs reluctantly)* .... So where are these girls now?

Dion: Down the street at the local Irish Pub waiting for me to cue their entrance.

Paul: By all means, call them. *Fixing the music and having a drink.* Meanwhile, Misha.... Shall we dance? *They begin the social dancing, accompanied by modern Greek lounge music.*

Euripides: Well then, it's settled. Bring on more girls. Let's pass the jug and get on with our symposium.

Scene 15— Romantic Duets

There is open dancing and the scholars dance with the Muses to a romantic ballad sung by EUTERPE. They all pair off in their couples for duets. Each couple performs a choreography with their dialogue. Apollo/Artemis; Pythagoras and Theoclea (Terp); Hesiod and Erato; Plato and Urania; Melpomene and Euripides.

Dion gets on the phone, while Clio, Polyhymnia, Calliope, and Thalia surround him.

Dion: *Calling the girls by phone at the local bar.* Hello, who's this? Samantha, what's going on? *He listens....* OK well bottoms up and load up the limo; they want to see the Bacchae over here at my brother's school of Muses right up the street from the pub. Samantha, how many drinks? Well, that's enough. — I will expect you in a half hour, OK? Put it on my tab and get in the car.

PYTHAGORAS AND TERPSICHORE (Theoclea)

Pythagoras: *Approaching Theo.* May I have the pleasure of this dance, Terpsichore?

Terpsichore/Theo: By all means……..*(they dance and their synchronization is exceptionally beautiful)*

Pythagoras: It doesn't take a genius to know that something unusual

is happening here.

Terpsichore/Theo: Yes, I'm melting in your arms … and it's happening so fast that it won't be long before I evaporate from sheer ecstasy.

Pythagoras: Already I feel like you follow me like a shadow.

Terpsichore/Theo: I am your shadow, and I can expand your power in the darkness.

Pythagoras: *Stops dancing to check his erotic attraction.* First, I must share my knowledge with you, and we must refine this wonderful talent you have, for I can see that you are an open channel, pure and of high light, but vulnerable, and you must be guided with proper wisdom. This is my mission, and we will dance together, *(Starts dancing again)* and study the cosmos, examine the numbers, and uncover the mysteries of prophecy and divination. Yes, I have found my muse.

Terpsichore/Theo: And I have found my Master. Introduce me to the Pythia. [21]*(Great Initiates Pg 292)*

PLATO and URANIA

Urania: Oh Mr. Plato I can't tell you what an honor it is to hear you speak, let alone be in the same room with you, and ultimately . . . what magic it is to be in your arms.

Plato: Urania, the pleasure is mine of course to be in the company of such beauty and intelligence combined in the same beautiful young woman, and smelling so delightfully, delightfully, . . .

Urania: Cosmic . . . that's the perfume. Thank you, Mr. Plato, the pleasure is mine to dance with you. You actually dance quite well, for a man.

Plato: I realize that women of your age and caliber are quite secluded, but my dear, you must look at it as if you are being saved in a rosebud of virtuosity until the stars unite to form the configuration for love.

Urania: Shall we go together to examine the stars Mr. Plato, and share our perceptions together in the world of astronomy?

Plato: Not only do I love the way you dance, but I actually feel something inside that could drive me irrationally to a romantic position under the stars with some of Dion's wine in complete fascination of your deep knowledge. Perhaps tomorrow. Of course, this is our secret.

Urania: Is that a date Mr. Plato? Or shall we just dance? By the way, are you a Virgo?

HESIOD and ERATO

Hesiod: Dear Erato, this has been such a wonderful, exciting, and romantic evening. It is clearly arousing for me because I must confess that all my love poetry has been inspired by you, and to hold you and look at you, and for you to be every bit and more beautiful than I could ever imagine, is a mystery beyond chance.

Erato: Mr. Hesiod, you have put the Muses on the map and have given me a job. I am the writer's Aphrodite, and I have responded to the most powerful desires of love in songs, diaries, letters, and books everywhere in the world. I search the deep, swollen realms of my heart to pour out this love. What I forgot, was how strong you make me feel in your arms, with your attention, your warmth, your fire— you regenerate me as a man does for a woman, for a goddess, for mother nature. Take my love and inspiration with you as you have blessed me with your gracious strength.

EURIPIDES and MELPOMENE

Euripides: Melpomene, your dark beauty envelops me, and I am lost in the mystery of your gaze. Do you speak only the truth of humanity, or can you also speak for yourself, sultry Muse of tragedy and darkness?

Melpomene: Do you really want to go there? I do know the darkness well, as you do, from the extent of the tragedy in your work. May I suggest that we go beyond the pain of heartbreak, to the pleasure of pure acquaintance and exchange, a quick dance, rebirth— attraction— romance— desire— passion

Euripides: Casual dating, maybe a kiss or two?

Melpomene: A loving, tender relationship, engagement, and marriage?

Euripides: Problems, betrayal

Melpomene: Counseling, separation

Euripides: Divorce, heartbreak

Melpomene: No . . . . let's go back to the beginning . . .

Paul: *Eves dropping while dancing* Misha, do you think that the girls are too sexually vulnerable to be dancing with these brilliant scholars??

Misha: I think that the brilliant scholars are too horny to be dancing with our naïve girls.

Paul: Yes, our girls are beautiful aren't they— absolutely perfect in every possible way— physically, emotionally, psychologically, artistically, academically, socially— *pause* – But you know their parents do not approve of this. Look at them whispering.

Misha: Paul, I think you better change the music.

Paul: OK and I'll ask Hestia to put on the coffee.

Scene 16 — Ceci returns

A voice is heard at the door. It is Ceci, the lost Terpsichore, dressed like a rock/ballet dancer. All the music stops.

Ceci: May I speak gentlemen?

Paul: Ahh Ceci!! My lost Terpsichore..........Yes, please come in.

She gently enters the stage area.

Ceci: Forgive my inexcusable absence from school today. I want to explain my actions and offer some defense of my need to withdraw from the Muses.

Pythagoras: Please feel free to speak. For I believe that an honest voice as a young, intelligent woman is what the school wishes to develop.

Ceci: Thank you, Mr. Pythagoras. I welcome the opportunity to express myself. First of all, I love ballet. I love my academic studies. I believe in deep intellectual and scientific thought. I am an A student, and yet . . . I am also a passionate young woman, who cannot live in a cage of rules day and night. If I am supposed to be groomed as the true Terpsichore, I must see the hidden side of human passion as well and be fully able to inspire and illuminate the raw passion of love. To be able to lift someone out of an immobile darkness, one must know the abyss for themselves. I swear Mr. Goodman . . . I did not want to walk out on any of my Apollonian studies. But . . . Friday night, something happened inside my body. I feel like I literally flew out of my cage. I heard Dion's music and saw those girls singing and dancing so freely, and knowing how much my soul wants to rock out, I could not control my body, a force had taken me over . . . I was ecstatic, joyful, full of desire, hungry, thirsty, dying to let it rip!!!!

Misha: Yes, and I heard that you showed those Maenads a thing or two about technique up on that stage!!

Paul: You mean you crashed the stage, Ceci? You know better than that.

Dion: That was you?!! This is Ceci Diaz? You know, I was wondering what happened to you after the show. This girl can dance!!!

Paul: Please Dion. This is a trained ballerina. Let's not forget that one must learn the rules before they break the rules.

Pythagoras: And without dreams, and alternate philosophies, where would civilization be?

Hesiod: I say that these young women need to study both doctrines and negotiate a balance from their inquiries.

Plato: This is only logical.

Hestia: I insist that Ceci remains with us for the evening, and we will discuss this all in the morning.

Paul: Very well Hestia . . . I think that is an excellent idea, confused as I am at this point.

Dion: *Clearing his throat.* If you don't mind, my band will be here any minute with three cases of wine and a show to clear your chakras. If you haven't already seen us, I suggest you stay on the magic carpet and just sit back and enjoy the entertainment. Cancel the coffee.

The wild Maenads arrive at the door.

Dion *continues:*

And here they are now, ladies and gentlemen, my gypsy caravan of rogues, artists, burlesque queens, and brujas. Watch your step, don't come too close, because they are conduits for the spirits of nature, and ready to take on all forms of paranormal magic. Stand back. I give you my brood of panthers, THE MAENADS, dark, wild, and sexy.

Paulo: Remember Dion….NO BLOOD!

Scene 17— Dion and The Maenads— Musical Number

This musical number is divided into seven little Acts.

The lyrics have been abstracted from Euripides's THE BACCHAE and carved into a musical rock score which sets up a dramatic catharsis. The music should make use of the "dithyramb", or hymn, using the iambic trimeter and trochaic tetrameter, which were the two chief meters in Greek tragedy, mostly attributed to Dionysus. (Greek Drama pg 880 Encyclopedia of Religion and Ethics)

**Bachhus = Dionysus; Bachantes = Maenads

<u>**ACT I – THE BACCHAE**</u> - *Dion takes the stage:*

Dion: I want to thank Euripides for being the pioneer in revealing my archetype to the world, as well as having written the lyrics to my rock symphony The BACCHAE. I am proud to be here in the presence of such learned scholars and fine young ladies, and hope that you can appreciate the extremity I represent, with all of its madness and midnight.

Dion sings:

"I'm back— a god standing on ground where I was born, in Thebes. Lightning ripped me from the pregnant body of Semele. That blast of flame was my midwife. I am Dionysus, son of Zeus.
Dion continues with verses from THE BACCHAE

I first gave joy to the people far from here, in the golden deserts of Phrygia and Lydia.

Then I left. Everywhere on my journey here I taught my holy dances, my mysteries, and everywhere, the people knew I was a god.

Let's go! My women who adore me! I'll overtake you dancing on the heights— I'll run you wild with ecstasy!" *Dion exits*

Act II

The stage of the school becomes transformed by the Maenad's wild, explosive entrance. They are a group of nine of the most powerful looking women you have ever seen, with tattoos, rings, tribal and punk regalia, like savage warriors, fearless and sexy.

The choreography begins as drums, cymbals, and flutes accompany the Maenads in joyous, carnival dancing and singing, sporting all of their religious paraphernalia. Then the electric sounds of guitar and piano kick in. With disheveled hair, and snakes for headbands, belts, and bracelets, they swing torches and carrying tambourines, and a "thyrsus" staff tipped by a pinecone wound with ivy. The furs of panthers, leopards and fawns cover their backs, and all of these natural elements contribute to their transformation into the savage.[28] *(Pantel, pg. 222).*

As these women enter in their urban/animal tribal regalia with their uninhibited struts, comments, and interactions, almost as if they own the place, Apollo and his guests and students are spellbound and step back. The roadies, dressed as satyrs, bring in a huge tree stump with an image of the head of Bacchus/Dionysus on top, grapevines winding around. Ceramic jugs of wine are placed near this makeshift altar where candles are lit, and flowers are placed.[29] *(Golden Bough pg. 449)*

The Muses and The Maenads

The Maenads sing:

"Who's with us out here in the streets?
Who's there in the dark house?
Come! All of you! Keep your mouths quiet and your minds pure.
Hear us sing to Dionysus, the living god,
all truths that will never die.
Bless the man, bless his luck,
who learns the mysteries of this god;
He lives in sacred joy,
Bless the dancers who give body and soul to Bacchus!
We take them with us into the holy body of god.
Bacchus will dance steep mountain joy into our
spirits until we are pure.

We keep Great Mother Kybele's rites—
twisting the ivy into our hair,
lifting the green wand to Dionysus our God.
Go out into the hills, Bacchantes!
 Find him! Bring home the God who cries out.
Guard the violence in your green wand—
respect its holy power.
This land will be dancing when God runs his pack out to the mountain,
pulling the women free from their looms,
their minds stung wild by Bacchus.
No question - we are carefree old women, young women,
and girls not yet married, —
all moving in perfect formation."

THE BACCHAE - *Euripides*

Euripides enters / and speaks more verse from The Bacchae:

Euripides: My God, one can hardly believe their eyes. "First, they loosen their hair down their backs and hitch their fawn skins up. Then we see animal belts around each woman, live snakes who twist up to lick their cheeks! And mothers whose new babies are left back home, ease their aching breasts by picking up gazelles and wild wolf cubs to suckle with their white human milk. Soon they weave leaf-garlands into each other's hair— of ivy, oak and bryony flowers. Then one strikes her wand to a rock— out jumps icy spring water!

Another pushes her wand gently into the pasture feeling for Bacchus— She finds the god who made wine flood up right there! Women, eager for milk, raked the meadow with their fingers until it oozes out fresh and white. Raw honey drips in sweet threads from their wands."

The girls sing again:

Will I ever again arch my throat back
with joy to dance barefoot in the dark dew of heaven
the nightlong dance of the fawn bounding out—
into the sheer green joy of a meadow
away from the hunters, away from the beaters closing in,
away from the closing nets, from the hounds.

Where is our Bacchus?
He who gives us our soul back,
Who refreshes our spirit with song and dance, fruit and meat,
Wine and sweet milk,
Give us our life force, O god of nature and sustenance!!

Act III – The Lenea Festival

Dion, as Bacchus, is then carried in on a grape-covered wine barrel boat with wheels. He is dressed like an aging grape vine, draped in leopard skins, and is escorted out of his throne-boat to sing his song. The satyrs carry him around as this God of Vegetation, in exaltation while the Maenads dance around joyously. There is a mimetic comedy to this festival, called The Lenaea,[30] (Farnell pg. 207) celebrating the death of the old god of vegetation in the fall. The dance soon turns into the tragic buffoonery of Dionysus becoming the grape that the satyrs stamp upon, linking hands, executing violent steps, making a game out of trampling him into the divine juice of the wine. When the life is "squeezed" out of him, Dionysus is placed back in his boat like coffin, drained and lifeless.

Act IV - The Anthesteria Festival

The sound and lights shift to that of winter coldness. The Maenads begin a ritual in which they call the spirit of Dionysus back as they remove ceremonial jugs of wine from the boat-throne and place them next to tree stump altar. This was originally called the Anthesteria festival which took place in the winter. They wail for him, and the mood shifts from the joyous to the ceremonial and tragic. They uncork the jugs, asking the ancestor spirits to come forth on this special evening of "All Souls" or "the Day of the Pots", promising assistance with fertility and the growth of crops.[31] (Farnell 221)

The steps of the dance grow wilder and wilder, the circle swifter and swifter, as the Maenads call up the power of the god returning to fill them with renewed vitality. The calling escalates musically until . . .

Act V – The Sacred Marriage

The young reborn Dionysus is revived, born again from his wine barrel. He sings. He sees Ceci as Persephone in the distance and calls her. (He actually calls Ceci from the audience who is brought on stage by the Maenads and decorated with flowers as the maiden Persephone.)[32] (Farnell 217) He then proceeds to court her in a ballet attended by the Maenads who encourage the enactment of a "Sacred Marriage" in ceremonial, erotic formality. The wedding is consummated with an elegant and ritualistically romantic pas de deux, and the couple dances off together. Paulo is clearly upset.

Act VI – The Dionysian Orgy

The music changes and the Maenads and the Satyrs (who are now wearing huge phalluses) begin to dance in a more savage and frenzied fashion. Through rhythmic movements they arrive in a trance using tremendous forward and backbends of the body, throwing their heads back, their hair flying. With great leaps, constant changing of rhythms, and then an abrupt change to slow voluptuous, sexual movements, the women dance insanely grabbing at the men and their huge phalluses.

The gathering turns into an orgy of women transformed into animals fighting and screaming. Next, they begin to throw around their snakes and fight overstuffed animals which they begin to tear apart.

A huge paper mache horned bull charges into the stage (carried by the satyrs) straddled by a paper mache image of Dionysus. The women see this and go crazy chasing after the bull. The sound of the drums builds and climaxes causing the women to abandon their mad choreography and attack Dionysus and the horned bull effigy (which has now become suspended like a pinata). They tear away madly at Dionysus and the bull, eating the contents of the pinata (maybe pieces of bread like the body of Christ) They begin to spin like whirling dervishes until one by one they fall asleep in slow motion as the music retards.

Act VII – The Emmeleia – Dance of Tragedy

*We can hear off stage the voice of Dionysus, singing his sad lament, the "Emmeleia", or the noble dance of tragedy, which brings the Muses to their feet. All
nine girls enter the stage with solemn gestures as they pick up the pieces of Dionysus and the Sacrificial Bull.[33] (Lawler pg 82)*

Scene 18 — The Pythia speaks

Ceci, who has been watching with trepidation as Dionysus's demise unfolds…., suddenly is thrown into a shaking tremor, and she begins a spastic dance which takes her onto the stage, into the role of the Pythia. Pythagoras rushes to her side.

Paul: *Who is completely freaked out —* What's going on here? What has happened to my brother? Is this theater or madness? And what is happening to Ceci? I should have never let this take place under my roof.

Pythagoras: The Pythoness must speak— the spirit wants to come through. Bring her the three-legged stool and let her transmit the words of the Gods.

One of the muses brings a small three-legged wooden stool.

Paul: The oracle has never revealed itself here, in public, without my priests. This is only permitted in the sacred cave with sacred priestesses, and Ceci isn't trained for this work. What is happening here? We must stop this. Look what you've done! This is sacrilege in the Temple of Delphi.

Misha has run to her side.

Misha: My dear brother— the forces of spirit come when they must. We have invoked the Gods and now they are here.

Plato: Let the Pythia speak. For the madness here clearly must be arbitrated by the Gods.

Ceci has been shaking and wailing and semi-consciously taking on spirit with difficulty. Finally, the spirit calms down, and we can see a divine light across Ceci's face as the Pythia speaks through her.

Pythia Spirit (Ceci): My sons, and daughters, I have waited for this moment for so long to take place. It is here tonight when you will witness the re-convocation of this great temple in the name of two great brother Gods, Apollo and Dionysus. I am the messenger of the gods' wishes, and you will hear their reasons.

The dialogue of the artistic expressions and philosophies revealed here tonight uncovers a great mystery for all of us. As we all desire to rise up to the knowledge and peace of the celestial heavens, we must also merge with the earth and with all of her unknown, mysterious darkness below.

"The development of art and science depends on the dual influence of Apollonian and Dionysian forces— as reproduction depends on the sexes, in their unrelenting conflict and only occasional— periodic reconciliation."[34] *(Campbell on Nietzsche— pg 334 Creative Mythology)*

Pythia (Ceci) *continues eyes closed:*

My dear Apollo— Striving for perfection creates individuality to seek the truth, to calculate the movement of the stars, to perfect the lines of a poem, a song, or a dance.

This constant search sets divine qualifications, defines limits, promotes competition, and reinforces the perimeters for expression. This magnificent precision distinguishes man from animal. These are all great contributions to the evolution of man and this work is honorable. But you must open your heart.... learn to listen carefully

The Pythia turns to Dion

Pythia (Ceci): And now, my Gypsy rogue child Dionysus, enchanted by the spirit of nature, the wine of the vine, the magic of dance, music, and love, the expression of passions and desires, the pain of loss, the ritual of death and rebirth. Yes, we must acknowledge your contributions.

But oh the madness, dear Dionysus, which frightens the powers that be— the loss of control; to drink the wine and forget life's restrictions, to live out one's desires, to fuse with your animal spirit— oh yes to go into the dark libido and drain out all fears, anger, and sadness— expel it by burning it out of you to the point of exhaustion, destruction ... dissolving all boundaries to merge with the natural savage. Oh, such dark mysteries Dionysus are too much for the ethical, public mind.

The Pythia (Ceci) continues

How can these two men stand side by side? — both the sons of the same great bull-headed Zeus— manifesting the polarities of the human soul. Here we have "The Birth of Tragedy" *(The Birth of Tragedy, Nietzsche)* and the indispensable use of poetry, song and dance to accommodate the emotionally charged dichotomy between such familiar opposites— perfection and madness— GRACE and FURY. It is the wish of the Great Mother Gaia, to unite these two brother gods through the compassion of the triple goddess— maiden, mother, and crone. So be it.

Plato: The Gods have spoken Paul, and there can be no contest. We must acknowledge this magical dialectic of "Grace and Fury".

Scene— 19 — Resurrection and Initiation of the Double God by the Triple Goddess

SONG of the Triple Goddess blessing the Apollo/Dionysus polarity—"Grace and Fury"

A. The Pythia spirit (Ceci), then makes a linked line of Theoclea (Maiden), Misha (the mother), and Hestia (Crone), as they sing a final consecration hymn. The Muses and the Maenads interweave to form the thread of a large, labyrinthic journey/ choreography around the three women.

During this song the temple statues are rearranged to accommodate a rebuilt statue of Dionysus on the bull, Artemis in the middle, and Apollo to the right. The Muses move their statues to surround the altar where the Maenads decorate them with their Bacchanalia regalia of furs, wreathes, wands, and offerings of wine, flowers, and incense.

B. Both the Muses and the Maenads form a united choreography in reverence to the altar incorporating their separate styles.

The two brothers are brought into the circle, face to face. They fight and wrestle stylistically in silence. Hestia and Misha referee. The Muses and the Maenads gather round and begin to sing out with the AAAAHS of the tragic Greek choruses. The two Gods wrangle it out. Dionysus dances around him like a clown until Apollo gets him down and serious. Dion outwits him with dexterity and reverses the pin; but not for long, when Apollo flips him over and takes his victory. He claims, "Too much wine my brother", and they embrace. Instrumental MUSIC continues, and the two brothers weave into the lineup of the Triple Goddess, with the company of the Muses, the Maenads, and the philosophers behind them.

C. The show ends with the singing and dancing, show stopping finale of perfection and madness— Grace and Fury.

THE END

BIBLIOGRAPHY

The Muses and The Maenads

Blake, Tyrell William, Athenian Myths and Institutions, NY Oxford U Press, 1991

Bonnefoy, Yves., Greek and Egyptian Myth, U of Chicago Press, 1992

Campbell, Joseph, Creative Mythology, Masks of God, Penguin, 1968

Dodds, E.R., The Greeks and The Irrational, Berkeley, U of Cal Press, 1951

Eliade, Mircea, editor, Encyclopedia of Religion, Macmillan Pub Co., NY, 1987

Encyclopedia of Religion and Ethics, Charles Scribner and Sons, NY

Euripides, The Bakkhai, trans. R. Bagg, University of Mass Press, Amherst 1978

Farnell, Lewis, The Cults of the Greek State, Vol 5, Clarendon Press, Oxford, 1909

Frazer, Sir James, The Golden Bough, Macmillan Pub. Co, NY 1922

Ginner, R., The Gateway To The Dance, Newman Neame, London, 1960

Grove, L., Dancing, A Handbook of the Terpsichorean Arts, Singing Tree Press, Detroit, 1969

Hesiod, Theogony, Invocation to the Muses, trans. S. Lombardo, Hackett Pub. Co, Inc. Ind, Camb. 1993

Kerenyi, Karl, The Gods of the Greeks, Thames and Hudson, London/NY 1951

Kraus, R., History of the Dance in Art and Education, Prentice Hall, Inc. Englewood Cliffs, N.J. 1969

Lawler, L. The Dance in Ancient Greece, Middletown, Conn.

Wesleyan University Press, 1965

Nietzsche, F., The Birth of Tragedy, Garden City, NY, Doubleday, 1956

Pantel, P., The History of Women, The Harvard U Press, Cambridge, Mass. 1992

Schure, E., The Great Initiates, Secret Study of Religions, Harper

& Rowe, SF 1961

Schure, E., <u>Pythagoras and The Delphic Mysteries,</u> trans. F. Rothwell, Health Research, Mokelumne Hill, Calif. 1964

Vuillier, Gaston, <u>A History of Dancing,</u> Boston, Milford House, 1972

EXTENDED BIBLIOGRAPHY

The Muses and The Maenads

Sachs, Curt, <u>World History of the Dance,</u> NY The Norton Company, 1965

Taylor, T., <u>The Eleusinian and Bacchic Mysteries— a dissertation,</u> NY JW Bouton 1875, reprinted by Health Research, Modelumne Hills, Ca. 1971

Meyer, Marvin, <u>The Ancient Mysteries— sacred texts,</u> SF, Harper and Rowe, 1987

Graves, R.— The <u>Greek Myths I,</u> London, Penguin Books, 1960 Nillson, Martin, <u>Greek Folk Religion,</u> Philadelphia U of Penn Press 1940

Wosien, MG, <u>Sacred Dance— Encounter With The Gods,</u> NY Thames & Hudson 1986

Fierz-David, Linda, <u>Women's Dionysian Initiation, The Villa of Mysteries in Pompeii</u> Dallas,

Spring Publications, Inc. 1988

Guthrie, WKC, <u>The Greeks and Their Gods,</u> Beacon Press, Boston, 1962

Pickard-Cambridge, Sir Arthur, <u>The Dramatic Festivals of Athens,</u> Oxford, Clarendon

Lewis, IC, <u>Ecstatic Religion-Study of Possession,</u> NY Routledge, 1989

Hall, Manly, <u>The Adepts, Part One, Initiates of Greece & Rome,</u> Philosophical Research Society, LA, Ca. 1981

ENDNOTES

The Muses and The Maenads

1. Ginner, pg. 39. "This was a small round temple, built in circular form in imitation of the household brazier, representing the hearth of the city. There any special national ceremonies took place conducted by the head of state. This temple of Hestia was attended by priestesses who were vowed to celibacy and, having entered her service between the ages of six and ten, served the goddess for thirty years. They wore white robes with purple borders, and their heads were closely bound and veiled. Their duty was to tend the sacred fire in the temple which must never go out, and to present sacrifices and prayers. The dances of the "vestal virgins" were among the most important of the sacred dances of Greece and later of Rome."
2. Ibid, pg. 154
3. Lawler, pg. 108
4. Encyclopedia of Religion and Ethics; Muses pg
5. Redfield, pg. 39
6. Lawler, pg. 12
7. Farnell, pg. 437
8. Encyclopedia of Religion, Muses pg 163
9. Kerenyi, pg. 149
10. Blake, pg. 21
11. Hesiod, Theogony
12. Schure, Pythagoras, Delphic Mysteries, pg 88
13. Schure, Great Initiates pg 294
14. Schure, Pyth, pg 92
15. Bonnefoy, pg 192
16. Ginner, pg 6—The Republic of Plato
17. Grove pg 36
18. Kraus, pg. 37

19 Vuillier pg. 48
20 Lawler pg. 96
21 Euripides, The Bakkhai
22 Dodds pg. 69
23 Ibid pg. 76
24 Lawler pg. 76
25 Schure, Pythag. Pg 34
26 Ginner pg. 57
27 Encyclopedia of Religion and Ethics; Greek Drama pg. 880
28 Pantel pg.222
29 Frazer, James, Golden Bough pg. 449
30 Farnell, pg. 207
31 Ibid pg. 221
32 Ibid pg. 217— "Here takes place the corporeal union and marriage of the wife of the king and Dionysus. The formal marriage was necessary to cement the union of Dionysos with the state of Athens through the person of the queen: and this becomes a sacred pledge of his political adoption oand hof his fellowship with the people's life. And the marriage was more than a formal ceremony: the actual consummation was enacted, but by what means we can only conjecture."
33 Lawler pg 82
34 Campbell on Nietzche pg 334

www.ingramcontent.com/pod-product-compliance
Lightning Source LLC
Chambersburg PA
CBHW080601170426
43196CB00017B/2874